Santo Daime

ALSO AVAILABLE FROM BLOOMSBURY

Santo Daime

A New World Religion

ANDREW DAWSON

B L O O M S B U R Y

LONDON • NEW DELHI • NEW YORK • SYDNEY

Bloomsbury Academic

An imprint of Bloomsbury Publishing Plc

50 Bedford Square	175 Fifth Avenue
London	New York
WC1B 3DP	NY 10010
UK	USA

www.bloomsbury.com

First published 2013

British Library Cataloguing-in-Publication Data
A catalogue record for this book is available from the British Library.

ISBN: HB: 9781441102997
PB: 9781441154248
ePub: 9781441157942
PDF: 9781441184375

Library of Congress Cataloging-in-Publication Data
Dawson, Andrew, 1966–
Santo Daime : a new world religion / Andrew Dawson.
pages ; cm
Includes bibliographical references and index.
ISBN 978-1-4411-0299-7 (hardcover) – ISBN 978-1-4411-5424-8 (pbk.) –
ISBN (invalid) 978-1-4411-5794-2 (epub) – ISBN (invalid) 978-1-4411-8437-5 (pdf)
1. Santo Daime (Cult) I. Title.
BL2592.S25D39 2012
299'.93 – dc23
2012032002

Typeset by Newgen Imaging Systems Pvt Ltd, Chennai, India
Printed and bound in Great Britain

For Maggie

Contents

Introduction

My first experience of Santo Daime occurred in 2005 during research for a book on the non-mainstream religious scene in Brazil (A. Dawson, 2007). Pretty much unprepared for the sensory feast of a Santo Daime ritual, I was visually struck by the colourful 'uniforms' and brightly decorated ceremonial space. The strongly rhythmical and fervently sung 'hymns' also made an impact, as did the powerful smell and bitter taste of the religious sacrament which practitioners call 'Daime'. A psychoactive beverage more commonly known as 'ayahuasca', the sacrament of Daime and its psychotropic effects further added to the intense sensory stimulation which abides as an enduring memory of my earliest encounter with Santo Daime. Staged within the mountainous terrain of a national park hundreds of miles north of São Paulo, the ritual contents and format originally forged in the Amazon region of north-west Brazil did not seem particularly out of place. However, unlike the poor, mixed-race community which first elaborated Santo Daime as part of its semi-rural subsistence lifestyle, the ritual participants with whom I was celebrating were overwhelmingly drawn from Brazil's predominantly white urban middle class. Whereas the uniforms, songs and sacrament were very much of the Amazon region, those wearing, singing and consuming the ceremonial accoutrements of Santo Daime certainly were not. By no means discordant, the juxtaposition of Amazonian origins and urban-professional appropriation nevertheless piqued my academic interest.

Subsequent to finishing the book which first took me to Santo Daime, a British Academy Research Grant followed by a Leverhulme Trust Fellowship generously provided funding which enabled the questions raised by my early encounters with 'the doctrine' to be pursued at length. And so it was in 2007 that a research project commenced that would take me initially to the Amazon region, then to a miscellany of states across Brazil before taking in parts of Europe and North America. As well as the usual academic engagement with written and electronic sources produced by or about Santo Daime, research chiefly comprised periods of participant observation during which formal interviews, impromptu conversations, casual interactions and ritual practice took place. Since its founding in 1930, Santo Daime has split into a variety of different branches, most of which remain relatively small and concentrated within the Amazon region of their birth. In contrast to other branches, however, the organization known commonly as 'Cefluris' is significantly larger, more geographically dispersed and, as a result, the most demographically diverse.[1] Except where explicit qualification is made, this book concerns Santo Daime Cefluris (hereafter, Santo Daime) which was originally led by Sebastião Mota de Melo (1920–90) and is today headed by his son, Alfredo Gregório de Melo.

Building upon questions raised by my first experiences of Santo Daime, the research undertaken from 2007 to 2011 primarily focused on three areas. First, research concerned the origins and ethos of Santo Daime as a religious system. Here, attention was paid to the socio-cultural conditions of the Amazon region that gave rise to Santo Daime, the historical trajectory of the movement (from its Amazonian beginnings to international status) and the various practical and symbolic components which combine to form its hybrid ritual repertoire and variegated religious world view. Second, consideration was given to the processes of transition and transformation associated with Santo Daime's initial expansion beyond the Amazon region and subsequent internationalization as part of the non-mainstream, alternative religious scene. Importantly, Santo Daime's geographical spread and ongoing growth is intimately connected with a significant shift in its demographic profile and concomitant modification of the practical-symbolic dynamics at play across its ritual repertoire and religious world view. In this respect, research focus rested upon the implications for traditional beliefs and behaviour of Santo Daime's progressive insertion within the alternative religious scene populated by middle-class members of late-modern, urban-industrial society. Third, attention was paid to Santo Daime's relationship (as a now established occupant of the non-mainstream religious landscape) with the overarching societal processes and socio-cultural dynamics constitutive of Western late-modernity in general and urban middle-class subjectivity in particular. Here, research centred upon the ways in which the practical-knowledge furnished by Santo Daime speaks to and articulates the life-experiences, aspirations and concerns of its urban-professional membership. It also engaged Santo Daime relative to the overarching interface between late-modern society and contemporary religiosity.

The end result of this research, the book before you now addresses each of these three sets of concerns. It does so by combining the data acquired during fieldwork with insights offered by a variety of academic disciplines and approaches, not least of which are the sociology of religion, religious studies, social anthropology and cultural studies. By way of overall balance across the following chapters, the second and third sets of concerns receive the lion's share of attention. The issues and questions comprising these concerns would not, though, make much, if any, sense without a prior and sufficiently thorough treatment of the origins, early trajectory and practical-symbolic composition of the ritual repertoire and religious world view of Santo Daime. As such, Chapter 1 and a considerable portion of Chapter 2 are given over to delineating these matters. After detailing the birth of Santo Daime at the hands of its founder Raimundo Irineu Serra (called 'Master Irineu' by his followers), Chapter 1 concentrates upon the organizational offshoot of Cefluris established by 'Padrinho Sebastião' (Godfather Sebastian) and led today by his son, 'Padrinho Alfredo'. In addition to identifying the most important religio-cultural sources on which Santo Daime draws, the opening chapter traces the initial spread and subsequent internationalization of Cefluris. Chapter 2 continues the introductory theme by describing the ritual repertoire of Santo Daime along with its use of ceremonial space and time. Employing the insights of Michel Foucault, Santo Daime's ritual repertoire is engaged as a disciplinary regime preoccupied with physical probity and symbolic order. The chapter then moves, by way of Pierre Bourdieu, to explore contemporary ritual space as a dynamic arena characterized as much by fluidity and contestation as by fixity and hierarchy. Here, the disciplinary regime of Santo Daime ritual is treated as a mutable and evolving 'field of force' which, at the hands of a now dominant urban-professional constituency, is undergoing a variety of practical and symbolic modifications typical of its newfound late-modern context.

Chapter 3 combines the concepts of 'dislocution' and 'performative utterance' to explicate Santo Daime's religious world view. Santo Daime's world view is thereby treated as a dislocutory speech act which situates believers (known as *daimistas*) in a relationship of constructive tension vis-à-vis society at large. Although relativizing *daimista* relations with their prevailing socio-cultural environment, Santo Daime's contemporary world view does not fully foreclose on the practical and symbolic possibilities made available by the late-modern, societal context. Exemplifying the principally apolitical character of Santo Daime, two important emphases are identified and treated as narrative leitmotifs which inform the *daimista* world view. While each orchestrating leitmotif embodies a countercultural stance in respect of the world at large, they articulate two relatively contrasting views of the triadic relationship between the Santo Daime community, its individual members and their overarching socio-cultural context. Whereas the more established leitmotif of an 'apolitics of social transformation' reflects a traditional communitarian ethos, the later but increasingly popular leitmotif of an 'apolitics of self-transformation' embodies the strongly subjectivized character of Santo Daime's urban-professional practitioners. Chapter 4 explores the growth of spirit-oriented practice across the contemporary *daimista* movement and explains why certain novel forms of spirit mediumship are gaining in popularity relative to established modes of supernatural engagement. Santo Daime's understanding of the self as 'possessable' by spiritual agencies is first outlined, along with the notion of 'alternate' rather than altered states of consciousness. The spiritual entities engaged by Santo Daime are then treated, followed by a detailed look at the ritual context, types and modes in and through which spirit-oriented practice occurs. In addition to highlighting the hybrid, variegated and rapidly evolving nature of the contemporary *daimista* repertoire, these discussions identify novel modes of expressivity and alterity (otherness) as instrumental to the progressive transformation of traditional belief and practice in respect of the self, the spirits and the overarching ritual context by which spirit-oriented activity is framed.

Concentrating on the urban middle-class constituency which now forms the overwhelming majority of the movement, Chapter 5 explicates the contemporary character of Santo Daime. It does so by linking Santo Daime's orientation to the world at large with the typically late-modern traits of its urban-professional membership; identified here as part of the 'new middle class' which emerged in the second half of the twentieth century across the urban-industrial landscape of Western late-modernity. The notion of 'entangled modernity' is used to describe both the prevailing dynamics and practical-symbolic implications of the societal context which, as members of the new middle class, urban-professional *daimistas* hold in common. Next, and by way of contributing to academic discussions about religion and the market, the concept of 'mystified consumption' is formulated as a means of exploring the manner and extent to which the commoditized subjectivity of the new middle class can be said to impact upon the contemporary *daimista* repertoire. Subsequent to considering how Santo Daime may be classified as a religious world view, the chapter closes by identifying the contemporary *daimista* repertoire as form a 'world-rejecting aestheticism'. A short Postscript concludes the book.

The book's title, *Santo Daime: A New World Religion*, is both indicative and slightly playful. *Santo Daime* baldly refers to the religious movement with which this book is concerned. Coined by the religion's founder, Master Irineu, the term 'Santo Daime' literally means 'Holy Daime' and refers to the sacramental beverage of Daime (i.e. ayahuasca). Of Portuguese origin, 'Daime' (or *dai-me*) literally means 'give me' and is understood by *daimistas* to function in a petitionary sense of, for example, 'give me light' (*dai-me luz*), 'give me strength' (*dai-me força*), 'give me love' (*dai-me amor*). The term 'New World' has a twofold meaning. First, it refers literally to the South American continent and thereby plays on traditional renderings of Latin America as the 'new world' (*nouvum mundum*). Santo Daime is, then, a religion *of* the new world. Second, the term refers figuratively to various countercultural strands of the *daimista* paradigm which reference a 'new world' as either imminent or desirable by virtue of the debased condition in which our planet and its inhabitants currently find themselves (see Chapter 3). Santo Daime is, then, a religion *for* a new world. The final phrase of the title, *New World Religion*, plays on established (though contested) categorizations which differentiate between 'world', 'ethnic' or 'indigenous' and 'new' religions. Setting aside the utility or otherwise of categorical distinctions such as these, the term 'New World Religion' is intentionally mixed and serves to underline the challenge to neat and tidy typologies issued by Santo Daime's hybrid, flexible and variegated ritual repertoire and religious world view.

Compared with 'world' or 'ethnic' religious traditions, and despite its ongoing growth and international expansion, Santo Daime remains a relatively small religion. While organizational factors and societal conditions (see Chapter 1) make numbers hard to determine, at the time of writing (July 2012) regular participation in Santo Daime is unlikely to exceed 20,000 individuals world wide. As with other new religious phenomena, however, the importance of Santo Daime resides not in its size but in its significance for understanding the respective character and dynamic interface of society and religion. It is for similar reasons that the founders of sociology as an academic discipline in its own right (e.g. Max Weber and Émile Durkheim) interested themselves in novel religious phenomena as practical-symbolic barometers of overarching social transformation. For example, the non-mainstream status and countercultural ethos of new religions such as Santo Daime furnish potential insight into the nature of both marginal and minority means of socio-cultural signification and collective practice. The academic study of novel religious phenomena also engenders appreciation of socio-cultural formation and change through engaging such things as new and alternative lifestyles, unconventional modes of social integration and corporate behaviour and innovative expressions of disenchantment and protest. Organizational and interpersonal dynamics can also be explored through the study of new religions, along with group formation, the maintenance of collective identity, membership and belonging, leadership styles and the making and acceptance of authority claims. In addition, the rapid emergence and growth (along with the sometimes equally rapid decline) of new religious movements furnishes a bounded opportunity to analyse the concrete impact of the otherwise extended processes and overarching dynamics of modern social change. All in all, the study of novel religious phenomena like Santo Daime promises to shed light not only upon the present status and possible future of religion, but also upon the nature and potential directions of the societal forces and dynamics which frame religious belief and ritual practice. Barometers of both religious change in particular and societal transformation in general, movements such as Santo Daime have an analytical significance well in excess of their actual numerical size.

Acknowledgements and thanks

Santo Daime: A New World Religion would not have been possible without the cooperation of many *daimistas*. I am indebted to those in authority who, as well as giving their time, facilitated access by way of introduction and bona fides. The warmth and welcome furnished by communities and individuals across the three continents where fieldwork occurred are also very much appreciated. Conscious of the vulnerable status and relative intimacy of the *daimista* movement, and aware of the discomfort which aspects of this book may cause some members, individual informants are given pseudonyms and the names or exact locations of communities (excluding the mother community of *Céu do Mapiá*) are deliberately unspecific. The fieldwork on which much of this book rests would not have been possible without the funding provided through the British Academy Research Grant scheme and the Leverhulme Trust Research Fellowship. I am particularly grateful to Jean Cater of the Leverhulme Trust for the support and flexibility afforded in the face of the bureaucratic machinations of university accounting. Acknowledgement should also be made of the Research Fellowship granted by the Arts and Humanities Research Council of the United Kingdom which permitted my release from the usual academic responsibilities and thereby allowed the time and energy necessary to writing this book.

Among others, I am intellectually indebted to fellow members of the Ayahuasca Research Network whose general reflections and particular insights have contributed to shaping some of what follows. All of the following, however, is my responsibility alone. The initial support and subsequent promotion of this project by Kirsty Schaper of Continuum (now Bloomsbury) is much appreciated, as is the helpful and prompt editorial advice given by Rachel Eisenhauer. Thanks are likewise due to Adam Bardsley for his design input and final production of the diagrams included in Chapter 2. Academic and administrative colleagues in various parts of Lancaster University have also provided support and encouragement of different kinds. I am particularly thankful to those colleagues who refused to be put off by the potentially controversial nature of the fieldwork undertaken as part of the broader research project. Above all, it is to my wife and best friend, Debbie, that I am most grateful and personally indebted. For her abundant support and positivity, along with her tolerance of my periodic absences (in body and/or spirit), I am appreciative beyond measure.

1

Historical origins and contemporary developments

Introduction

The opening section of what follows details the birth of Santo Daime at the hands of its official founder Raimundo Irineu Serra (1892–1971), known to his followers (*daimistas*) as 'Master Irineu'. In addition to reproducing some of Santo Daime's foundational narratives, the most formative religious influences drawn upon by Master Irineu and the early *daimista* community are identified and described. Focus then turns to the branch of Santo Daime, founded by Sebastião Mota de Melo (1920–90), with which this book is concerned. First outlining the conversion of 'Padrinho Sebastião' (as he is known to his followers) to Santo Daime, the next section details the most important religious sources with which his fledgling religious community augmented the ritual repertoire inherited from Master Irineu. Santo Daime's spread beyond the Amazon region and subsequent internationalization at the hands of an increasingly influential urban-professional cohort is then delineated. The chapter concludes by identifying a range of transformative dynamics associated with Santo Daime's changing demographic profile and progressive insertion within the non-mainstream religious scene of late-modern, urban-industrial society. Given the broader focus of the overarching narrative within which this chapter sits, much of what follows uses broad brushstrokes on a somewhat limited canvas. It is, though, sufficient to provide both the historical context and general orientation necessary to getting the most from the book as a whole.

Amazonian origins

The beginnings of Santo Daime are officially dated to a religious ritual of 26 May 1930 held in a neighbourhood on the outskirts of the Amazonian city of Rio Branco, the capital of what is now the Brazilian state of Acre. Of the three adults who gathered for the religious ritual, by far the most important was Raimundo Irineu Serra, the founder and undisputed 'Master' of Santo Daime. Of Afro-Brazilian parentage, Irineu Serra was born in the town of São Vicente Ferrer in the north-east state of Maranhão. Attracted by the employment opportunities offered by the first national rubber boom (c.1890–1920), Irineu Serra moved to Acre in 1912. For the next two decades, he worked as a rubber tapper (seringueiro), a frontiersman staking out the borders between Brazil, Peru and Bolivia, and, latterly, a member of the territorial guard from which he retired with the rank of corporal in the early 1930s (MacRae, 1992: 61). Unlike the religious repertoire in place by the time of Master Irineu's death in 1971, the intimate and relatively short ritual of May 1930 lacked many of the repertorial components (e.g. hymns, uniforms and battalions) which so readily distinguish Santo Daime from most other forms of organized religion; excluding, perhaps, Brazil's other 'ayahuasca religions' of A Barquinha (The Little Boat) and A União do Vegetal (The Union of the Plant) (see A. Dawson, 2007: 67–98).

The word 'ayahuasca' derives from the north-Andean Quechua language and means 'soul vine' or 'vine of the dead'. Although also serving social and therapeutic ends, as the literal translation of the term indicates, ayahuasca plays a key role in the spiritual practices of the indigenous South American cultures from which its production and consumption originates. Traditionally consumed in liquid form throughout the upper reaches of the Amazonian river system (i.e. Bolivia, Brazil, Colombia, Ecuador and Peru), ayahuasca is a generic term given to the preparation of the mildly psychoactive vine Banisteriopsis caapi.[1] In its indigenous context, B. caapi is processed by communities belonging chiefly to the Aruák (e.g. Ashininka and Machiguenga), Chocó (e.g. Emberá and Noanamá), Jívaro (e.g. Aguaruna and Shuar), Pano (e.g. Kaxinawá and Marubo) and Tukano (e.g. Desana and Siona) peoples (Luna, 1986: 167–70; Luz, 2004: 37–68). Owing to their ability to intensify and prolong the psychotropic event, a range of other natural substances are combined with the vine. Although tree barks and coca or tobacco leaves are used, a common additive is the foliage of plants which contain the psychoactive agent N,N-dimethyltryptamine (DMT); not least among which is the shrub Psychotria viridis.[2] The term 'ayahuasca' is generally applied as much to these latter concoctions as it is to preparations using only the vine as its sole psychoactive agent.

The passage of ayahuasca consumption from indigenous to non-indigenous contexts is thought to have occurred through the formation of mixed-race (*mestiço*) communities and by way of sporadic contact between indigenous peoples and non-indigenes (such as Irineu Serra) working in remote parts of the Amazonian forest (Franco and Conceição, 2004). Prior to the emergence of the ayahuasca religions of Brazil, the most popular form of non-indigenous ayahuasca consumption occurred principally among *mestiço* communities living on the borders between Brazil, Colombia, Peru and Bolivia. Known most popularly by the term *vegetalismo*, the *mestiço* consumption of ayahuasca is orchestrated by specialists who claim the spirits of certain plants (*vegetales*) as their teachers (*professores*) (Luna, 1986: 14–15). As with their indigenous counterparts, *vegetalistas* (known also as *ayahuasqueros*) use ayahuasca to invoke the presence of or facilitate interaction with the spirits of plants, animals and other supernatural forces.

Addressed as 'Master' (*mestre*), the *vegetalista* consults different plants, animals and supernatural agents relative to the specific task at hand. While used for other purposes, such as artistic inspiration and divination, the consumption of ayahuasca within the context of *vegetalismo* has primarily served therapeutic ends. On account of their focus upon the ritual pursuit of healing (*cura*), *vegetalistas* may also be known as *curandeiros*. As with its ritual consumption by indigenous peoples, ayahuasca is taken on its own or along with other substances. It may also involve the invocation of spirits to possess the body of the Master or employ the shamanic motif of soul-flight in which the, now disembodied, spirit of the healer seeks supernatural guidance by visiting the heavenly realms of the world beyond. Likewise in tandem with indigenous contexts, *vegetalista* practices are commonly accompanied by dietary restrictions, the use of songs (whistled or sung) and employment of rhythmical instruments such as the maraca. The use and spraying of alcohol or blowing of tobacco smoke throughout ritual space and over those being treated is also widespread (Mabit, 2004).

Founding narratives

Daimista tradition tells of Irineu Serra's initiation into the ways of ayahuasca at the hands of Dom Pizango (also Don Pizon), a Peruvian *ayahuasquero* whose knowledge and practice claimed a direct line of descent from the mythical Incan king Huascar (MacRae, 1992: 62). While initiatory association with the Incan heritage is beyond historical confirmation, it is certainly true that owing to the demands of his employment, Irineu Serra moved regularly along the borderlands of Brazil, Peru and Bolivia occupied by *mestiço* and indigenous communities within which ayahuasca was regularly consumed. Although it is highly likely that he took ayahuasca during his trips to the more remote parts of the borderlands, it was in the Acrean frontier town of Brasiléia that Irineu Serra regularly consumed ayahuasca in a formal ritual context. Attended by Irineu Serra chiefly during the 1920s, the Brasiléia community was known both as the 'Circle of Regeneration and Faith' (Círculo de Regeneração e Fé) and the 'Queen of the Forest Centre' (Centro da Rainha da Floresta). Beside a few key personalities (most notably Irineu Serra's cousins, André and Antônio Costa) and its use of ayahuasca, relatively little is known of the religious repertoire of the CRF. It is thought, however, that its beliefs and practices comprised an amalgam of popular Catholic, European esoteric, vegetalista and Afro-Brazilian discourse and practice (Silva, 1983). Founded around the time of Irineu Serra's arrival in Acre, disputes among the leadership led to the eventual break-up of the community. Certainly, Irineu Serra had distanced himself from the group by the time of the aforementioned ritual of 26 May 1930.

Whatever the actual historical circumstances of Irineu Serra's eventual break with existing modes of mixed-race ayahuasca consumption, daimista tradition narrates this period as a time of calling in which he is commissioned as both a healer and one who, as a mestre in his own right, would moralize ritual ayahuasca consumption through its Christianization. An important element of ayahuasca consumption's moral rehabilitation involved Irineu Serra renaming the psychoactive beverage 'Daime' (see Introduction). As told by Luiz Mendes do Nascimento, disciple of Master Irineu and highly respected member across the Santo Daime community, two key episodes exemplify this period (see www.mestreirineu.org/luiz.htm). The first episode concerns Irineu Serra's initial experience with ayahuasca.

It was at this time that he first encountered ayahuasca at a rubber plantation near Peru . . . Only there, those taking the drink had a Satanic pact in order to bring fortune and ease to their lives . . . [Irineu Serra] took the drink and when the others started to work they put their mouths to the ground, calling the demon. He also started to call [chamar], but the more he called the demon, only crosses [i.e. Christian] would appear. So many crosses that he felt suffocated. Then the Master began to analyse things: 'The Devil is scared of the cross and the more I call him, the more the crosses appear. There's clearly something in this . . .'

The second event is narrated as occurring sometime later and relates Irineu Serra's commission by a heavenly being initially introduced to him as Clara by his cousin Antônio Costa.

The next time, after taking the Daime [ayahuasca], he arranged himself so that he could see the moon. It was full or almost full and the night was clear, very beautiful. When the visions became strong [*começou a mirar muito*], he looked toward the moon and saw her coming, until she came very close to him before stopping at rooftop height. Within the moon he saw a beautiful woman seated. She was so visible that everything was defined to the smallest detail, even her eyebrows. She said to him: 'You dare to call me Satan? . . . Do you think that anyone else has ever seen what you are now seeing? . . . Now tell me, who do you think I am?' Faced with such light, he said: 'You are the Universal Goddess!' 'Very good [she said]. Now you are going to subject yourself to a diet so that you may receive what I have to give you' . . . After the diet, she came to him as clear as the light of day and said that she was ready to attend to his request. He asked that she make him one of the best healers in the world . . . [and] that she combine everything to do with healing [*a cura*] in the drink [i.e. ayahuasca] . . . 'It is already done [she said], everything is in your hands.'[3]

In other accounts of subsequent visions (*mirações*), the heavenly being initially introduced as Clara, but soon identified as the 'Universal Goddess' (*Deusa Universal*), is also referred to as the 'Queen of the Forest' (*Rainha da Floresta*), 'White Moon' (*Lua Branca*), the Virgin Mary (*Virgem Maria*) and 'Our Lady of the Immaculate Conception' (*Nossa Senhora da Conceição*).

Variations on the popular religious theme

The *vegetalista* traditions of the upper-Amazonian basin undoubtedly played a formative part in the emergence of Santo Daime. Many of the motifs central to *vegetalista* practices (e.g. dietary restrictions, visions of animals, gift of cure, initiation by trial, spirit calls [*chamados*] and celestial bodies), for example, appear throughout Santo Daime's foundational narratives. Likewise, and in tandem with his *vegetalista* contemporaries, Irineu Serra's healing practices involved the blowing of tobacco smoke over the cup of ayahuasca, the issuing of medicinal prescriptions (*receitas*) and, in more extreme circumstances, the removal of foreign objects or errant spirits from the bodies of those seeking a cure.[4] It cannot be ignored, though, that *vegetalismo* shared key components of its world view and ritual repertoire with other forms of popular cultic practice around at the time. Consequently, while Irineu Serra's indebtedness to *vegetalismo* should not be underestimated (not least in respect of ayahuasca), a number of beliefs and practices present within *vegetalista* traditions may well have been derived by Santo Daime from religio-cultural sources other than *vegetalismo*. For example, both Galvão (1955) and Maués and Villacorta (2004) identify a range of spirit-oriented and plant-based ritual activities (e.g. peasant shamanism, *pajelança cabocla*) in other parts of the Amazon, the beliefs and practices of which share many similarities with those of *vegetalismo*.[5] At the same time, it should be noted that few, if any, of the early members of Santo Daime were born and raised in the north-west Amazon region. Indeed, the overwhelming majority were economic migrants from the north-east. Consequently, although Santo Daime first emerged in the Brazilian north west, it is naive to assume that exposure to the kinds of beliefs and practices outlined above occurred solely at Santo Daime's geographical point of origin.

A point not lost on others tracking the emergence of Santo Daime (e.g. Goulart, 2004), the influence of beliefs and practices from north-east Brazil has, perhaps, been most thoroughly examined by Labate and Pacheco (2004). Focusing upon Maranhão, the state of Irineu Serra's birth, Labate and Pacheco treat a range of possible influences to which Master Irineu and other foundational members of Santo Daime may well have been exposed. As with Galvão (1955) and Maués and Villacorta (2004), the authors identify popular religious practices which, by virtue of their indigenous heritage, share some of their key beliefs and ritual activities with those of *vegetalismo* (Labate and Pacheco, 2004: 318–24, 337). Importantly, however, and in addition to the highly formative influence of popular Catholicism (see below), Labate and Pacheco highlight a number of possible Afro-Brazilian influences which, like so many north-east states, pervade Maranhão by virtue of its former plantation system and historical concentration of the slave population (2004: 312–15). I use the word 'possible' to underline the uncertain, and no little contentious, nature of the evidential chain; principally as it concerns Afro-Brazilian influences, but also in respect of ritual practices from other sources.

Noted above, *vegetalista* traditions include forms of spirit-oriented activity which involve both bodily occupation of the practitioner by the spirits engaged and shamanic notions of soul-flight. Also present in the kinds of 'peasant shamanism' (*pajelança cabocla*) mentioned above, possession motifs are, however, strongly to the fore in the Afro-Brazilian practices (e.g. *Tambor de Mina*) to which Irineu Serra may have been exposed, but of which he was surely aware (see Moreira and MacRae, 2011). Irineu Serra's exposure to or awareness of such ritual activities do not in themselves establish these practices as formative elements of the emerging Santo Daime religious repertoire. Indeed, and as noted earlier by Luiz Mendes' comments, Irineu Serra is portrayed by these narratives as both regarding such practices as 'satanic' and calling up the Christian 'cross' instead of the 'demon'. Foundational narratives such as these, however, are laden with ideological weighting which portrays Irineu Serra and the religion he founded in a way which accords more with what they subsequently became than what they actually were during the formative years of their development. In tandem with the extreme paucity of corroborative documentation and virtual absence of otherwise independent historical sources, the narration of early *daimista* belief and practice offers, at best, a selective reading through which favoured components are emphasized while less favoured (if not, unfavourable) elements are downplayed, overlooked or completely expunged from the record.

To a significant extent, Santo Daime's extended struggle for political recognition as a legitimate religious practice has been commonly reinforced by its association with forms of indigenous ritual activity historically tolerated, if not now legally protected, on account of their established socio-cultural provenance. This strategy of continuity represents Santo Daime as evolving naturally from long-standing beliefs and practices which derive legitimacy from their roots in pre-conquest South American culture. Furthermore, official *daimista* narratives offer a value-added element by way of Santo Daime's purported Christianization of pre-existing practices customarily viewed by many in authority as backward and overly superstitious. In effect, Santo Daime is portrayed as being in continuity with, yet improving upon, what has gone before. By way of complementarity, there also exists a strategy of discontinuity. Perhaps driven more by internal identity-politics than external dynamics, the strategy of discontinuity distances Santo Daime from practices and beliefs which may once have been part of its ritual repertoire but no longer reflect existing doctrinal concerns or contemporary socio-cultural composition. By virtue of its explicit linkage with spirit possession and lowly socio-cultural status, for example, the kind of Afro-Brazilian religiosity identified by Labate and Pacheco (2004) is ideally placed to be targeted as an undesirable element to be downplayed or ignored by some official narratives.[6] The absence of evidence in respect of certain beliefs and practices playing a formative part in Santo Daime's initial development should not, then, be straightforwardly read as evidence of their absence.

Setting aside the extent of Afro-Brazilian influence upon the nascent ritual repertoire of Santo Daime, it is clear that by the late 1940s Irineu Serra (or Master Irineu as he was now called) and his fledgling community intentionally sought to minimize association with particular forms of popular religious expression; not least those prone to accusations of base superstition or black magic (MacRae, 1992: 65–6). At least in part, this move probably represented a response to escalating persecution orchestrated by resurgent Catholic authorities. Revitalized through its post-1890 reintegration within the international (i.e. Roman) ecclesiastical network and reinvigorated by the favoured legal-political treatment enjoyed under the Getúlio Vargas presidency (1930–45), the Catholic hierarchy in Brazil set about eradicating what it regarded as the outdated and superstitious excesses of much popular religious practice (Oliveira, 1985). Already susceptible to unwanted attention by virtue of its use of ayahuasca, Santo Daime's weeding out of potentially controversial, but expendable, elements of its religious repertoire thereby made perfect sense at a time of increased persecution.

Acknowledging the impact of persecution upon the early *daimista* community, Goulart nevertheless stresses the importance of socio-economic change in shaping the ongoing transformation of Santo Daime's nascent ritual repertoire (2004). Whereas the earliest phase of Santo Daime's existence was most closely associated with the rural context of the forest, she argues, the end of the rubber boom and increasing urbanization of Rio Branco and its outskirts presented *daimistas* with a new set of experiences in want of a different religious articulation. Faced with a receding dependence upon the forest and the particular lifestyle it afforded, the forces, symbols and practices which most directly corresponded to Santo Daime's originary frame of reference were subsequently reinterpreted, adapted or replaced in a manner most effectively dovetailing with a new set of socio-economic circumstances (also Silva, 1983). For Goulart, the religious consequences of the socio-economic changes experienced by the early *daimista* community are most clearly reflected in a decreasing reliance upon popular cultic practice and spirit-oriented activity and progressive recourse to ostensibly universal symbols and rituals of an explicitly moral tenor (Goulart, 2004). Above all, the beliefs and practices of European esotericism furnished the vehicle by which this transition was made. Before exploring the impact of European esotericism, however, something should be said of Santo Daime's relationship with the popular Catholic world view to which its early members were exposed from birth.

Popular Catholic roots

Oliveira defines popular or folk Catholicism as 'the body of religious practices and representations developed by the popular imaginary starting from the religious symbols introduced to Brazil by Portuguese missionaries and colonists, to which certain indigenous and African religious symbols have been added' (1985: 122). According to Mello e Souza, the form of Catholic Christianity established in Brazil was an admixture of late-mediaeval and early-modern religiosity 'imbued with paganism' and accustomed 'to a magical universe' in which 'people could barely distinguish between the natural and the supernatural, the visible and the invisible, part and whole, the image and what it represented' (2003: 48). The strong correspondence between the supernaturalized world of popular Catholicism and those of indigenous and African-derived belief systems readily lent itself to much by way of overlap and outright syncretism. The popular Catholic identity at the core of Santo Daime belief and practice is somewhat removed from the Catholic Christianity of the modern West.

Exemplified by practices such as the *promessa*, *novena*, pilgrimage and festival, popular Catholicism was principally structured around the ritualized interaction of supplicant and saint. A figure too remote for meaningful exchange, God the Father ceded place to the holy family (i.e. Mary, Jesus and Joseph) who, in turn, sat within a broad spectrum of saintly intercessors and heavenly agents to whom appeal was made. Popular Catholic ritual and daily devotions embodied an unabashedly pragmatic religiosity in which overwhelmingly mundane objectives were sought through a combination of saintly patronage and thaumaturgy (i.e. use of charms, spells, offerings, amulets and curses). Orchestrated through domestic shrines, local chapels and strictly segregated associations (e.g. *irmandades* and *confrarias*), popular Catholicism drew upon a raft of lay functionaries (e.g. *benzedores, rezadores* and *festeiros*) whose daily ministrations attended the social rhythms and hardships of everyday life (Azzi, 1978: 155).

Given the nature of popular Catholicism, not least its overlap with aforementioned belief systems, the Christianization of ayahuasca traditions envisioned by Irineu Serra preserved much by way of their pragmatic ethos and supernaturalized world view. Consequently, while the names used and the modes of supplication may have changed, the pantheon of Catholic saints and heavenly forces to which appeal was now made served much the same purpose of securing healing, security and everyday well-being as the spirits and supernatural agents formerly engaged. At the same time, while the curative ministry of Irineu Serra may be most closely associated with *vegetalista* traditions and ayahuasca healing practices, the influence of the popular models offered by Catholic lay-practitioners cannot be discounted. For example, the festival events of the popular Catholic calendar furnished something of a template by which a number of Santo Daime's most important rituals were both organized and scheduled. Detailed in the next chapter, some of the key elements of *daimista* ritual practice (e.g. dance, uniforms, regimentation and hymns) may well have been appropriated from popular festival formats. Celebrated in June, the Feast of Saint John was the occasion of Santo Daime's first formal Hymnal ritual (*hinário*), and many of popular Catholicism's most significant saintly festivals have furnished dates on which the movement's most noteworthy Hymnal rituals are sung and danced (e.g. Christmas, Holy Week, Our Lady of the Conception, Saint Peter). To minimize persecution, rituals such as baptism and marriage were initially left to local Catholic auspices. Over time, however, *daimista* rites of passage were developed by appropriating and adapting existing liturgical models.

Esoteric influences

By the time of the founding community's move in the early 1940s to the site it occupies today, many of the foundational components associated with Santo Daime had been incorporated within its nascent ritual repertoire.[7] Hymns, ceremonial dancing, uniforms and the regimentation of ritual participants (see Chapter 2) were now well-established components of the growing community led by Master Irineu; as was Irineu Serra's title of 'Chief of the Juramidam Empire' (*Chefe do Império Juramidam*).[8] Likewise, most of the key personnel with whom Master Irineu worked closely had now joined the Santo Daime community.[9] It was during this period that the influence of European esotericism came increasingly to the fore in a manner which reshaped existing beliefs and practices as well as adding new elements to the *daimista* world view (Goulart, 2004: 57). On account of their diffuse influence upon popular Catholic beliefs and presence within the ritual repertoire of the aforementioned CRF, esoteric motifs and traditions would not have been unknown to Irineu Serra prior to this time. As such, his formal association in the late 1940s with one of Brazil's foremost esoteric organizations, the 'Esoteric Circle of the Communion of Thought' (*Círculo Esotérico da Comunhão do Pensamento*), might best be seen as reflecting rather than initiating a long-standing interest with esoteric traditions. In contrast to the magical emphases of popular esoteric sources such as the 'Cross of Caravaca' (*A Cruz de Caravaca*), for example, the kind of esotericism mediated by the Esoteric Circle (and the Rosicrucian Order of which Irineu Serra was also a member) was of a much more rational and moralistic kind.[10]

Founded in 1909, the Esoteric Circle was based in São Paulo but enjoyed a fairly extensive national reach through a variety of publications, the most notable of which was its magazine 'Thought' (*O Pensamento*) to which Irineu Serra subscribed. Associated with a variety of alternative 'philosophies' and non-mainstream 'scientific' world views, the Esoteric Circle was principally a vehicle for the dissemination of and instruction in European esoteric traditions such as Anthroposophy, Rosicrucianism and Theosophy (Moura da Silva, 2006). The adjective 'esoteric' is derived from the Greek word for 'inner' (*esoteros*), and when applied to the European traditions which became popular from the late 1800s it denotes two relevant characteristics. First, the term 'esoteric' is used in contrast to 'exoteric' and distinguishes between an exclusive corpus of *inner* knowledge and practice available only to initiates and a general body of *outer* knowledge and practice available to all and sundry. Esoteric discourse and practice thereby embodies elements of exclusivity, custodial responsibility, secrecy, initiation and hierarchy. Second, the word 'esoteric' connotes an emphasis upon interior states of mind, experiences and dispositions which are awakened through access to particular esoteric knowledge and practice. These interior realities are nurtured through a range of disciplines and techniques (e.g. meditation, introspection and regression) and provide access to further truths located deep within self, known here as the 'higher' or 'true' self (Faivre, 1986: 156–63). These two aspects of the term 'esoteric' come together in an understanding of esotericism as a privileged form of practical-knowledge ('science') whose learning and execution permits a reading of reality and oneself as they truly are. This reading, in turn, facilitates the development of previously dormant powers or hidden subjective faculties said to reside in the 'higher-self'.

Underwriting these 'scientific' processes are a number assumptions foundational to esoteric repertoires, the most relevant of which are the principles of *correspondence* and *manipulation* (Faivre, 1992: xv). The principle of *correspondence* sees the visible, natural world as a direct correlate of an all-embracing invisible, supernatural reality. In effect, the material (i.e. physical, chemical and biological) processes that combine to constitute the visible, natural world are direct reflections of overarching immaterial dynamics constitutive of the cosmos as a whole. Summed up in the esoteric maxim 'as above, so below', the universe as we know and experience it is held to be no more than a material effect of immaterial causation. The immaterial forces and dynamics constituting the universe are understood by esoteric thought to be encapsulated in a series of 'laws' such as karma (known also as 'reciprocity') and reincarnation (known also as 'perpetual return'). As with most of these laws, esoteric representations of karma and reincarnation are modelled analogically on scientific laws such as magnetism or gravity. Embodying typically modern preoccupations, these laws encapsulate an ameliorative vision of the cosmos in which human consciousness evolves through the pedagogical opportunities afforded by successive incarnations within which a meritocratic ethic of just deserts (i.e. karma or reciprocity) ensures the appropriate dispensation of merit and punishment from one incarnation to the next. Pervading the entire universe, and thereby operating at both immaterial and material levels, these laws impact directly upon the spiritual and physical well-being of every rational entity. Given the principle of correspondence between the visible, natural world and invisible, supernatural reality, knowledge of these laws is available to those who know how and where to look. It is here that esoteric knowledge comes in.

The principle of *manipulation* is the practical outworking of the principle of correspondence. Given the causal nature of immaterial forces and dynamics, the ability to harness and control their creative energies engenders limitless possibilities for the transformation of the material world and those who inhabit it. Within traditional esotericism, this quest for material transformation through the manipulation of immaterial forces was typified by the science of alchemy and its attempts to transmute lead into gold. Typical of their ameliorative moralistic bent, modern esoteric repertoires articulate the manipulation of immaterial forces in terms of the inner transmutation of human consciousness (here, higher-self) and its subsequent ascent up the evolutionary chain of being. Informed by esoteric knowledge as to the nature of these universal forces and the manner of their impact upon the world and its inhabitants, initiates of esotericism use techniques such as meditation and introspection to harness and subsequently manipulate these forces for their own and the greater good (Faivre and Needleman, 1992).

Whatever the respective technique applied, its principal dynamic involves the eradication of defective aspects of the self (understood as the 'ego' or 'lower-self'). Such defects may be accumulated in this life by way of improper thoughts and behaviour or be inherited (as bad karma) from prior incarnations. Commencing with self-scrutiny, the ameliorative process involving the annihilation of the lower-self is both gradual and cumulative. By way of concentrated self-scrutiny (in both daily life and ritual practice), details of subjective routines, thoughts, feelings and dreams are individually identified, along with the basic mechanisms and motives by which they are driven. Such practices, thoughts and feelings are then subjected to critical analysis by means of sustained reflection upon their moral status and spiritual propriety. If practised properly, this process gives way to self-understanding as particular defects, their causes and place in the self are identified. Once identified, the subjective defects which collectively make up the ego or lower-self are incrementally eliminated as they become the focus of specific prayers and ritual action. Understood and applied correctly, esoteric practical-knowledge thereby results in the gradual eradication of the ego, which in turn permits the development of the higher-self. In so doing, the esoteric practice of self-scrutiny engenders the discovery, awakening and channelling of forces residing deep within the individual (i.e. higher-self) but ultimately grounded in the cosmic energies of the surrounding universe.

Formalizing the Santo Daime repertoire

The progressive adoption of esoteric themes impacted most clearly upon the ritual repertoire of Santo Daime through adaptations made to the ceremony now known as the Concentration (*concentração*); the evolutionary precursor to which was the foundational rite celebrated by the first *daimistas* on 26 May 1930. In addition to being rescheduled to dates considered propitious by the esoteric community (the 27th of the month), the narrative and practical framing of the ritual imbued it with an increasingly subjectivized tenor oriented to the inward looking preoccupations of an ameliorative self-scrutiny. In effect, the ceremonial framing of cure, with which the originary ritual was chiefly concerned, moved from being something obtained as a grant from another to become something achieved on the grounds of individual endeavour and the merit (*merecimento*) acquired by it. Some of the key invocations of the Esoteric Circle were also adopted at this time (e.g. 'Consecration of the Room' and 'Key of Harmony'), as were its characteristically rationalizing universal principles of, for example, harmony, love, truth and justice (see Chapter 2).

Typical of the changes taking place, the ritualized calling upon traditional spiritual agencies was incrementally exchanged for or complemented by the ceremonial appropriation of cosmic forces and universal moral principles. Such was the influence of esotericism that Master Irineu's eventual break from the Esoteric Circle in the 1960s (caused by his refusal to give up the ritual use of ayahuasca) had only a superficial effect upon Santo Daime's now well-established and thoroughly esotericized ritual repertoire.

Coinciding with the increasing appropriation of esoteric themes and preoccupations, Santo Daime beliefs and rituals were progressively formalized as the movement and its members distanced themselves from popular cultural practices with which they were once closely associated. Over time, for example, the use of rum and tobacco in rituals involving the consumption of ayahuasca (a characteristically *vegetalista* practice) was banned in favour of the sole presence of the 'sacrament' of Daime. Likewise, festival dances which allowed alcohol, popular music and couples dancing in hold were replaced by formal religious rituals comprising the consumption only of Daime, singing of hymns and strict segregation of the sexes (MacRae, 1992: 137). Although outbreaks of persecution continued to impact the *daimista* community, Master Irineu gained something of a reputation across Rio Branco as both a folk healer and man of deep-seated wisdom. As well as providing respite from the intermittent bouts of persecution, if not a full-blown sense of legitimacy, the support of well-placed public dignitaries certainly furnished the new religion of Santo Daime with a growing sense of security. Indeed, by the time of his death on 6 July 1971, Master Irineu had secured both an enduring religious legacy and widespread public respect; as evidenced by the many non-*daimista* mourners at his funeral, including representatives of local government and Rio Branco high society.

In addition to the movement of Cefluris, the originary community known as Alto Santo has spawned a number of breakaway groups in the decades subsequent to the death of its founder. Excluding Cefluris, not all of these groups remain geographically close or in complete doctrinal harmony with the founding community. Nevertheless, and not least to distinguish them from the version of Santo Daime propagated by Cefluris, these groups are often collectively referred to as 'Alto Santo' or 'of the Alto Santo line' (Labate and Pacheco, 2010: 18). Although a few of these new communities are located outside of the north-west states of Acre and Amazonas, the organization of Cefluris founded by Sebastião Mota de Melo is overwhelmingly responsible for the expansion of Santo Daime beyond the confines of the Amazon region. The emergence and growth of Cefluris not only represented a geographical change to the traditional profile of Santo Daime, but also involved doctrinal transformation and demographic transition beyond the theological world view and socio-cultural make-up of the foundational community of Alto Santo.

Transition and expansion

Cefluris was founded by Sebastião Mota de Melo (1920–90) and began life
as a breakaway from Santo Daime's mother community of Alto Santo in
1974. Cefluris stands for the 'Raimundo Irineu Serra Eclectic Centre of the
Universal Flowing Light' (*Centro Eclético da Fluente Luz Universal Raimundo
Irineu Serra*) and represents both continuity with and movement beyond the
foundational repertoire bequeathed by Master Irineu. Mota de Melo was born
in the Upper Juruá Valley of the state of Amazonas and was a renowned
canoe maker and practising medium in the Spiritism of the Kardecist tradition
(see below). Having moved to Acre in 1957, Mota de Melo visited Master
Irineu in 1965 in search of a cure for a long-term liver condition. According
to Mota de Melo, Master Irineu suggested that he participate in the ritual
of Concentration scheduled for later that day. Subsequent to taking Daime
and feeling the onset of its psychotropic affects, Mota de Melo recounts the
following experience of being healed of his ailment.

> It was then that it happened. The world fell away and my body was below!
> My body was on the ground and I, now on the outside of my body, was
> looking down at it . . . Then, two men presented themselves; they were
> the two most beautiful things I had ever seen in my life! They shone like
> the sun [and] . . . were made only of fire . . . They brought an apparatus that
> seemed very heavy. Upon reaching me they took my entire skeleton in their
> hands and pushed on all of my bones . . . separating the rib from the spine,
> taking everything out; turning, cleaning and showing me everything . . .
> They turned over the remaining carcass and broke it into pieces, hanging
> everything on hooks. They pulled out the intestines and then took my
> liver, cutting and opening it before showing me three creatures [*bichos*],
> each the size of a beetle. It was their movement up and down which was
> causing all that badness. One of the men came close to me . . . and said:
> 'Here they are; it was these that were killing you. Do not fear, you won't
> die now.' After they returned my skeleton and organs, I awoke back in my
> body. Not knowing where the doctors [*doutores*] had gone or where I had
> been, I stood up and brushed the dust from my clothes. (Polari, 1998: 60)

The spiritual surgery of which Mota de Melo speaks was executed in the astral
realm (*no astral*) and understood to have been performed by supernatural
agents identified here as 'doctors'. Derived from indigenous traditions, the
removal of foreign bodies as a means to healing is a common motif occurring
in popular curative practices across the Amazon region. Raised in the Juruá
Valley, Mota de Melo was exposed to many of the popular practices previously
discussed and commonly expressed belief in the kinds of enchanted beings

and spiritual forces widespread within Amazonian culture (see Araújo, 2004: 44–8; Polari, 1999). Whereas the term 'doctor' is used by a number of popular curative traditions to refer to spirits who heal, Mota de Melo's training in the Spiritist repertoire of Kardecism is the most likely influence by which the preceding conversion narrative has been shaped. Given the formative impact and ongoing influence of Kardecist Spiritism upon the ritual repertoire of Santo Daime Cefluris, a relatively extended examination of its beliefs and practices is warranted.

Spiritist mediumship

The Spiritist tradition known as Kardecism was partly inspired by the events of 1848 in Hydesville, New York, which subsequently gave rise to the similarly named but otherwise discrete paradigm of Spiritualism (McGarry, 2008). Influenced by European esoteric traditions and indebted to the works of Franz Mesmer (1734–1815) and Emanuel Swedenborg (1688–1772), Hippolyte Rivail (1804–69) systematized his Spiritist world view along the lines of 'modern' scientific approaches (Hess, 1991: 72). Assuming the name under which Rivail (as Allan Kardec) published, Kardecism offered itself as the 'third codification' of spirit-inspired revelation for a modern era; in effect, superseding earlier 'first' (Judaism) and 'second' (Christianity) attempts (Cavalcanti, 1983: 21). Kardec's first and major work, *The Book of the Spirits* (1857), represents a codified distillation of moral teaching, philosophical instruction and 'scientific' insight gleaned from a range of eminent spirits (e.g. Socrates, John the Baptist and Benjamin Franklin) through his work with a number of Spiritist mediums. The information provided by these spirits was further elaborated in Kardec's other major works, *The Book of the Mediums* (1859) and *The Gospel According to Spiritism* (1864).

Akin to its esoteric counterparts, Kardecism was formed through an eclectic trawling of marginal, alternative and Eastern world views (e.g. Mesmerism, Swedenborgianism, Hermeticism, homeopathy and Hinduism) which were merged with moralized Christian teachings and selected insights from prevailing ethical, scientific and philosophical opinion. Employing the latest in rational argument and scientific method, Kardecism presented itself as an inclusive, universal alternative to purportedly outdated and divisive traditional religions (Santos, 2004: 62). As such, it offers a quasi-religious world view in which traditional beliefs (e.g. heaven, hell and miraculous intervention) are replaced with universal moral principles (e.g. love and charity) and scientific insight (e.g. cause and effect) conducive to the modern, liberal classes of urban-industrializing Europe. Kardec's emphasis upon spiritual freedom of choice, responsibility for prior actions and meritocratic advance through reincarnation is indicative of a modern conception of religiosity as a field of autonomous self-expression bounded by an ameliorative ethic of just deserts.

The Kardecist world view holds the universe to be composed of 'universal fluid' which is an all-encompassing energy force that alters its form to constitute the different components of the cosmos. At its densest, universal fluid forms the 'material plane', of which the earth is one among many habitable worlds. Framing these habitable, material worlds is the 'spiritual plane', comprising any number of sub-planes which are progressively less dense relative to their distance from the material plane. The relationship between these planes is regulated by a series of 'laws' (e.g. sympathy, karma and charity) which are known by spirits to different extents relative to their respective evolutionary status. Originally created equal and endowed with free will and intelligence, different spirits inhabit different spheres of the universe in accord with their respective evolutionary trajectory from the material to the ethereal. Generally speaking, three classes of spirit inhabit the Kardecist cosmos: 'pure spirits', whose evolutionary advance has placed them beyond the influence of matter; 'good spirits', whose evolutionary status allows for the predominance of the spiritual over the material; and 'imperfect spirits' whose relatively lowly evolutionary position reflects the predominance of matter over spirit. As all spirits are more or less good, Kardecism does not acknowledge the existence of evil spirits (Cavalcanti, 1983: 39).

Spirits evolve from the imperfect to the perfect by means of reincarnation. When in a disincarnate condition, every spirit is wholly aware of itself and its evolutionary status. In so being, each spirit is fully free and able to choose for itself an appropriate material world into which it is to be incarnated. Upon assuming corporality, the previously disincarnate spirit is now known (at least in this world) as the 'higher-self'. In choosing the material conditions into which it is to be born, each spirit has in view the range of trials and tribulations through which its probity is to be tested, prior misdemeanours expiated and sufficient merit earned to enable its evolutionary ascent up the cosmic hierarchy of existence. The better the life lived by an incarnate spirit in this world, for example, the broader its range of options in the spiritual plane when next choosing a (less material) world in which to undergo a subsequent set of tests. The worse the life lived, however, the less the options available and, consequently, the more delayed the ascent up the evolutionary ladder. Minimizing the inevitable disorientation brought on by incarnation and its potentially damaging consequences for the spirit's evolutionary well-being, Kardecism regards itself as a scientific philosophy oriented to aiding spirits (incarnate or otherwise) on their evolutionary ascent.

Kardecism arrived in 1850s' Brazil as an avant-garde pastime of the Francophile saloon culture of the educated elite. Quickly referred to as 'Spiritism' (*Espiritismo*), Kardecism was soon adopted by the popular classes and practised as a principally religious repertoire oriented to engaging the spirits for chiefly therapeutic ends (Stoll, 2002). In so being, Kardecism spread quickly across Brazil and was subsequently merged with or stood alongside other forms of cure-centred popular religious practice. As with aforementioned religious repertoires, Kardecist Spiritism is rarely encountered within popular Brazilian culture in a form free from addition, amendment or hybridism with other spiritual practices (Bastide, 1985: 433). Consequently, when Mota de Melo describes himself as working within the Kardecist tradition, this is best regarded as an overarching orientation including elements of belief and practice appropriated from a variety of aforementioned popular world views. Mota de Melo's mediumistic experiences began at the age of eight when he started hearing voices (Polari, 1998: 56). According to Spiritists, every person enjoys, by virtue of their composition, certain mediumistic qualities. For some people these qualities remain undeveloped but may be glimpsed at times through such things as dreams, sleep walking and extrasensory perception. For others, however, such mediumistic qualities are, by virtue of their evolutionary maturity, quite strong and allow for concerted interaction with the spiritual plane. With the appropriate mediumistic training and morally disciplined lifestyle, this latter type of person can function as a trained medium capable of not just communicating with occupants of the spiritual plane but actively receiving ('incorporating') them into the body in a controlled fashion. Such was the case with Mota de Melo who was trained in the Spiritist tradition by Master Oswaldo, a Kardecist medium originally from São Paulo (MacRae, 1992: 71). In addition to receiving the gift of cure (which, he claims, came unsought), Mota de Melo worked with a number of the most important supernatural entities of Brazilian Spiritism (e.g. Doctor Bezerra de Menezes and Professor Antônio Jorge).

As a medium in the Brazilian Spiritist tradition, two of the most significant elements of Mota de Melo's work with the spirits involved moral instruction and therapeutic practice. In respect of moral instruction, Mota de Melo served as a medium through which the spirits could offer morally uplifting and spiritually edifying insight that served to orient and assist incarnate spirits as they undergo the trials and tribulations of life on the material plane. While exhorting individuals to proper behaviour towards their fellow human beings, such instruction also involved entreaties to constant vigilance lest unbecoming thoughts and unwary actions open the subject to unwanted spiritual attention. On the material plane, every deed and thought produces its own range of vibrations, each of which reverberates across the spiritual plane. Lower thoughts and baser deeds produce inferior vibrations which penetrate only the denser, lower strata of the spiritual plane inhabited by less evolved spirits. In contrast, higher thoughts and deeds generate superior vibrations which penetrate higher spiritual strata occupied by purer spirits. Whereas the coarser vibrations generated by morally debased thoughts and actions leave an individual vulnerable to the unwanted attentions of lower spirits, morally upright thoughts and deeds create a purer, and thereby further reaching, range of vibrations through which cosmic merit (karma) is engendered. The moral instruction offered by the spirits and mediated by the likes of Mota de Melo is thereby a necessary adjunct to incarnate spirits optimizing their time on the earthly material plane.

Complementing the moral component of his Spiritist repertoire, Mota de Melo employed a therapeutic regime of diagnosis, prescription and cure attending to a broad range of issues connected with physical well-being and everyday concerns. In many cases, the therapeutic intervention provided by Spiritist mediums involves no more than the spirit-assisted diagnosis of a particular problem and subsequent prescription of homeopathic treatments (*receitas*) and/or lifestyle changes. When faced with more serious or prolonged issues, however, such mediumistic prescription is complemented by a more robust set of Spiritist techniques involving direct action upon the patient. A lesser form of therapeutic intervention involves use of the 'pass' (*passe*). Having diagnosed the energy field which surrounds each incarnate spirit as, for one reason or another, imbalanced, the medium recalibrates the sufferer's vital force through a series of hand gestures and arm movements around or upon the patient's body. In more serious cases, direct action upon the patient may also involve the kind of spiritual surgery described earlier or, what has perhaps become the primary signifier of popular Spiritism in Brazil, the practice of 'disobsession' (*desobsessão*). Disobsession comprises the removal of a lower or disoriented spirit which has, for a variety of reasons, erred into the body or latched onto the energy field of an already incarnate spirit. Severely disruptive to the effective functioning of the body – spirit relationship, the intrusion of an errant spirit results in a range of physical, emotional and psychological problems which will continue, if not worsen, until the intrusive spirit is ritually persuaded or coerced into returning to the spiritual plane (see Chapter 4).

A new branch sprouts forth

Cefluris tradition records Mota de Melo as reducing his mediumistic practices subsequent to his encounter with Daime and resulting alliance with Master Irineu and his community (Polari, 1999: 69). Regularly participating in *daimista* rituals at Alto Santo, Mota de Melo nevertheless continued to live on family lands to which he had moved with his wife and children upon arrival in Acre in the late 1950s. Known as 'Colony 5000', this family holding gradually became a focal point of communal ritual activity which not only used Daime as a religious sacrament but also manufactured it on site. While subsequent disputes between Alto Santo and Cefluris have given accounts of this time an explicitly ideological tenor, evidence points to Mota de Melo having secured permission from Master Irineu both to practise particular rituals and produce Daime; half of which was then sent to Alto Santo (see Goulart, 2004; MacRae, 1992). The subsequent breakdown in relations between Alto Santo and Colony 5000 occurred a few years after the death of Master Irineu and was occasioned by a bout of renewed political concern with the activities of Santo Daime. Already strained by Mota de Melo's earlier and unsuccessful claim to succeed Master Irineu as the spiritual head of Santo Daime, relations between the two communities came to the boil in 1973 over a dispute about the unfurling of the national flag during a ritual to which local authorities had been invited by way of allaying their concerns. Citing a recently received hymn ('I Raise this Flag'), Mota de Melo claimed to have received instructions from the astral plane to raise the Brazilian flag as a sign of Santo Daime's loyalty to the nation. Upon being refused by the then leader of Alto Santo, Leôncio Gomes, Mota de Melo severed relations with the mother community and, taking 70 per cent of the membership with him, subsequently established Colony 5000 as a fully independent *daimista* centre (Gregorim, 1991: 65–7).

The organization of Cefluris was formally instituted soon after the break with Alto Santo and remained headquartered at Colony 5000 for the next six years. During this time, Mota de Melo became known as Padrinho Sebastião; the term 'Godfather' (*Padrinho*) having both cultural and spiritual connotations. The ritual repertoire of Alto Santo was adopted almost entirely by Cefluris, with the esoteric emphases of Master Irineu's later years remaining in force.[11] As such, Padrinho Sebastião continued prior instructions about the nurturing of the higher-self through critical self-scrutiny and the spiritual transformation to which it gives rise (Polari, 1998: 123). At the same time, Padrinho Sebastião went on receiving the hymns which members of Cefluris would ultimately come to regard as a 'new gospel' for new times. Resuming the full suite of his mediumistic practices after the break with Alto Santo, Padrinho Sebastião recommenced his work with the spirits. Now, though, he augmented his mediation of the traditional entities of Brazilian Spiritism by also engaging the heavenly beings and supernatural agencies lauded by Santo Daime under the leadership of Master Irineu.

The move of Cefluris headquarters from Colony 5000 to the remoter lands of Rio do Ouro in the state of Amazonas was completed in 1980. Official narratives attribute the move both to the growing scarcity of the constituent plants of Daime brought on by local deforestation and the movement's rapid growth beyond the abilities of Colony 5000 to sustain it. No doubt important factors in informing the move, there is something to be said for the issues raised by the growing significance of cannabis to Cefluris as playing a part in its desire to decamp to an altogether less accessible, and thereby more private, location. One of the earliest 'southerners' (*sulistas*) to join Santo Daime, Lúcio Mortimer claims credit for introducing cannabis (*Cannabis sativa*) soon after his arrival in 1975 (2000: 115–38). Attracted by the psychoactive qualities of ayahuasca, Mortimer was part of a growing band of visitors drawn to Colony 5000 as part of their ongoing quest for alternative spiritual experiences. Known variously as 'backpackers' (*mochileiros*), 'long-hairs' (*cabeludos*) or 'hippies', a number of these middle-class 'wanderers' (*andarilhos*) stayed on to become prominent members of Cefluris (Goulart, 2004: 86). Upon confessing to Mota de Melo that he was not only smoking cannabis in private but that cannabis plants were being clandestinely cultivated in Colony 5000, Mortimer tells how Padrinho Sebastião responded by informing him of a dream he had experienced some years before. Within the dream, Padrinho Sebastião claimed, he was led by a heavenly being to a clearing in which cannabis was growing. Upon entering the clearing, the supernatural entity handed the Padrinho a cannabis plant and told him to use it as part of his curative repertoire (Mortimer, 2000: 123–8). To distinguish the therapeutic use of this 'sacred herb' (*erva sagrada*) from the worldly smoking of marijuana (*maconha*), it was to be called 'Holy Mary' (*Santa Maria*) and referred to as a 'sacrament'.[12]

The role and implications of cannabis (Holy Mary) consumption within the ritual repertoire and lifestyles of the contemporary *daimista* movement is addressed in later chapters. In respect of its earliest phase, however, such was the rapid growth of the importance of cannabis to Cefluris that its increasing consumption created a range of issues and tensions, not least in respect of the wider context of Rio Branco with which Santo Daime members regularly came into contact. Matters came to a head in October 1981 when a police raid upon Colony 5000 found the cultivation of cannabis to be widespread and its consumption extended across broad sectors of the community (MacRae, 1992: 74). Although the move of headquarters to Rio do Ouro had already been completed by this time, the invasion of Colony 5000 (still active as a Santo Daime centre) and the resulting legal indictments of Mota de Melo and other key members served to reinforce the Padrinho's increasing desire to found a religious community remote from the mundane preoccupations of the material plane. At the time more than two days' journey from the city of Rio Branco, the isolated former rubber plantation of Rio do Ouro appeared to meet these needs.

Umbanda

Cefluris was headquartered at Rio do Ouro for three years (1980–3), during which time the community of less than 200 *daimistas* sustained itself chiefly through tapping remaining rubber reserves, arable and livestock farming and timber production. In respect of the movement's ritual repertoire, the most significant development during this period was the construction of the 'Star House' (*Casa de Estrela*) within which ceremonies influenced by the Afro-Brazilian religion of Umbanda took place. The founding of Umbanda is popularly attributed to practising Spiritist Zélio de Moraes (d. 1975) who received a series of visitations during a prolonged illness in 1920s' Rio de Janeiro. Such visitations were contentious, however, in that some of the spirits engaged by Moraes were of an Afro-Brazilian and indigenous origin and consequently regarded by Spiritism as of lowly evolutionary status and thereby lacking in ritual utility. Rebuffed by fellow Spiritists, the story goes, Moraes was subsequently charged by the spirits of a Jesuit priest and an indigenous chief to found an authentically Brazilian religion that might better meet the needs and aspirations of a modern nation. To be called 'Umbanda', this authentically Brazilian religion was to reflect the modern-day fusion of the nation's three founding races: the indigenous peoples, white Europeans and black Africans. While the historical veracity of this founding myth is questionable, its overall tenor contains a number of relevant themes. First, Umbanda emerged in Brazil at a time of self-conscious nation-building during which the themes of national identity, modernization and racial harmony were linked through their combined political promotion. Second, Umbanda was formed in the centre-south of Brazil, subsequently spreading to other regions as they underwent the urban-industrializing processes of government-orchestrated 'modernization'. Third, Umbanda developed through the fusion of Spiritist and Afro-Brazilian religiosity, each of which contained elements of popular Catholic and esoteric origin (Bastide, 2001; Giumbelli, 2002).[13]

The Umbanda world view situates the earth and its inhabitants between higher and lower spiritual planes. Occupied by a remote creator god, the higher spiritual plane is subdivided a number of times, each tier of which is populated by a complex assortment of lesser spirits including popular Catholic saints, Afro-Brazilian deities and figures from everyday life and the popular cultural imaginary. By virtue of their proximity to the material plane of the earth, the most ritually active of these spirits are the *caboclos* (Amerindians) and *pretos velhos* (black slaves) whose work is complemented by numerous other entities stretching from 'cowboys', 'street people' and 'children' to 'gypsies', 'sailors', 'Turks' and 'European aristocrats'. Understood as an act of charity performed to ascend (*evoluir*) the spiritual hierarchy, Umbanda spirits temporarily possess trained mediums to offer healing, insight and advice to supplicants in need of cure, counselling or some form of supernatural intervention. As with Spiritism, natural causation and medicinal remedies play a part. By and large, though, causes and solutions are most commonly attributed to the supernatural realm, with the occupants of the spiritual underworld (e.g. *Exu*) or the spirits of recently deceased human beings (*eguns*) commonly blamed for things that go wrong. Eager to visit the material world to enjoy its pleasures or cause mischief and suffering, inferior spirits of the lower realms may be attracted to individuals on account of their bad thoughts and misdemeanours or, as is common in many kinds of popular religiosity in Brazil, summoned by third parties seeking to cause trouble for the individual targeted. As with Spiritism, problems caused by the spirits of recently deceased human beings are generally attributed to their post-mortem disorientation or reluctance to move on from their former life. Given the range of causes and degrees of spirit infestation by 'obsessor' or 'suffering' spirits, its treatment is varied. In contrast to Spiritism, however, the heavily therapeutized ritual repertoire of Umbanda employs a much greater engagement with inferior and suffering spirits and does so through a more pronounced reliance upon mediumistic possession (D. D. Brown, 1994).

The Star House constructed at Rio do Ouro owed its existence to events which occurred during the final years of Cefluris being headquartered at Colony 5000. In 1977, Padrinho Sebastião allowed the practising Umbanda medium Jose Lito, known commonly as Ceará, both to stay at Colony 5000 and to practise rituals in which Mota de Melo and many of his community participated (Junior, 2007). As a medium, Ceará incorporated a number of spirit-guides, the most important of which were the *caboclo* spirits Tranca Rua and Ogum Beira Mar. Over time, the consumption of Daime was included within these rituals which now involved its administration to inferior and suffering spirits by way of the medium through whom these spirits were incorporating (see Chapter 4). According to official Cefluris accounts, Tranca Rua and Ogum Beira Mar were eventually converted to Santo Daime as part of a spiritual battle of wills between Padrinho Sebastião and the subsequently vanquished Ceará. Now indoctrinated into the *daimista* way and incorporated by Mota de Melo, Tranca Rua ordered the construction of a Star House so that the application of Daime to the spirits of Umbanda might continue in the embryonic rituals then known as 'star works' (*trabalhos de estrela*) (Polari, 1999: 114–17). Such works, however, were not long practised at Rio do Ouro, for the entire community was forced to move when its occupation of the former rubber plantation was disputed by an industrial corporation claiming ownership of the land. The hardships entailed by uprooting the whole community and starting afresh in a new location were thereby repeated in 1983 as Rio do Ouro was abandoned and Cefluris moved 150 kilometres to what eventually became the village of Mapiá. Traditionally referred to as *Céu do Mapiá* (Heaven of Mapiá), this location remains the organizational headquarters and spiritual home of Santo Daime Cefluris.[14]

Mapiá is the name of a tributary which branches from the river Purus in the state of Amazonas. Today, Mapiá village is approximately half a day's journey by motorboat downriver from the border town of Boca do Acre; itself eight hours in the dry season by car from Rio Branco, the capital of Acre.[15] At the time of its founding, the journey from Rio Branco to Mapiá took little less than a week, with the final leg (from Boca do Acre) made by canoe and taking three days to complete. Established in 1983 by a vanguard of 70, Mapiá village today has about 1,000 permanent residents, with a greater number again spread along the banks of the tributary from which the village takes its name (Arruda et al., 2006: 30). These numbers are intermittently swollen in festival periods by an influx of Brazilian and international *daimistas*. While many are repeat visitors, a good number of those attending the festivals at Mapiá do so as pilgrims fulfilling what they regard as a spiritual obligation to undertake at least one visit to the mother community and all that it entails by way of personal sacrifice and hardship. By the time of my visit to Mapiá in 2007, a money economy had been in existence for just over a decade and a dirt road had recently been driven through to the village from the point near which the Mapiá tributary meets the river Purus.

Near where I lodged in Mapiá stands a building whose architectural style reflects that of the Star House originally constructed at Rio do Ouro. In Mapiá, however, this building is now known as the 'Little Star House' (*Casa de Estrelinha*) to distinguish it from the main church (*igreja*) building, the starred shape of which is responsible for its popular designation as the Star House (*Casa de Estrela*). While potentially confusing to the uninitiated, the fact that the main church building was constructed in the shape of a star is highly indicative of the extent to which Umbanda had impacted Cefluris by the time of its design and commencement in 1987. By this time, and starting in 1984, Padrinho Sebastião had made a number of visits to the centre-south of Brazil during which he participated in rituals explicitly designed to cement the place of Umbanda belief and practice within the now expanding Santo Daime movement. Indeed, such was the desire to promote the relationship of Santo Daime with Umbanda that the term 'Umbandaime' was coined by those eager to further this association (Junior, 2007: 16).

Heading south

Over the course of the final few years of his life, Padrinho Sebastião participated in a number of ceremonies in central-south Brazil within which Umbanda practitioners and Santo Daime members shared elements of their respective ritual repertoires. While Mota de Melo's involvement in these rituals clearly reflected a sincere interest in Umbanda belief and practice, his search for a cure for the illness which would eventually kill him may also have served as a motive. As with other accounts of this period, Guimarães' informative treatment identifies the Umbanda medium known popularly as 'Baixinha' as an influential source of practical and theological input. She also identifies the increasingly important role played by members of the urban middle classes of Rio de Janeiro and São Paulo who had recently converted to or taken an interest in Santo Daime (1992: 34). Noted earlier in respect of the ritual adoption of cannabis, from the mid-1970s, Santo Daime became an increasing source of interest to middle-class participants in the alternative religious scene. Having converted to Santo Daime after spending varied amounts of time living among the Cefluris community, some of these individuals returned to the central-south region to found communities of their own. Founded in 1985 by the writer and former political activist Alex Polari de Alverga, the community of *Céu da Montanha* (Heaven of the Mountain) was heavily involved in orchestrating the earliest ritual exchanges between the Umbanda medium Baixinha and Padrinho Sebastião. Indeed, it was during one of these joint rituals that the *caboclo* spirit Tupinambá (incorporated by Baixinha) announced both his alliance with Santo Daime and desire to work with Padrinho Sebastião (Junior, 2007: 24).[16]

By the time of Padrinho Sebastião's death on 20 January 1990 there were approximately ten *daimista* communities outside of the Amazon region. The oldest of these was *Céu do Mar* (Heaven of the Sea) which was founded in the city of Rio de Janeiro in 1982 by the daughter and son-in-law of Padrinho Sebastião. Located on the border with São Paulo and Minas Gerais, the aforementioned community of *Céu da Montanha* was founded in the state of Rio de Janeiro in 1985. Other noteworthy communities founded around this time were, for example, *Rainha do Mar* (Queen of the Sea, Rio de Janeiro), *Flor das Águas* (Flower of the Waters, São Paulo), *Céu do Patriarca* (Heaven of the Patriarch, Florianópolis) and *Céu do Planalto* (Heaven of the Planalto, Brasília).[17] Indicative of the overwhelming majority of those drawn to Santo Daime during and after this time, the founders of these new communities were members of the urban-industrial middle classes. Furthermore, a significant number of these *daimista* pioneers had prior and long-standing experience of participating in non-mainstream religions and alternative spiritualities. Taking *Céu do Mapiá* (or an idealized version thereof) as their template, many of Santo Daime's new communities were founded in rural locations intentionally remote from major urban centres. In addition to furnishing a sought-after proximity to nature and the spiritual forces inherent to it, these isolated locations guaranteed much by way of privacy for a ritual repertoire still prone to the unwanted attentions of state agencies. Founded as alternative communities intended not just to live in but to live off nature, some of the earliest settlements attempted to forge a self-sustaining and cooperative lifestyle conducive to the promotion of simplicity and communalism. Over time, however, the issues engendered by a lack of skills, financial insecurity and lifestyle hardships led to the abandonment of nascent experiments with subsistence lifestyles. As one informant put it after recounting the early abortive experiments of his south-Brazilian community, 'this type of stuff was not in our blood . . . I mean, I'm an administrator; it's what I do, what I'm good at'.

Today, some of the older communities outside of the Amazon area continue on a quasi-cooperative basis, with individual households and communal arrangements supported through a mixture of salaried incomes, profits from small-scale artisan industries, government subsidies of land management schemes, inherited wealth and private investments. This is generally not the case for younger groups, the overwhelming bulk of whose membership (while economically secure by Brazilian standards) cannot afford to adopt the lifestyles of some of their older counterparts. Furthermore, and although a number of contemporary communities continue to exist in remote locations, urban spread, movement expansion and the desire to enhance accessibility for those travelling to *daimista* rituals have resulted in a greater willingness to locate on the peripheries of or in rural pockets within Brazil's increasingly sprawling conurbations. Consequently, whereas most Santo Daime rituals in Brazil continue to occur in relatively private rural locations, the majority of Brazilian *daimistas* undertake their ceremonial practice at a distance from where they live and work. Effected through its spread beyond the Amazon region, Santo Daime's demographic shift to an increasingly urban-professional profile was thereby complemented by the movement's transition from a principally static communal base to a predominantly mobile gathering of ritual practitioners. With the gathered community model forming the basis of almost every group founded outside of Brazil, Santo Daime's international expansion consequently involves its progressive congregationalization.

Organizational transformation

The organizational implications of Santo Daime's movement beyond its Amazonian base were the subject of much discussion at the first national gathering of CeflUris churches at *Céu do Mapiá* in 1989. Although officially established soon after the break with Alto Santo, Cefluris was reconstituted in 1989 as a legal entity of national standing and international aspirations. As the movement continued to grow both at home and abroad, further changes to institutional statutes and organizational structures ensued over subsequent years. The most significant of these changes was perhaps the formal separation (at the tenth national gathering in 1998) of the 'religious and doctrinal' responsibilities of Cefluris from its institutional concerns with the 'social, economic, ecological and cultural organization of its people'. The first set of responsibilities is now executed by the formal legal entity of the 'Church of the Eclectic Cult of the Universal Flowing Light' (Iceflu – *Igreja do Culto Eclético da Fluente Luz Universal*), while the second falls to the

'Institute of Environmental Development' (IDA – *Instituto de Desenvolvimento Ambiental*). Although legally separate, the management of both entities is overseen by virtually the same group of people, headed by the spiritual leader of Santo Daime Cefluris, Padrinho Alfredo Gregório de Melo, and his chief administrative counsel, Padrinho Alex Polari de Alverga (www.santodaime. org.br; www.idaCefluris.org.br).[18]

The establishment of IDA-Cefluris was intended to optimize organizational access to financial resources and professional expertise progressively being channelled to the Amazon region on the back of increasing domestic concerns and international preoccupations with raising local living standards and promoting environmental preservation. Organizationally focused upon the upper Amazon region, IDA-Cefluris is principally concerned with sustaining the population and surroundings of the village of Mapiá. Made under the institutional auspices of Iceflu, organizational developments within the 'spiritual and doctrinal' mission of Santo Daime respond to a number of dynamics both internal and external to the movement. In respect of external dynamics, a significant impetus to the formalization of institutional structures has been the need to address state concerns to monitor and regulate the socio-political implications of the ongoing expansion of ritual ayahuasca consumption beyond its traditional geographical range. Although regional authorities had expressed concern or acted against the ritual consumption of ayahuasca in the decades subsequent to its emergence among the non-indigenous population, it was not until the 1960s that the federal government of Brazil turned its attention to this matter (Araújo, 1999: 54). An official state investigation, however, would not be instigated until the mid-1980s when, in response to political lobbying, the government listed the ingredients of ayahuasca (i.e. *Banisteriopsis caapi* and *Psychotria viridis*) on its register of proscribed narcotics. Two years after their proscription, though, the 1987 report commissioned by the 'Federal Narcotics Council' (Confen – *Conselho Federal de Entorpecentes*) recommended that these ingredients be removed from the list of banned substances (MacRae, 1992: 79–83).

There have over the years been a series of further investigations and reports about the ritual consumption of ayahuasca in Brazil, the most recent of which (at the time of writing) was issued in January 2010 by Confen's successor, the 'National Council on Drug Policies' (Conad – *Conselho Nacional de Políticas sobre Drogas*). As with all prior reports since the Confen recommendation of 1987, the most recent official pronouncement affirms the continued legality of ritual ayahuasca consumption in Brazil. Likewise in line with previous statements on the subject (see Labate, 2004: 97), the Conad report makes a number of stipulations in respect of the productive processes, distributive mechanisms and organizational arrangements which make possible and frame the ritual consumption of ayahuasca. As well as highlighting the uncertain legal status of the recommendations made by the 2010 Conad report, Labate records their concern with inhibiting ayahuasca consumption's commercialization (e.g. advertising and selling), ensuring its dissociation from illicit drugs, regulating its environmental impact and enforcing its explicit association with religious use in formal ritual contexts. The report also suggests that first-time users be appropriately screened and prepared, religious groups form registered legal entities and scientific investigation into the therapeutic potential of ayahuasca be undertaken (2011: 301). Faced with reports and expectations such as these, the development of formal institutional structures and coherent organizational processes was essential to the possibility of Cefluris demonstrating sufficient compliance with state regulation of ritual ayahuasca consumption.[19]

Engendered also by its increasing geographical spread, Cefluris today has the kind of bureaucratic organs (e.g. Administrative, Doctrinal and Financial Councils) and representative mechanisms (e.g. Regional, National and International Assemblies) found in most traditional and mainstream religions. Exemplified by the 'Higher Doctrinal Council' (CSD – *Conselho Superior Doutrinário*), these institutional structures are helping manage the operational and religious issues implicated in the movement's continuing and rapid expansion across Brazil and throughout the urban-industrialized world. The CSD undertakes its work, for example, with an eye to addressing potential issues and actual concerns raised by Santo Daime's interface with external bodies and organs of state. In so doing, the CSD promulgates norms and directives intended to ensure institutional compliance with the regulatory demands and expectations in respect of the ritual consumption of ayahuasca and all matters pertaining immediately to it. Such matters include, for example, regulating the production and distribution of Daime, the screening and preparation of first-time attendees of *daimista* rituals and the ceremonial framing of ayahuasca consumption. The CSD also works to promote repertorial coherence by promoting such things as the standardization of official hymnals, harmonization of ritual form and content and shared practices in respect of, for example, the training of spirit mediums (see Chapter 4). In addition, the CSD looks to maintain organizational cohesion by addressing the challenges and tensions raised by different communities and interest groups across the now global Cefluris movement.

Internationalization

In many respects, the international expansion of Cefluris has generated the same kinds of organizational challenges as those engendered by its initial movement beyond the Amazon region. Importantly, though, almost all of the countries to which Santo Daime has spread do not have the socio-cultural conventions which facilitate Brazil's political and legal tolerance of ritual ayahuasca consumption. Noted above, DMT is the most active psychotropic ingredient of the ayahuasca brew produced and consumed as 'Daime' by the Santo Daime religion. DMT, however, was designated a 'controlled' substance by the 1971 United Nations' *Convention on Psychotropic Substances* (Tupper, 2009). Consequently, DMT is defined as a Class 1 (or Class A) narcotic by national jurisdictions across the world who thereby treat it in the same manner as they do cocaine or heroin. In view of the fact that its religious sacrament contains what many countries regard as a dangerous narcotic, the international expansion of Cefluris has been fraught with difficulties.

The international expansion of Cefluris was by no means the only medium through which the ritual consumption of ayahuasca spread to other parts of the world. Facilitated by the cultural flows of late-modern globalization and influenced by writings such as the aforementioned work by Harner (1972), ayahuasca was being consumed by alternative practitioners and non-mainstream religionists as part of a broader new-age psychedelic regime by the mid-1970s. Whether already using ayahuasca or not, the desire of a number of otherwise independent alternative practitioners to augment their existing ritual repertoires with practices informed by the *daimista* paradigm furnished one of the earliest platforms upon which Cefluris expanded beyond its native South American context. Having recently entered the non-mainstream religious scene of the Brazilian middle classes, the alternative networks made available were subsequently mobilized in the late 1980s as the means through which (urban-professional) Cefluris representatives were invited abroad to conduct formal *daimista* rituals and therapeutic ayahuasca workshops. Even before the death of Padrinho Sebastião in 1990, *daimista*-led rituals were practised as early as 1987 in Argentina and the United States and in 1989 in Belgium and Spain.[20] The relationships established through these early rituals and the subsequent visits to Brazil by those involved in them later gave rise to the founding of some of the most important Santo Daime churches in Europe and North America.

The internationalization of Santo Daime through existing ayahuasca and alternative networks was further aided by the migration of Cefluris members to other parts of the world and an increasing succession of foreign visitations made by groups (*comitivas*) of Brazilian *daimistas* intended both to consolidate existing growth and sow the seeds of future organizational expansion. Combined with those drawn to Santo Daime on the back of its gradually expanding profile, these factors ensured the relatively rapid creation by the late 1990s of fledgling groups (known as 'nuclei' or 'points') and full-blown churches both across the United States and in a significant number of

European capitals and urban-industrial centres (Balzer, 2004; Groisman, 2004; Labate 2004: 73). Overwhelmingly represented by communities affiliated to Cefluris, Santo Daime today has an organizational presence throughout South and North America, in most of the countries of Western Europe (and some to the east), in parts of the Middle East, South Africa, and in some of the more industrialized countries of Australasia (e.g. Australia, Japan and New Zealand). Unlike Brazil, however, the presence of Santo Daime in most of these contexts manifests through an extremely low, if not clandestine profile. Although some *daimistas* see the low profile of their religion as something in keeping with its non-mainstream, alternative ethos (see A. Dawson, 2010: 180), for most it is regarded as an act of necessity born of the unwanted attentions of state authorities.[21]

The first recorded arrests relating to Santo Daime outside of Brazil occurred in France, Holland and the United States, all in 1999, and Spain in 2000. While the Spanish arrest was carried out at an airport in respect of undeclared attempts to import ayahuasca, the other three sets of arrests occurred in relation to the undertaking of ritual practices involving the *daimista* sacrament. Judicial actions and appeal processes following these arrests have since resulted in the legalization of Santo Daime's ritual use of ayahuasca in Holland and the US state of Oregon (Haber, 2011; van den Plas, 2011). The juridical situation in Spain, however, remains relatively less well defined (López-Pavillard and de las Casas, 2011). Paralleling the international spread of Cefluris, the decade following these first four sets of arrests has seen an increasing number of police actions and, at least in the northern hemisphere, subsequent legal battles. At the time of writing, police have recently raided church members in France and Portugal, the trial of two Santo Daime leaders in the United Kingdom is currently under way and an appeal against the criminal conviction of a church leader in Ireland is being processed. Prior state actions in France and Germany have resulted in the unequivocal criminalizing of Santo Daime's use of ayahuasca, while similar processes in Italy, although not resulting in full legalization, have nevertheless concluded with the acquittal of those charged with criminal offences (Bourgogne, 2011; Menozzi, 2011; Rhode and Sander, 2011). In view of these developments, the legal and policy ramifications of Santo Daime's continuing global spread are being carefully watched by scholars concerned with the internationalization of ayahuasca consumption in both its ritual and therapeutic modes. In tandem with the legal cases involving the Union of the Plant (UDV), the court actions and ensuing public debates provoked by Santo Daime's internationalizing profile promise further developments in respect not only of the ritual consumption of ayahuasca but also its manufacture and distribution beyond Brazil (see Labate 2005; Labate and Feeney, 2012; Tupper, 2008, 2009; Tupper and Labate, 2012).

Institutional diversification

I have elsewhere compared the religious world view of Cefluris to a palimpsest, the earlier usage of which, though overwritten by subsequent writings, nevertheless remains visible to the trained eye (A. Dawson, 2012a). The Cefluris repertoire has been formed through the successive appropriation of beliefs and practices drawn from a broad range of socio-cultural contexts, religious traditions, spiritual paradigms and non-mainstream world views. Before its full-blown integration within the alternative religious spectrum of the urban-industrial middle classes, the Cefluris repertoire comprised an amalgam of ritual and theological elements drawn from Afro-Amazonian, popular Catholic, esoteric, Spiritist and Umbanda paradigms. The inclusion of the word 'eclectic' within the name of Cefluris was intended by Sebastião Mota de Melo to signal an organizational willingness not just to acknowledge the validity of a broad range of beliefs and practices but to be actively disposed, where fitting, to their incorporation within the ritual repertoire of Santo Daime. On the one hand, the eclecticism of Cefluris reflects the pragmatic concerns and hybridizing dynamics of aforementioned modes of popular religiosity in which the theological niceties of truth and falsity are relativized by an altogether more pragmatic preoccupation with religious utility and ritual efficacy. Born of this characteristic pragmatism, popular Brazilian religiosity tends to a hybridizing inclusiveness rather than a doctrinaire exclusivity. On the other, the openness of Cefluris to entertain beliefs and practices not traditionally part of its repertoire expresses the foundational influences of the esoteric and Spiritist paradigms; influences embodied by another part of the Cefluris name (viz. 'Universal Flowing Light'). Inherent within these typically modern traditions is a relativizing universalism in which otherwise discrete beliefs and practices are viewed as historically contingent and thereby partial refractions of an all-inclusive cosmic Whole (see Chapter 3). Although embedded in varied, if not contrasting, world views and ritual contexts, the beliefs and practices of different spiritual traditions are regarded as complementary in their underlying nature and, as such, unproblematically transposable from one religious repertoire to another. Imbued with this characteristic holism, esoteric and Spiritist traditions tend to inclusive expropriation rather than exclusive demarcation. From its very beginnings, then, Cefluris has been marked by an inclination not simply to tolerate the beliefs and practices of others but to appropriate them within a holistic world view characterized by hybridism and fluidity.

Importantly, however, the orchestrating principles by which the amalgamation of different influences has been directed have traditionally reflected the everyday life experiences of a typically mixed-race, peasant (*caboclo*) culture and its subsistence lifestyle. This is no longer the case. Begun gradually after the arrival of the first young 'backpackers' from central-south Brazil, the orchestrating principles of the Santo Daime community have since been radically reshaped thanks to the expansion and subsequent internationalization of Cefluris. As well as its increasing integration within the alternative religious scene both in and beyond Brazil, Santo Daime has come under the growing influence of an urban-professional constituency drawn from the 'new middle class' spawned by late-modern society in the latter part of the twentieth century (see Chapter 5). The change in Santo Daime's geographical profile has thereby been accompanied by the transformation of its demographic profile. The implications of this transformation are widespread and, indeed, the vast majority of the pages that follow are taken up with its explication. A number of introductory points are, though, well worth making here.

First, the expansion of Cefluris beyond its regional homeland has involved the ongoing pluralization of the *daimista* world view through its exposure to an almost vertiginous assortment of beliefs and practices most closely associated with urban-professional occupants of the alternative and non-mainstream religious scene. While many of those joining Santo Daime from the urban middle classes have experienced some form of tangential or committed involvement with mainstream traditional religions (not least Christianity), the most significant influences comprise a miscellany of beliefs and practices culled from the alternative scene. In no particular order of priority, many of those encountered during fieldwork had prior or continuing associations with Western esoteric traditions (e.g. Anthroposophy, Rosicrucianism, Spiritism, Spiritualism and Theosophy), new-age repertoires (e.g. Druidism, Kabbalah, neo-shamanism, paganism and Wicca), self-realization systems (e.g. the Human Potential Movement) and modern Eastern paradigms such as the International Society for Krishna Consciousness (ISKCON), Japanese new religions (e.g. Church of World Messianity and Soka Gakkai), Osho-Rajneesh movement, Sathya Sai Baba organization and Transcendental Meditation. Furthermore, and in addition to the supernatural agents of traditional religious repertoires, many expressed belief in both a miscellany of spirits and mystical forces indigenous to various regions of the globe and a range of preternatural entities such as Atlanteans, elves, extraterrestrials and fairies.

Such associations and beliefs are complemented by the practice of corporal regimes such as bio-dance, meditation (e.g. Transcendental and Zen), tai chi and yoga (e.g. bhakti and kundalini) and use of divinatory techniques involving, for example, astrology, crystals, I-Ching, numerology, palm-reading, runes, shells and tarot cards. In the same vein, middle-class members of Santo Daime champion a range of therapeutic treatments, among the most popular of which are acupuncture, bio-energy harmonization, chakra realignment, colour therapy, cranial-sacral integration, homeopathy, hypnosis, iridology,

Jungian psychodynamics, massage (e.g. ayurvedic, reiki and shiatsu) and past-life regression. Furthermore, and in addition to the ritual consumption of ayahuasca, a significant portion of the *daimista* community uses a variety of natural substances including, for example, cannabis, psychedelic mushrooms, peyote and San Pedro cacti, iboga (psychoactive tree bark), kambô (poison frog secretion), mapacho (unprocessed Amazonian tobacco which is smoked or taken as snuff) and wild plant extracts of a more or less psychotropic kind.

Treated at length in subsequent chapters, the contemporary *daimista* repertoire is increasingly orchestrated by a range of principles and dynamics which directly reflect the life experiences, values and beliefs of the urban-professional constituency now dominant across the movement. By way of anticipating what follows, these orchestrating principles comprise: the *subjectivized* valorization of the individual as the ultimate arbiter of religious authority and the primary agent of spiritual self-transformation; an *instrumental* (i.e. strategic and reflexive) religiosity oriented to the goal of absolute self-realization; a *holistic* world view which both grounds the individual self in an overarching cosmic Whole and relativizes religious belief systems as contingent expressions of otherwise universal truths; an *aestheticized* demeanour characterized by strong experiential preoccupations manifest through inward self-exploration and outer self-expression; a *meritocratic-egalitarianism* which is expectant of rewards for efforts expended and qualifies traditional hierarchical structures; and a *this-worldly* ethos which looks for the benefits of spiritual transformation as much in the here and now of this life as in the there and then of any future incarnation. Demonstrated in the following chapters, these now dominant characteristics of the contemporary *daimista* repertoire combine to induce the progressive transformation of received practices and established beliefs at the heart of Santo Daime tradition.

Second, and in common with many institutions undergoing rapid and relatively large-scale expansion, Cefluris organizational structures have been subject to a typically centrifugal dynamic whereby executive power and authority are incrementally dispersed outwards from the traditional centre of operations. Certainly, the family and close associates of Padrinho Sebastião, *Céu do Mapiá* and the broader Amazonian matrix continue to exert considerable influence across the Cefluris network. In addition to the supply of Daime and formal institutional support given to those in need, the veneration of 'authentic' Amazonian spirituality personified by the leadership of Cefluris plays a significant part in continuing to uphold their status and authority throughout the now global Santo Daime community. At the same time, however, the development of local community structures and regional networks in various parts of the world is increasingly giving rise to organizational arrangements which, of necessity, have their own executive powers and alternate authorities. The power and authority traditionally concentrated in the administrative and spiritual heart of Cefluris is thereby being progressively dispersed and, in effect, weakened in its ability to influence the shape and direction of the international *daimista* movement and its religious repertoire. The movement's traversing of successive geographic and socio-cultural domains is also engendering a diverse constituency with variegated experiences, needs and aspirations which find voice and direction in progressively heterogeneous modes of local expression and regional organization. While outright conflict between the institutional centre and local bodies remains relatively rare, the formation of regional networks nevertheless constitutes an organizational counterpoint to inherited structures of administrative power.

The mode of authority still very much dominant across Cefluris is what sociologists (following Max Weber) tend to label 'charismatic'. In contrast with other forms of authority (e.g. 'rational-legal' and 'traditional'), charismatic authority is intimately connected with the personality and status of an individual regarded by his or her followers as being of an extraordinary quality and exceptional nature (Weber, 1991b: 245–52). Exemplified within Santo Daime by its founder Master Irineu, the authority wielded by Padrinho Sebastião was likewise of a charismatic kind. Although by no means of the same degree, charismatic modes of authority continue to be employed by the contemporary leadership of the movement and those who have founded or now lead Cefluris communities of whatever age, size or status. The personalized form through which charismatic authority manifests is soon evidenced in conversation with *daimistas* from all parts of the world. Santo Daime members, for example, frequently recount their most meaningful encounter with Daime or entrance into membership by referencing key persons, locations and dates (usually significant anniversaries connected with *daimista* dignitaries) by whom, where and when the sacrament was served or their membership star was awarded. In the same vein, spending time at Mapiá and receiving Daime from the hands of Cefluris leaders played an important part in establishing my bona fides with *daimistas* and facilitating access to communities and their members.

Combined with the institutional youthfulness of Cefluris and the ongoing centrifugal dispersal of executive power and status, the prevalence of charismatic modes of authority within Santo Daime facilitates a decentralized style of leadership in which the local community and its leaders enjoy a considerably broad scope of self-determination. The directive latitude enjoyed by the local leadership thereby allows the development of relatively diverse community identities as each individual leader impresses a range of discourse and practice which, at points, reflects idiosyncratic predilections as much as broader organizational expectations. Indeed, at the same time in which some local leaders are underlining their charismatic authority by stressing their connections with the Cefluris leadership (often reinforced by regular visits to Brazil), they are modifying the *daimista* repertoire in ways similar to, if not as far reaching as, those visited by Padrinho Sebastião upon the heritage of Master Irineu. Furthermore, and while for many members of Cefluris repertorial evolution is by no means necessarily bad, the relative newness of groups often entails an absence of those able to distinguish between *daimista* discourse and practice rooted in received traditions and repertorial modifications instigated at a local level.

Third, the diversification of the *daimista* repertoire is further reinforced by the traditional operation within Cefluris of what I have elsewhere termed a 'minimal orthodoxy' (A. Dawson, 2007: 94). Minimal orthodoxy contrasts with maximal orthodoxy which demands conformity in all matters of official belief and practice across an entire institution. The minimal orthodoxy operated by Cefluris, however, requires the conformity of its communities only in respect of particular components of its ritual repertoire. As Chapter 2 notes, such components include, for example, calendrical schedules, particular ritual content and certain ceremonial form. In effect, as long as affiliated groups meet designated requirements relating to these components they are, within reason, free not only to modify existing rites but also to celebrate beliefs and practices totally unconnected with the traditional *daimista* repertoire. Combined with the diversifying ramifications of rapid pluralization, centrifugal power flow and charismatic self-determination, the threshold dynamics of minimal orthodoxy further catalyse the ongoing variegation of the Santo Daime movement.

In the earliest years of the movement, personal devotion to Padrinho Sebastião and the Amazonian heritage, the mutual dependence of fledgling communities and the relative youthfulness and modest size of the Cefluris network combined to limit the extent of both organizational diversification and repertorial variegation. As each of these factors is eroded or cedes precedence to other influences, traditional constraints upon the modification of organizational processes and the *daimista* ritual repertoire are incrementally diminished. Certainly, within the overwhelming majority of Santo Daime communities, the beliefs and rituals inherited from Padrinho Sebastião furnish a much revered template by which local discourse and practice are orchestrated. Contemporary commitment to and passion for 'authentic' beliefs and practices bequeathed by prior generations is beyond question. However, while some communities pride themselves on their level of adherence to the ritual repertoire espoused by the Cefluris leadership, others regard it as by no means definitive; preferring instead to view the alterations and additions they make as legitimate variations on the *daimista* theme. Whereas some communities, for example, are shaped by a variable mixture of esoteric and Spiritist themes, others are inspired by a fluid assortment of Afro-Brazilian influences. At the same time, the ritual repertoires of some communities are oriented by indigenous shamanic motifs, while others articulate a range of explicitly new-age preoccupations or demonstrate a distinctly autochthonous emphasis upon regional themes native to their own locale. The contemporary ritual repertoire of Cefluris is thereby a progressively variegated one.

The ongoing variegation of the *daimista* repertoire is, though, neither blind nor random. Intimately associated with a now dominant urban-professional constituency, the progressive transformation of the Santo Daime movement and its world view reflects a range of processes and dynamics which owe far more to the contemporary landscape of late-modern urban-industrial society than they do to the Amazonian context in which the *daimista* repertoire was first forged. While urban-professional *daimistas* continue to articulate a deep-seated respect for the structures, beliefs and practices inherited from the Amazonian context, they view and occupy the world in ways which are markedly different than those of their *caboclo* counterparts. Imbued with values, concerns and aspirations not straightforwardly compatible with established traditions, the now dominant urban-professional constituency is, albeit at many points unintentionally, incrementally transforming Santo Daime in a manner which renders it increasingly conducive to meeting the needs and expectations associated with its typically late-modern, urban-industrial existence. As real as the commitment and loyalty of contemporary *daimistas* to established beliefs and practices, the ongoing transformation of Santo Daime's ritual repertoire and religious world view is no less significant.

2

The *daimista* ritual repertoire: Disciplinary regime and dynamic field of force

The stocky young man was no more than 25 years old, though his physical appearance and bodily demeanour spoke of an age somewhat greater. Distorted by an animalistic grimace, the young man's face had glassy eyes beset with a remote, almost lifeless, stare. Distributing his weight from one foot to the other, he lolled from side to side. Combined with the jutting jaw, hunched shoulders, gently swinging arms and almost clenched fists, these features comprised an ape-like, bestial characterization of the 'low' or 'inferior' spirit by which he was being possessed. In contravention of the ritual strictures governing most Santo Daime practices, the young man (or, perhaps, the possessing spirit) refused to maintain the place to which he had been assigned; attempting instead to move across other parts of the ritual space. Constantly accompanied by at least one of those charged with maintaining ritual order, the young man was shepherded and, at times, corralled by up to four individuals in an effort to return him to his designated place or, when failing, at least to limit his movement to a particular area at the back of the section within which he should have been sitting. Besides guiding his physical placement in ritual space, no other kinds of interaction occurred with the young man. Commencing about 90 minutes into the ritual of 'Cure' (*cura*) then being celebrated in the Brazilian state of Minas Gerais, this unscheduled game of cat and mouse continued for most of the remaining 5 hours.

The ritual order so readily transgressed in this episode is believed by *daimistas* to be grounded on internal discipline and external regulation; an equation in which the latter comes to the fore when the former is found wanting. Of an individual and collective nature, these factors combine to constitute a ritual repertoire which, this chapter argues, might fruitfully be understood as a disciplinary regime responsible for the maintenance of physical and symbolic order. In respect of the episode above, and by way of introducing what follows, two complementary points are worthy of note. First, a good deal of the interaction between the young man and those charged with upholding ritual order centred upon the physical management of ceremonial space. As well as striving to ensure that he remained in the section to which he had been assigned, the 'inspectors' (*fiscais*) responsible for maintaining order worked hard to preserve the integrity of those parts of ritual space deemed off-limits to the young man.[1] In effect, the young man was as much being kept out as he was being kept in. Second, an important element of the encounter comprises the refusal of the *fiscais* to entertain any form of symbolic exchange with the possessed individual. On the one hand, the relatively skilled manner in which the young man presented the stylized gestures and stereotypical characteristics of a low/inferior spirit indicated a degree of practised experience with ritualized possession motifs. On the other, his lack of 'uniform' (*farda*), designated position in the 'ranks' (see below) and prolonged ritual infraction signalled a relative newness to Santo Daime. Although the young man was clearly well versed in the practice of spirit possession in other religious contexts, his relative inexperience of and lowly status within the *daimista* cultic arena combined to undermine any form of constructive symbolic exchange between him and his ritual co-participants.

As indicated, this chapter explores the ritual repertoire of Santo Daime through its framing as a disciplinary regime characterized by a preoccupation with physical and symbolic order. Informed by the insights of Michel Foucault, the opening section explores the spatial, temporal and symbolic dimensions of the *daimista* ritual repertoire. In so doing, the physical constitution of ceremonial space and the temporal ordering of cultic practice, along with its major rituals and their foremost components, are each treated in turn. The spatial and temporal ordering of the *daimista* ritual repertoire is further explored by next explicating the manner in which the regulation of cultic space-time impacts upon the physical and symbolic experiences of ritual participants. Drawing upon the work of Pierre Bourdieu, a closing section engages the ritual space of Santo Daime as a dynamic arena characterized as much by fluidity and contestation as it is by fixity and hierarchy. Here, the disciplinary regime of *daimista* ritual is treated as a mutable and evolving 'field of force' which, at the hands of the now dominant urban middle classes, is undergoing a variety of practical and symbolic transformations typical of its newfound late-modern context.

Ritual order

Charting the rise of the 'modern institution' (e.g. prison, school and factory), Foucault identifies the formulation of a new 'technology of power' through which the human body is regulated in relation to space, time and miscellaneous forces. Understood by Foucault as a 'political anatomy' or 'instrumental coding of the body', the modern institution's regulation of the individual serves to ensure his efficient control and maximal use-value (1991: 135–9, 193–4). Although Foucault overplays the 'docility' and pacification of the body which is subjected to modern techniques of power (see below), he makes a number of observations which prove insightful when used to reflect upon the context, structure and content of Santo Daime ritual.[2] Among these observations is Foucault's identification of the 'disciplinary methods' through which institutional order is created and maintained by way of the spatial, temporal and symbolic regulation of individual behaviour and collective contexts. The following employs a number of these disciplinary methods to frame the most important components of the *daimista* ritual repertoire and, in so doing, explicate it as a disciplinary regime oriented to the maintenance of physical and symbolic order.

Ritual space

The ritual space within which *daimista* cultic activity occurs is regimented through a spatial ordering which, à la Foucault, is both 'real' and 'ideal' (1991: 148). Once ordered relative to its real and ideal qualities, ritual space is then populated by cultic participants according to a very specific political anatomy. The real ordering of *daimista* ritual space involves its literal reading as something defined in respect of its outer boundaries and partitioned in respect of its inner divisions. In part, then, the spatial ordering of the ritual environment comprises a set of literal distinctions between, on the one hand, inside and outside and, on the other, *this* (e.g. my) place and *that* (e.g. your) place. The literal arrangement of real space is complemented by an ideal ordering through which ritual space is read both normatively and hierarchically. The ideal ordering of ritual space furnishes an evaluative rationale (the 'why') which justifies and articulates existing spatial arrangements (the 'where', 'what' and 'how'). Real and ideal orderings of ritual space thereby combine to distribute and rank ritual participants in a way which explains both why one should be where one is and how one should behave relative to what one is.

In reality, there is a great variety of architectural configurations within which Santo Daime rituals take place. Principally, but not solely, in Brazil, *daimista* rituals are practised in purpose-built structures (often, but not always, called 'churches') which sit in their own grounds. In countries where Santo Daime is relatively young or practised clandestinely, however, rituals usually occur in makeshift locations which, when borrowed or rented, are temporarily converted for the task at hand. Either way, *daimistas* make an explicit spatial demarcation which distinguishes the inner area sanctified for formal ritual practice from both a liminal area in which auxiliary and associated activities occur and an outer area at which point ceremonial space is considered to end. Effected relative to prevailing architectural circumstances, the inner area of *daimista* ritual space is equally divided into two halves; respectively occupied by male and female cultic participants. As shown later, however, the 'ideal' reading of ritual space implicitly invokes a threefold division which adds the space occupied by the central table to the two halves respectively occupied by male and female participants.

Illustrated by Figure 2.1, *daimista* ritual space is most commonly organized hexagonally, with one half of the floor occupied by male participants and the other by female practitioners. Indicative of the millenarianism at the heart of Santo Daime's origins (see Chapter 3), these cohorts are commonly referred to as the male and female 'battalions'. As shown, the male and female battalions are divided into three sections. Traditionally populated relative to

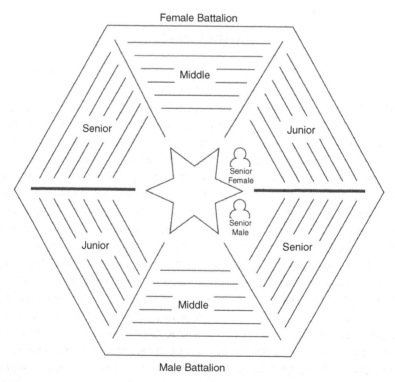

FIGURE 2.1 *'Real' ritual space.*

ritual experience and marital status, age is now a key criterion determining the section into which ritual participants are placed. These sections are oriented as spokes around a central hub occupied by a table; preferably, though not always, shaped as a six-pointed star (the esoteric 'Star of Solomon').[3]

Most Santo Daime rituals are undertaken with participants facing inward towards the 'star-table'. The star-table is commonly laid with 'the cruzeiro' (i.e. two-sparred cross) draped by a rosary, statuettes of Mary and Jesus and photographs of significant figures such as Master Irineu and Padrinho Sebastião. Representing the elemental forces of earth, water, wind and fire, the table is also laid with flowers, a jug of water, incense sticks and candles. Some groups include, for example, statuettes of Catholic saints and a Christian Bible, while others may use crystals, representations of Afro-Brazilian entities and the icons and scriptural excerpts of assorted Eastern religions and non-mainstream spiritualities. Ritual space is likewise decorated in a manner which speaks of the palimpsestic character of the *daimista* cultic repertoire. Within spaces permanently set aside for ritual use, great effort is often made to reproduce the forest canopy through material or paper decorations hung overhead. In the same vein, and commonly used to decorate temporary locations, pictures, paintings and murals are pinned to the walls with representations of, for example, Santo Daime leaders, Jesus, Mary and the Catholic saints, Iemanjá and other Afro-Brazilian deities, indigenous motifs most relevant to context (e.g. eagles and feathers) and miscellaneous Eastern imagery (e.g. the Buddha and Hindu 'Aum' symbol).

In addition to providing the literal centre around which the male and female battalions are ordered, the star-table is the metaphysical hub of *daimista* ritual space. As the nodal point of ideal ritual space, the star-table is occupied by those ultimately responsible for managing ceremonial activity. The respective heads of the male and female battalions occupy the prime space at the star-table, as do those principally charged with leading the singing and providing its musical accompaniment. While traditional modes of gender stereotyping are progressively being eroded by Santo Daime's expansion among the urban middle classes, those responsible for leading the singing in ritual space remain overwhelmingly female. Given the centrality of hymnody to the Santo Daime religion, however, the task of 'pulling' the hymns during ritual practice is one of the most important, and thereby prestigious, roles occupied in ceremonial space. Although a growing range of instruments is being used to guide and accompany the singing of hymns, as the most traditional musical tool in Santo Daime the guitar remains the most popular.[4] In contrast to the singing of hymns, but again undergoing gradual erosion, responsibility for musical accompaniment has traditionally fallen to the male battalion.

Oriented in relation to the star-table, each of the three sections of the male and female battalions is subdivided into rows or 'ranks' (*fileiras*) according to various criteria.[5] Although applied in different ways across the movement, the most used criteria by which the sections are internally organized comprise membership status (i.e. 'uniformed' or 'non-uniformed'), length of membership or ritual experience, marital or partnership status and organizational status (see below). Likewise, but increasingly less so, the height of a ritual participant may be employed to determine location on a particular row, with participants ranged from the shortest at the beginning to the tallest at the end. Although such ordering embodies more of an aesthetic than religious dynamic, the unusually tall nature of Master Irineu (1.98 m/6 ft 5 in.) involves for some an association of height with spiritual stature.[6] In effect, and however employed, the criteria used for the internal organization of each section should result in the most senior participants being situated in the rows nearest the star-table.

Orchestrated through the application of these criteria and oriented with reference to the star-table, the distribution of ceremonial practitioners across and within their respective battalions results in three complementary flows of ritual status which are illustrated by Figure 2.2. As can be seen, at the heart of ritual space a central status-flow moves around the star-table. The

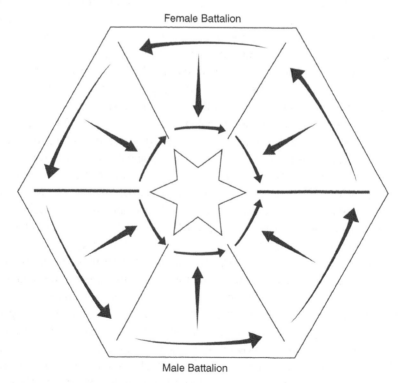

FIGURE 2.2 *'Ideal' ritual space.*

status-flow culminates with the respective female and male heads of the cultic event where ritual authority and the ceremonial spiritual force are believed to be most concentrated. In the same vein, the status-flow from the junior, through the middle, to the senior section of each battalion combines to create an anticlockwise pattern which likewise circulates around the axial centre of ritual space. Moving towards rather than around the star-table, a third status-flow is formed within each battalion section by a centripetal movement from the most distant (and junior) row to the (most senior) row nearest the centre.

Just as movement between the male and female halves of ritual space is technically forbidden except in very particular circumstances, passage between and within each battalion section is strictly governed and occurs solely at the instigation of those in authority. In principle, and upon first entering ceremonial space, ritual attendees are expected to present themselves to the relevant fiscal/guardian whereupon they are assigned a place in which they should remain unless or until told otherwise. In practice, however, I have seen *daimistas* use a number of tactics to try and obtain a more prestigious place than that which they had been or might otherwise be allocated. Those charged with the proper ordering of ceremonial space are, though, not only wise to such gambits but also undertake their roles without fear of moving cultic participants to the place adjudged to be in keeping with their ritual status. Once a ritual is under way, and in order to maintain 'balance' within the ranks, it is commonplace for practitioners to be moved within and across rows throughout the course of a ceremony.

Ritual time

As with the organization of ritual space, the disciplinary ordering of ritual time includes real and ideal dimensions. Exemplified perhaps by the 'time-table' (Foucault, 1991: 149), the real ordering of ritual time involves its scheduling as a liturgical calendar. Real ritual time is calendrical time; time as *chronos*. Ritual time is likewise subjected to an ideal ordering through the normative 'elaboration of the [ceremonial] act' (Foucault, 1991: 151). Ideal ritual time is metaphysical time; time as *kairos*. Through the scheduling of ceremonial practice and the temporal formatting of the cultic act, the 'where' of ritual space is complemented by the 'when' of ritual time.

The ritual calendar

The real-time scheduling of *daimista* ritual practice is ordered through the 'Official Calendar of Works' (*Calendário Oficial de Trabalhos*) issued by the mother community of *Céu do Mapiá*. The official calendar comprises

19 'Hymnals' (hinários) and 24 'Concentrations' (concentrações) which all affiliated centres classed as a 'church' are expected to fulfil.[7] Inherited from Santo Daime's popular Catholic legacy, the calendrical scheduling of official Hymnal rituals (known as 'Festivals') maps onto a template provided by the major festivals and feast days of Brazil's Luso-Christian heritage (Goulart, 2004).[8] The daimista ritual calendar is oriented around two major festival periods; the first from December to the back end of January and the second comprising June and July. In addition to the Saints' Days of Sebastian (19 January), Joseph (18 March), Anthony (12 June), John (23 June) and Peter (28 June), official Hymnals also occur at Christmas, New Year, Holy Week, All Souls (1 November) and the Feasts of the Three Kings (5 January) and Our Lady of the Conception (7 December). Two Hymnals relate to Mothers' Day (second Sunday in May) and Fathers' Day (second Sunday in August) respectively, while the dates of the remaining official Hymnals are determined by anniversaries important to Santo Daime: 7 January (birthday of Padrinho Alfredo), 25 June (birthday of Madrinha Rita, wife of Padrinho Sebastião), 6 July (death of Master Irineu), 6 October (birthday of Padrinho Sebastião) and 14 December (birthday of Master Irineu).[9] Whereas Hymnal rituals may be practised sitting down, all of those included in the official calendar are executed as a 'dance' (bailado). Influenced by esoteric rather than popular Catholic scheduling, the Concentration ritual is timetabled for the 15th and 30th of every month.

While the official calendar lists a total of 43 rituals (19 Hymnals and 24 Concentrations), it is common for the larger Santo Daime churches to celebrate as many as 80 to 90 rituals in the calendar year (excluding rites of passage such as funerals and weddings). The most common and important of the rituals which complement those of the official calendar are non-official Hymnals, healing 'works', the daimista 'Mass' (missa), the feitio (at which Daime is made) and the 'Prayer' (oração) ceremony. The 19 Hymnals included within the official calendar are complemented by a good many more, the scheduling of which is often locally determined relative to special dates (e.g. anniversaries) and ad hoc arrangements such as ceremonial visits. As Chapter 4 demonstrates, the healing works which cater most explicitly for ritualized spirit possession (e.g. 'Cure', 'White Table' and 'Saint Michael') are becoming increasingly popular but do not have a universally acknowledged schedule. The daimista Mass is scheduled for the first Monday of each month. Though regarded as an important ritual by older communities, its indebtedness to the Catholic Mass results in its avoidance by some of the younger communities uncomfortable with explicit expressions of Christianity within the ritual repertoire of Santo Daime. Formerly tied to the lunar cycle, the ritual of feitio (from the Portuguese fazer, to make) at which Daime is produced is now usually practised when stock levels and demand dictate.

Although practised daily at *Céu do Mapiá*, the ritual of Prayer is less popular elsewhere as an event scheduled in its own right. It is, however, integrated into the rituals of the Hymnal, Concentration and Mass to form the opening section of these ceremonies. Official and non-calendrical rituals may be further complemented by the practice of ceremonies appropriated from other religious traditions or created through the merging of *daimista* cultic elements with assorted components from other paradigms. All in all, the ritual commitment of most Santo Daime churches is not only comparable to that of many mainstream religions but also relatively onerous when the length and demands of its rituals (see below) are taken into account.

The published ritual calendar stipulates that the 19 Hymnals classed as 'official' should commence at sunset and continue 'all night until the dawn of the festival day'. For some communities, however, the logistical issues raised by such scheduling result in alterations to the timetabling of some of the longer Hymnals. As a result, some Hymnals are moved to the nearest date (usually a weekend) when such demands can be met or staged during the day with commencement in the morning and the close towards or around the onset of night. While the shorter of the official Hymnals last no more than 8 hours, their longer counterparts can take over 12 hours to complete. The Concentration ritual is likewise scheduled to commence usually after dark, while the rituals of Mass and Prayer generally fall towards the end of the working day but not always after sunset. I have attended Concentrations lasting little over 3 hours but also known this ritual to extend to 6 hours. The Mass may take 2 or 3 hours to perform and the Prayer ritual about an hour. In contrast to most Santo Daime rituals, the *feitio* opens in the early hours of the morning and, although a great deal of its content is heavily ritualized, there is little by way of explicit liturgical direction. In effect, the duration of the *feitio* ritual is usually determined by the amount of Daime the *feitores* wish to produce or, conversely, the amount of time it takes to process the materials harvested. While I have been involved in *feitios* lasting no more than two days, I have also known them to last more than two weeks (see A. Dawson, 2012a).

As Cemin maintains, the rituals of the Hymnal, Concentration, Mass and *feitio* are the most traditional of those practised across the *daimista* movement (2004). There are, however, a good number of established and historically recent rituals which combine with traditional ceremonies to inform the cultic activity of contemporary practitioners. The aforementioned Prayer ritual (*oração*), rites of passage and membership ceremony, as well as the healing works mentioned in Chapter 4, are among the most prominent of these. At the same time, and in addition to official and non-official *daimista* ceremonies, different communities practise a miscellany of rituals of a hybrid and improvised form forged through the mixing of various cultic components from any number of different regions, traditions and sources. Whereas some of these rituals contain components of a recognizably *daimista* provenance, others bear little, if any, resemblance to established rites or elements thereof. Some take place within designated ritual space and some do not; some use Daime and/or other psychoactive substances, while others don't; and some enjoy regular scheduling, while others occur on an ad hoc basis.

The Hymnal ritual involves the singing of a complete hymnal, part of a hymnal or collection of shorter hymnals. The Hymnal may be practised sitting down or, as is more common, undertaken as a 'dance' (*bailado*) without recourse to seating except during a mid-ritual break. Hymnals typically last between 7 and 12 hours and involve participants employing three kinds of dance step, respectively to the rhythms of the march, mazurka and waltz. All aforementioned modes of ritual regulation remain in force for the danced Hymnal, while the seating used for other rituals is removed to provide each participant with a dance space of less than one square yard. As with the singing of hymns, the correct execution and attendant coordination of the dance is of the utmost importance. Although embellished by narrative and practical components appropriated from esoteric and Spiritist repertoires, the *daimista* Mass is chiefly derived from popular Catholicism and embodies a principal concern with the souls (here, disincarnate spirits) of the dead. Unlike the Hymnal and Mass, the ritual of Concentration owes little to the popular Catholic heritage of its creators. Instead, both the scheduling and intellective preoccupations of the Concentration reflect the patterns and processes of the esoteric paradigm. As if further to underscore its contrasting provenance, the Concentration has little by way of festive ethos and is, unlike the Hymnal, always undertaken in a seated position conducive to the esoteric disciplines of introspection and self-scrutiny. While prayers are said and hymns are sung in parts of the ritual, most of the Concentration is spent in silence and dedicated to the reflexive nurturing of the higher-self. To further emphasize its introspective intent, much of the Concentration is undertaken with the lights turned down. As with the spirit-oriented rites engaged in Chapter 4, and in contrast to the Hymnal ritual, the relatively stronger doses of Daime served at the Concentration inform the 'heavier' spiritual current generated by this ceremony.

In many ways the archetypal *daimista* ritual, the *feitio* is believed to generate a spiritual current all of its own. The already well-established use of ayahuasca by the time of the proto-Concentration ceremony of 1930 makes the *feitio* the oldest *daimista* ritual. The fact that this ritual involves the production of Santo Daime's sacramental tea also makes it the most important. As well as being the oldest and most important ritual, the *feitio* is the longest and, at points, the most arduous. Owing to its unique combination of sacramental production and psychophysical exertion, the ritual of *feitio* is regarded as highly efficacious in respect of the spiritual, moral and psychophysical benefits which ensue from ceremonial participation. The importance of the *feitio*, however, goes beyond the production of Daime. The fact that many Santo Daime churches rely upon others for the provision of their sacrament gives the *feitio* a strategic importance. In addition to bestowing status upon those communities with sufficient resources to stage it, the *feitio* plays an important part in the establishment of alliances, along with their inherent hierarchies and dependencies. Given the difficulties in cultivating the constituent vine and leaf in most places outside South America, the international spread of Santo Daime has, to date, replicated the status and strategic importance of the *feitio* (see A. Dawson, 2012a).

Ritual components

The ideal ordering of ritual time involves the temporal configuration of individual cultic components to form a normative template through which the unfolding of ceremonial activity is structured and, as such, deemed propitious. Demonstrated below, the proper unfolding of cultic time is something zealously upheld by the Santo Daime religion and forms an integral part of the subjective discipline and collective regulation upon which ritual order is founded. Among the individual ritual components which feature prominently in *daimista* ritual practice, the three most important are the 'sacraments' of Daime (i.e. ayahuasca) and Santa Maria (i.e. cannabis), the hymns through which the 'sacred doctrine' of Santo Daime is manifest and the prayers by which the 'heavenly beings' are petitioned. Within most *daimista* communities, teaching or instruction for the purposes of spiritual and moral edification is something minimally employed within formal ritual contexts. While one interviewee told me that 'the Daime and the hymns are all you need', another said that he very much valued the absence of 'sermons' in Santo Daime as he could 'get on with thinking' what was most on his mind. By and large, the verbal edification used during cultic activity tends to involve reading out a short passage from a revered text (usually in the middle of a ritual) or offering a brief narrative by way of an epilogue.

Sacraments

The Amazonian peoples from whom the psychoactive properties of ayahuasca were first learnt believe its constitutive components (i.e. the leaf and vine) to contain 'plant spirits'. Outlined in Chapter 1, such indigenous beliefs were appropriated by mixed-race *vegetalista* healers who hold the knowledge and force of the 'plant teacher' ayahuasca to be accessed through its processing and subsequent ingestion. Within the contemporary *daimista* movement, talk of Daime as literally containing or embodying a plant spirit or teacher is most popular within the more traditional communities located in or near the Amazon region. Certainly, *daimistas* around the world continue to use the terms 'plant spirit' and 'plant teacher'. When asked to explain what they mean by these terms, however, the responses given indicate their metaphorical employment as tropes whose usage is grounded more in a nostalgic reference to Amazonian origins than it is in a metaphysical reference to given ontological realities. In actuality, most *daimistas* conceive of Daime in a way which owes more to esoteric and new-age holistic paradigms than it does to traditional Amazonian world views. Daime is thereby regarded as a substance in which a sacred, universal and all-embracing cosmic life-force is found in an especially (but not exclusively) concentrated form. In so being, Daime is understood as a privileged medium whose concentration of cosmic spiritual energy allows it to serve as an 'entheogen', 'catalyst' or 'short cut' which facilitates and enhances human interaction with the universal life-force variously interpreted as the 'sacred', 'supernatural', 'divine' and 'holy'.[10]

Noted in the preceding chapter, the psychoactive effects of Daime result from the combination of beta-carboline alkaloids contained in the vine *Banisteriopsis caapi* and the alkaloid DMT inherent to the shrub leaf *Psychotria viridis*. As well as the age, quality and type of plants used, the psychotropic potency of Daime varies relative to the environmental conditions in which they are grown and the ratio of their combination at the point of manufacture (i.e. *feitio*). The potency of ayahuasca may be increased through the addition of other ingredients or the concentration of its strength in boiled-down reductions. Although Santo Daime uses only the vine, leaf and water in the manufacture of its sacrament, it does employ (and increasingly so) reductive processes to produce successively stronger decoctions. Daime is manufactured as a beverage and has an initially light-brown colour which deepens as the liquid ages. Daime is slightly syrupy in consistency, very strong in odour and rather bitter to the taste (especially the older it gets).[11] The amount and strength of the Daime 'despatched' during cultic practice varies within and across rituals. Within the Hymnal and Mass, for example, the strength ('grade') of the Daime used tends to be weaker than that employed in the Concentration and healing works detailed in Chapter 4. In the same vein, the weaker doses of Daime tend to be larger (about 80–100 ml) than those containing a more potent concentration (approximately 40–60 ml). Although of a weaker strength, the actual amount of Daime consumed during the average Hymnal ritual exceeds that consumed in the relatively shorter Concentration ceremony. It is also common practice to use differing strengths of Daime within the same ritual, with stronger doses commonly served before weaker ones.

Daime is generally despatched at the beginning of rituals and at intervals thereafter of anything between 90 minutes and 2 hours. Although I've seen

Daime despatched upon request to individuals towards the close of ritual proceedings, it is more common for the last despatch of Daime to be made no later than approximately 2 hours before the end of a ceremony. Distributed from a fixed location within ritual space, Daime may be simultaneously despatched from separate points serving the male and female battalions respectively or by dispatchers working at a single position but serving two separate lines. Some dispatchers make slight modifications relative to the size of the individual being served and unless explicit request is made, newcomers are generally served the same amount of Daime as that given to experienced members. Indeed, in some contexts newcomers are given a sizeable dose intended to facilitate their 'encounter' with 'the Daime' (see A. Dawson, 2010: 178).

Relative to strength, amount and individual physiology, Daime begins to make itself felt between 20 to 30 minutes after first being drunk, with subsequent doses consolidating its psychotropic effects.[12] In my experience, the psychotropic effects of an average dose of medium strength Daime increase gradually through successively stronger waves which peak approximately 1 hour after initial consumption and plateau for the next 20 minutes before incrementally declining in force but still being felt for at least another 45 minutes. The earliest effects of the beverage tended to be a warming of the stomach followed by feelings of physical relaxation and mental calm; yet, with no loss of vigour or alertness. The weaker forms of Daime consumed produced a mild intellectual detachment from my body and surroundings which allowed both the objectification of feelings, thoughts and memories (some long forgotten) and their sustained examination through a systematic scrutiny of even the most seemingly insignificant of matters. In addition to such detachment, moderately potent grades of Daime stimulated an enhanced sensitivity to the ritual environment which, at points, endowed it with an almost forbidding atmosphere and its contents (e.g. noises and sudden movements) with an ability to startle. Such grades also engendered periods of meditative tranquillity and, especially towards the end of the psychotropic event, mild elation. As they waxed and waned in their impact, the highest grades of Daime gave rise to the same experiences as those provoked by weaker- and mid-strength doses. At their peak, however, the effects induced by high-grade Daime included thoughts and images ranging from the serene to the frightening, the matter of fact to the insightful and the ordinary to the unearthly. Such effects also involved bouts of dizziness, nausea and impaired motor function.

The 'visions' (*mirações*) experienced at the height of Daime's psychotropic effects are variously interpreted by *daimistas*. From the verb 'to look upon' (*mirar*), the traditional term *miração* encompasses a variety of dimensions. Appropriating traditional, esoteric and neo-shamanic notions of psychical dislocation (e.g. soul-flight and astral projection), some *daimistas* describe their 'visions' as involving journeys to other realms and dimensions where an assortment of spiritual beings are met and engaged. For others, the visions made possible by Daime are interpreted through Spiritist concepts which include experiences of previous incarnations or mainstream esoteric and psycho-spiritual models which reference the inner workings of the self in both its lower and higher forms. Discussed at length in Chapter 4, spirit possession motifs are becoming an increasingly popular means of articulating the psychotropic events engendered by the ritual consumption of Daime. Whatever the experiences had or interpretative frames used to explicate them, *daimista* custom traditionally militates against individuals sharing their visions except in cases where the communication of their contents promises some degree of enlightenment or edification for others. Consequently, the disclosure of an individual's *miração* has customarily been discouraged and, when divulged, it is bounded by a reservation framed by humility and bordering on reticence. Noted below, established restrictions upon the sharing of personal visions are being gradually eroded as the movement continues to expand beyond its traditional homeland.

Especially with stronger grades, the emetic qualities of Daime may induce vomiting and, less often, the need to defecate. Whereas all communities I have practised with permit those needing to defecate to transit from inner ritual space to a liminal zone, some groups required those being sick to remain within the inner space and thereby vomit into buckets and bags or out of the window. It has been my experience, however, that the vomiting induced by ayahuasca tends to be far less disagreeable than that brought on, for example, by bad food, travel sickness or an excess of alcohol. This is just as well because some communities expect those who have just vomited to present themselves immediately for another dose of Daime. Whereas practical experience indicates the continued presence of Daime's psychoactive agents subsequent to vomiting, the immediate consumption of another dose is believed to reinforce bodily tolerance, signal commitment on the part of the individual and ensure continued participation in both the 'force' of Daime and the 'spiritual current' enabled by it. Although the emetic effects of Daime may be moderated by pre-ritual dietary practices, the purge it produces is regarded positively as a physical manifestation of inner spiritual cleansing. This spiritual cleansing applies as much to the bad karma accrued in previous incarnations as it does to the guilt engendered by the moral misdemeanours of this life.

Concern with ensuring that ritual practitioners remain in the force and help maintain the spiritual current means that every ceremonial participant is expected to consume Daime during a cultic event. There are no ritual bystanders in Santo Daime. Great care is thereby taken by many communities to ensure that all ceremonial participants present themselves at each despatch. Within some rites, the final despatch of Daime may be optional but only on condition that the stipulated number of despatches for that particular ritual has already been reached. During a post-ritual discussion with a community leader, he expressed his view that a minority of people 'do not work best with a full dose of Daime' as, for one reason or another, they may be overly sensitive to its effects and thereby easily overpowered and unable 'to work properly'. Instead, such people are better taking 'smaller doses but more often' so that by the end of the ritual they have had 'the same amount as everyone else'. He also added, however, that some individuals ask for a smaller dose because they are 'scared of the Daime and what it will do to them'. In cases such as these, smaller doses are 'not acceptable'.

Detailed in Chapter 1, the traditional sacrament of Daime was joined by the sacrament of 'Santa Maria' (Holy Mary) through Padrinho Sebastião's adoption of cannabis in the mid-1970s. As discussed by MacRae, subsequent police action in respect of cannabis cultivation and ongoing controversy regarding ayahuasca's legal status resulted in the official withdrawal of Santa Maria from formal cultic contexts in the late 1980s (1998: 336). Whether temporary or 'official' for the sake of appearances, this move neither negated the status of Santa Maria as a sacrament nor impeded its use by *daimistas* in subsequent decades. Today, the place of Santa Maria within Santo Daime is again provoking debate across the movement. Allied with the ongoing pursuit of legal protections for Santo Daime in various parts of the world, some *daimistas* argue that the continued use of Santa Maria in formal ritual practice is open to 'misunderstanding' and thereby makes the movement vulnerable to continued state persecution. This opinion has resulted in certain communities barring the use of Santa Maria in formally constituted ritual contexts; a practice argued by some to have played an important role in securing the legal recognition of Santo Daime in the US state of Oregon. Indeed, I have been told a number of times by those espousing this view that certain sectors of the Santo Daime movement reject the pursuit of legal recognition on the grounds that the ritual proscribing of Santa Maria is too high a price to pay.

By no means universally smoked across the Cefluris movement, Santa Maria nevertheless remains an important part of the lifestyles and ritual practices of many *daimistas*. For these individuals, Santa Maria is as much a sacrament as Daime, and, as with ayahuasca, the sacramentalization of cannabis includes the articulation of an attendant sacralizing discourse. Within traditional *daimista* narrative, the vine and leaf from which Daime is made are believed respectively to contain 'masculine' (e.g. power and strength) and 'feminine' (e.g. light and subtlety) qualities. As the union of these complementary qualities, the sacrament of Daime is held to combine two fundamental cosmic forces and thereby ministers to the needs of men and women alike. With the advent of Santa Maria, however, traditional discourse in respect of Daime has been modified to make room for the new sacrament. Daime is now presented as embodying a universal masculine force, while Santa Maria is regarded as the embodiment of a complementary feminine energy. Consequently, whereas the sacrament of Daime once ensured access to both masculine and feminine cosmic forces, such metaphysical complementarity is now believed by some to be best captured by the sacramental partnership of both Daime and Santa Maria.

Within contemporary *daimista* circles, four types of Santa Maria use are most in evidence. First, Santa Maria is smoked in non-cultic contexts both individually and collectively. As the term intimates, non-cultic usage occurs outside of formally constituted ceremonial activity. The term non-cultic, however, should not be taken to suggest that the smoking of Santa Maria outside of formal ceremonial contexts is regarded as lacking in ritual significance. On the contrary, the non-cultic use of Santa Maria usually employs a number of explicitly ritualizing practices which distinguish its sacramental employment from the profane usage of the 'drug' marijuana by those outside the movement. Santa Maria may be used privately as an aid to meditation, smoked at regular intervals both individually and collectively or consumed at the beginning of the day prior to leaving home. Employed in this latter sense, Santa Maria serves as a kind of spiritual prophylactic deployed as protection against the ills of the world at large. In so being, its use parallels the traditional practice of taking a spoonful of Daime at the beginning of the day or upon first exiting the home. Although not always employed, the non-cultic use of Santa Maria is often preceded by ritualizing actions such as the recital of a prayer, singing of a hymn or making the sign of the cross. The ritualization of Santa Maria use is further underlined by *daimistas* talking of 'consecrating' rather than 'smoking' it. To the best of my knowledge, Santa Maria is not consumed at the same time as alcohol.

The remaining three types of Santa Maria use involve its consumption in connection with formal cultic activity.[13] The second type of employment involves the smoking of Santa Maria immediately before and upon completion of a ceremonial event. This usually occurs in an area near but recognizably discrete from the actual ritual space set aside for cultic activity. The third type of Santa Maria use occurs during cultic activity but includes those involved leaving inner ritual space and moving to an adjoining area set aside for sacramental consecration. In view of the cultic responsibilities (see below) and aforementioned hierarchization of ceremonial participants, the third type of Santa Maria use is, unlike the second type, generally reserved for the most senior or high-status occupants of ritual space (i.e. those nearest the central table). As with so much else implicated in *daimista* ritual practice, the timing and order of transit between inner and liminal ceremonial space involved in this type is highly regulated. In view of the controversial nature of Santa Maria and presence of non-members within many rituals, those consecrating the sacrament around or during ceremonial activity are expected to do so out of plain sight. To a certain degree, the second and third types of Santa Maria use are compromises which permit the continued consecration of the sacrament while allowing rituals to remain open to those whose inexperience of the doctrine or lack of sacramental appreciation might result in some form of 'misunderstanding'. The fourth type of Santa Maria use makes no such compromise. Instead, the use of Santa Maria as an integral part of ritual practice is secured by excluding non-members from any kind of cultic participation. As such, rituals in which Santa Maria is smoked within inner cultic space are generally closed to the uninitiated. In addition to facilitating the undertaking of rituals ('Santa Maria works') explicitly oriented to the sacrament of Santa Maria, the closure of ritual space to non-members permits its untrammelled consecration within some of the more traditional rites mentioned above.

The sacramental status accorded Daime and Santa Maria by no means translates into a monopoly on *daimista* engagement with psychoactive substances. Rather, the difference bestowed by the sacramental status of Daime and Santa Maria is more one of degree than of kind. Perhaps greater than the first among equals, the import of Santo Daime's sacraments is nevertheless gained by virtue of being 'power plants'; an attribute shared with a relatively broad range of psychoactive flora. Characteristic of the relativizing holism discussed in Chapter 3, the belief that only two sacred plants could encapsulate the entirety of what the cosmic Whole has to offer is anathema to most *daimistas*. Consequently, I have met few members of Cefluris whose relationship with their sacraments is an exclusive one. As with Santa Maria, *daimistas* consume a variety of psychoactive substances beyond and within formal ceremonial contexts. Unlike Santa Maria, however, the majority of these substances are consumed in cultic practice which does not form part of Santo Daime's established ritual repertoire. Among the psychoactive substances I have known *daimistas* to use in non-cultic and ritual contexts are: varieties of cactus (e.g. peyote and San Pedro) and mushroom (e.g. fly agaric), kambô (poison frog secretion), iboga and jurema (kinds of bark), fermented wheat beer, unprocessed tobacco (e.g. mapacho) and concentrated extracts of miscellaneous flora.[14] In keeping with their homeopathic tendencies, it is important to many *daimistas* that the psychoactive substances they consume be readily categorized as a 'natural' material and not one artificially manufactured through pharmaceutical processes.

Hymns

The 'force' accessed through the individual consumption of the *daimista* sacraments is harnessed, integrated and focused into a collective 'spiritual current' by the shared singing of 'hymns' (*hinos*).[15] In addition to their liturgical function, hymns have traditionally been the principal medium through which *daimista* doctrine has been elaborated. Broadly speaking, the hymns of Santo Daime appear in two liturgical settings. First, hymns exist as part of a collection known as a 'hymnal' (*hinário*). Although some hymnals contain hymns donated ('offered') as gifts by others, most hymnals are authored by a single individual and are arranged chronologically in the order in which the hymns have been 'received' from the astral plane. Exemplified below by Padrinhos Sebastião and Alfredo, hymnals may be declared 'closed' by the author and a new one 'opened' in its stead. Second, hymns are arranged as compilations which form complete or otherwise discrete sections within rituals such as the Concentration, Cure, Prayer, Saint Michael and White Table. Most of the hymns used in these compilations are extracted from Santo Daime's most important hymnals, while others have been written with specific liturgical functions in mind (e.g. despatch of Daime or calling of the spirits). Of the 19 Hymnal rituals sung as part of the official calendar, 13 of these rites use the hymnals of Master Irineu, Padrinho Sebastião and Padrinho Alfredo. Of the remaining five Hymnals: two use the aforementioned *Hymnal of the Dead*; one is a Mass (sung on Good Friday); one sings the hymnal of a prominent *daimista* (Maria Brilhante) noted for healing a son of Padrinho Sebastião; and one employs the hymnals of three prominent women of Cefluris (Madrinhas Rita, Julia and Cristina).[16]

The hymnal of Master Irineu is called 'The Cruzeiro' (*O Cruzeiro*) and has 132 hymns set to the rhythms of the march and the waltz; two rhythms commonly danced to in popular Catholic festivals (Galvão, 1955: 77).[17] *The Cruzeiro* is populated throughout by the figures of 'Divine/Eternal Father', 'Jesus Christ the Redeemer' and the 'Virgin Mother/Mary'. The 'Divine Beings' who occupy the 'celestial court' also appear frequently, with early reference to regional spirits and popular supernatural agencies fading in frequency until eventually disappearing before the end of the hymnal. The astral bodies of the sun, moon and stars are also commonplace and are complemented by frequent reference to the elements (e.g. earth, wind and sea) and the flora (e.g. flowers and vine) and fauna (e.g. butterfly and birds) of the forest. Master Irineu appears often in the guise of a 'Teacher' entrusted by the Virgin Mother (commonly referred to as the 'Queen of the Forest') with 'sacred doctrines' to be conveyed by way of the 'hymns' being sung. Daime is likewise referred to as a 'Teacher' and 'Holy Light' whose consumption engenders 'force', 'power', 'cure' and 'cleansing'. 'Truth', 'love', 'wisdom' and 'understanding' appear throughout and are particularly connected with the community of 'brothers and sisters' whose consumption of Daime sets them apart from the world of 'sin' and 'illusion'. *The Cruzeiro* identifies the community of Santo Daime as the 'family' of 'Juramidam' and situates it within a millenarian world view framed by the cosmic battle between good and evil. Master Irineu is the 'Imperial Chief' whose 'soldiers' are led by 'commanders' and organized into 'battalions'. The members of the community constituted by the mutual consumption of Daime are much 'misunderstood' by the world of illusion but assuredly on the 'way'/'journey' towards 'salvation' and 'another incarnation'.

In one way or another, all of the themes present within *The Cruzeiro* are reproduced in the two hymnals of Padrinho Sebastião and three hymnals of his son, and current leader of Cefluris, Padrinho Alfredo. The two hymnals of Padrinho Sebastião are 'The Justice Maker' (*O Justiceiro*) and 'New Jerusalem' (*Nova Jerusalém*). Begun before his break from Alto Santo, *The Justice Maker* is the earlier of the two hymnals and comprises 156 hymns. *New Jerusalem* has 26 hymns and was being added to by Padrinho Sebastião up until the time of his death. 'The Little Cross' (*O Cruzeirinho*) is the first and longest of Padrinho Alfredo's three hymnals and contains 160 hymns. Closed with only 31 hymns having been received, 'New Age' (*Nova Era*) is Padrinho Alfredo's second hymnal, while (at the time of writing) 'New Dimension' (*Nova Dimensão*) has just been commenced with three hymns to date. Like *The Cruzeiro*, these hymnals are written both in praise of Santo Daime's supernatural pantheon and to instruct and encourage the *daimista* community. In the same vein, the hymns 'received' articulate general doctrinal material, offer concrete moral guidance and arise from specific events impacting either the author in person or the movement as a whole. Just as the hymnals of Padrinho Sebastião cement the status of Master Irineu as the reincarnation of Jesus of Nazareth, so those of Padrinho Alfredo reinforce *daimista* belief in his father as the reincarnation of John the Baptist and 'General' in command of the battalions of Juramidam. The hymnals of Sebastião and Alfredo add the mazurka to the rhythms of the march and waltz and make more explicit reference to esoteric themes and Spiritist concepts and motifs than *The Cruzeiro* of Master Irineu.[18] Santa Maria and the spiritual entities of Afro-Brazilian religiosity are referenced by Padrinho Alfredo and many of Santo Daime's most influential hymnals.[19] Indicative of the growing popularity of non-traditional forms of spirit mediumship, spiritual agencies and supernatural forces indigenous to other traditions or regions of the globe, along with extraterrestrial beings, are also more frequently referenced by contemporary hymns (see Chapter 4).

The importance of hymns to the Santo Daime religion is reflected in the fact that every leader of a community is expected to possess a hymnal of his or her own. Indeed, in cases where a leader is not particularly musical, a hymnal may be chiefly constituted through the donation of hymns 'offered' by others. Traditionally, the reception of hymns from the astral plane was something associated with high-status membership. Nevertheless, those receiving hymns were expected to pass them before individuals charged with evaluating their spiritual provenance and thereby rejecting or confirming their viability for communal use. (Inevitably, the higher the status, the greater a person's chance of having a hymn cleared for use.) Once cleared for communal use, hymns were memorized through their collective singing and subsequently transmitted as oral tradition. With the arrival in the mid-1970s of the 'backpackers' from the south, oral transmission was complemented by the use of pen and paper which, in turn, has given way to both mechanized and digital modes of recording and distributing hymns. Given the acute importance of singing hymns exactly as received from the astral, the use of digital media and attendant commentary is playing an increasing role in ensuring the correct (and thereby uniform) performance of hymns across the progressively dispersed *daimista* community.

Santo Daime's spread beyond the Amazon region has resulted in a number of other changes which impact upon its hymnic traditions. Detailed below, non-traditional dynamics operating within urban-professional communities are eroding established conventions which restricted the number of those deemed eligible to receive hymns. In tandem with the practical and economic ease with which hymns can now be recorded and distributed, the democratization of hymnic reception is giving rise to an increasing number of hymns by a growing number and range of people. At the same time, the geographical spread of Santo Daime exposes the movement to new socio-cultural themes and motifs which are subsequently articulated through hymns with an explicitly regional orientation or non-traditional content. In addition to being received in local languages, for example, such hymns may deviate from established formats, introduce previously unreferenced spiritual agencies or employ rhythms other than the march, mazurka and waltz. Despite these changes, though, the processes connected with the reception and subsequent validation (or otherwise) of hymns continue to reflect long-standing dynamics relating to both collective and individual identity. The processes of hymnic production continue to play a vital part in shaping the religious repertoire and interpersonal relations at play within single communities and the movement as a whole. On the one hand, and while reflecting the personal aspirations of the subject in receipt of a hymn, these processes continue to reinforce existing communal hierarchies and reflect changing patterns of individual status. On the other, discussion and debate surrounding hymnic production facilitate the modification of prevailing discourse and practice as existing patterns are reinterpreted or novel materials added in the light of fresh challenges and new experiences. Alongside their performative role in guiding *daimista* ritual practice, hymns are sites of symbolic contestation in and through which individual trajectories and collective modes of religious reproduction are negotiated, confirmed and transformed.

Prayers and recitations

The overwhelming majority of the prayers and recitations used in ceremonial practice originate outwith Santo Daime, although they are sometimes adapted for use within *daimista* ritual contexts. Every *daimista* ritual with a formal liturgy employs some kind of prayer or recitation. The most used prayers and recitations derive from the Roman Catholic tradition and include the 'Our Father', 'Ave Maria', 'Salve Regina', 'Apostles Creed', 'Prayer of Saint Francis' and 'Gloria'. Excluding the Mass, in which some of these prayers are cited throughout the rite, these generally appear at the beginning and close of the ceremonial liturgy. It is commonplace for those outside of Brazil to express surprise (and, for some, discomfort) at the extent of explicit Christian content found both in these prayers and Santo Daime's traditional hymnals. The 'Key of Harmony' and 'Consecration of the [Sacred] Space' were appropriated from the aforementioned Esoteric Circle of the Communion of Thought during Master Irineu's time. The Key of Harmony (*Chave de Harmonia*) is recited near the beginning of the ritual and invokes the formation of corporate union founded on the universal values of harmony, love, truth and justice. Appearing later in the ritual, the Consecration of the [Sacred] Space (*Consagração do Aposento*) likewise appeals to various universal values but does so as a means of claiming ritual space for 'Goodness' and thereby barring the entrance of 'evil'.

The Spiritist tradition of Allan Kardec, in which Padrinho Sebastião was trained as a medium, furnishes a number of prayers and recitations. The most popular of these is the 'Prayer of Charity' included in the Concentration ritual. This prayer both petitions God the Father for traditional religious goods (e.g. charity, consolation and repentance) and invokes the universal forces of 'Beauty', 'Goodness', 'Power' and 'Perfection'. Used principally in the mediumistic rituals of the White Table and Saint Michael, other prayers appropriated from the Spiritist paradigm include, for example, the 'Prayer for the Mediums', 'Prayer to Remove Evil Spirits' and 'Prayer for the Beginning of the Meeting'. Among the very few prayers and recitations deriving wholly from the Santo Daime tradition, the 'Decree of Master Irineu' (read out during the ritual of Concentration) is by far the most important. The Decree articulates the martial tenor of traditional millenarianism by addressing the battalion members to whom it is read out as the 'General Staff' (*Estado Maior*). It opens by calling for 'sincerity and respect' towards one's 'neighbour' before reminding those who drink the 'Holy Beverage' that they should 'correct' their 'defects' and work towards the 'perfection' of their 'own personalities'. The

Decree then outlines a number of matters to be addressed on the 'days of works' and undertaken through the course of 'our meditation'. Appeal to the 'Eternal Spirit of Goodness and the Sovereign Virgin Mother Creator' reflects a typical mixture of popular religious, Catholic and esoteric motifs; as does the meritocratic tenor of the assertion that 'desires' are 'realized according to what you deserve'. In perhaps a perfect summation of the collective responsibilities implicit in ritual participation with Santo Daime, Master Irineu decrees that the masculine and feminine battalions 'have the same obligation . . . and whoever has an obligation has a duty to fulfil it'.[20]

Ritual regulation

The combination of organized ritual space with ordered ritual time gives rise to an 'anatomo-chronological schema of behaviour' (Foucault, 1991: 152) through which ritual participants are regulated through their psychophysical subjection to the practical and symbolic demands of corporate ceremonial practice. Real and ideal orderings of ritual space-time thereby combine to distribute, rank and regiment cultic participants in a way which articulates their location, status and behaviour. Noted above, the ritual regulation achieved through Santo Daime's spatial and temporal ordering of cultic activity may fruitfully be understood as a disciplinary regime oriented to the production and upholding of physical and symbolic order. Perhaps more than most religious paradigms, the disciplinary regimentation of ritual practitioners is of major import to Santo Daime on account of the great emphasis it puts upon the necessary correlation of individual cultic activity and collective ceremonial practice. Such correlation is vital because it focuses the 'force' engendered by the individual consumption of Daime to create and maintain the collective 'spiritual current' which underwrites the religious efficacy of *daimista* ritual practice. The collective generation of the spiritual current is thereby reliant upon the sustained and focused contribution of individual ritual actors, while the individual participant is understood to be woven within a web of corporate obligation which both delimits autonomous action and corrects, if not censures, individual behaviour relative to the wider dynamics of communal ceremonial practice.

The necessary correlation of individual application and collective discipline is obtained through the symbolic and practical regulation of ritual activity. Symbolic regulation is most commonly achieved through cultic practitioners internalizing a range of discursive motifs which serve to normatize individual behaviour during ceremonial activity. A number of these motifs have already been mentioned in respect of the ideal ordering of ritual space and the various forms of regimentation to which it gives rise. The designation of rituals as 'trials' or 'works' is another form of symbolic regulation through which the 'obligations' implicated in *daimista* ritual practice are driven home. Employed by older generations of *daimistas*, the designation of rituals as trials (*provas*) reflects their demanding and often arduous nature. The now commoner term 'work' holds similar connotations. On the one hand, the psychoactive effects and physiological impact of Daime engender a range of challenges and discomforts for the individual which require vigilance and, at times, careful management. Corporal control in an alternate state of consciousness is a skill in itself. On the other hand, and in combination with these factors, the physical demands of often prolonged ritual participation predicated on sustained coordination with collective ritual dynamics makes for a doubly demanding experience. *Daimista* ritual space is no place for the faint-hearted.

The symbolic motifs of trial and work are complemented by the espousal of particular ritual virtues which cultic practitioners are expected to acquire and subsequently nurture. The words 'discipline' and 'firmness' are often used when talking about individual comportment during ritual activity and, like other forms of symbolic regulation, appear regularly in hymns. Traditional restrictions upon diet and sexual activity which circumscribe ritual involvement further reinforce the need for discipline and firmness in relation to cultic practice.[21] In tandem with other modes of symbolic regulation, cultic virtues have a dual character which refers both to the subjective benefits accrued by their possession and to the collective dynamics which their presence in ritual space makes possible. In the same vein, ritual practitioners are exhorted to 'remain in your place' and 'pay attention' to what is occurring. In so doing, the individual meets the corporate responsibilities of ceremonial participation while reaping the subjective rewards ('merit') of individual focus and application.

The merit accrued through individual focus and application is underwritten by a mechanistic causal dynamic jointly derived from popular religious and esoteric milieus. Articulated today through the meritocratic concept of 'reciprocity' (or 'law of return'), the spiritual efficacy of *daimista* practice is underpinned by a direct correlation of the amount of effort expended with the manner and extent of the reward returned (in this life or the next). In respect of its subjective benefits, the most common expressions of Santo Daime's spiritual efficacy relate to individual experiences of healing. Accounts of healing are common to all *daimista* communities and stretch from leg sores that wouldn't close, through addictions to drink and drugs, to cancers which conventional medicine had diagnosed as terminal. In many cases, healing occurred soon after the individual commenced participation in Santo Daime. At the same time, many of these accounts include episodes of relapse brought on by breaks in ritual attendance ('moving away from the Daime') or failures of 'vigilance' and the ensuing erosion of everyday religio-moral regimes. The subjective rewards earned through ritual practice rely also upon individual application in all walks of life. Grounded both in the popular religiosity of the Amazon region and the religious moralism of esoteric and Spiritist paradigms, the concept of vigilance informs *daimistas* of the need to be constantly alert to the ethical pitfalls and spiritual dangers of everyday life in the world of 'illusion'. Strong parallels are thereby drawn between the disciplines and exertions employed within the formal ritual arena and those to be used within the course of daily living. As with corporate ceremonial practice, the benefits accrued in everyday life rest ultimately upon the continued alertness and disciplined application of the individual.

The subjective discipline encouraged by symbolic regulation is complemented by the practical management of ritual space. As with symbolic regulation, certain elements of practical control during cultic activity have already been mentioned in relation to the ordering of ceremonial space. Not least among these are concerns with maintaining clear divisions between the male and female battalions and ensuring the appropriate distribution of ritual practitioners across their respective sections and within their designated ranks. In the same vein, transit between the various spheres (i.e. inner, liminal and outer) of *daimista* ritual space is closely monitored during cultic activity by those (i.e. inspectors/guardians) charged with surveilling and, where necessary, correcting ceremonial behaviour. Once a ritual has commenced (and especially so after the first 'despatch' of Daime), movement between the inner and liminal areas is only permitted on strictly qualified grounds, while passage to the outer sphere is reserved only for exceptional circumstances.[22]

Upon taking their place in the ranks, ceremonial practitioners are expected to remain there until either called to the despatch of Daime or instructed by the inspector to move from one place to another. No attempt to communicate with ritual co-participants should be made (unless absolutely necessary) and behaviour must be sufficiently reserved so as not to distract one's neighbours. While in one's place, arms and legs should not be crossed as this inhibits the flow of astral energy which, in turn, impedes the formation and maintenance of the collective spiritual current. As with much else, ritual inspectors correct inappropriate behaviour and, where necessary, censure those who should know better. Leaving the ranks is permitted only in very specific circumstances (e.g. vomiting and defecation) and hedged by particular practices which regulate the exiting and entering of both the ceremonial ranks and inner ritual space. Ideally, an individual should be absent from her place for no more than three hymns. When this amount of time has been exceeded, order is re-established in the ranks by moving people around to fill gaps deemed to impede the communal flow of astral energy. At the same time, and relative both to the needs of the individual and pastoral sensitivity of the inspector, those absent from the ranks are encouraged to return to their place as soon as possible.[23]

In combination, the symbolic and practical regulation of cultic participants involves the 'instrumental coding of the body' (Foucault, 1991: 153) in a way which ensures its ready calibration with the assorted demands of collective ritual practice. As one informant put it: 'Yes, it's necessary that we work on ourselves, our own journeys here and there. But, in Santo Daime this must be done in a way that is synchronized with those around you.' On the one hand, the constant need to correlate individual discipline and communal practice engenders a generic form of cultic regulation which, irrespective of the ritual in question, ensures that participants are aligned vertically with the supernatural plane and bound horizontally with each other. Within every ritual, then, there is a common set of obligations incumbent upon all who enter ritual space. On the other, the fact that the spiritual current generated through shared cultic activity is nuanced relative to the rite in question demands that the bodily coding achieved through ritual regulation comprise slight variations from ceremony to ceremony. As well as symbolizing these variations, the two ritual uniforms employed by Santo Daime further underline the instrumental coding of the body implicated in its cultic practice.[24]

The 'white uniform' (*farda branca*) is worn at all but three of the official Hymnals and was introduced by Master Irineu in 1936, one year after the first Hymnal ritual was celebrated by the nascent *daimista* community. The white uniform reflects the festive and celebratory tenor of the danced Hymnals at which it is worn. Likewise, the lightness of its colour embodies the lighter spiritual current thought to be generated at such events. Introduced in 1972 after the death of Master Irineu, the 'blue uniform' (*farda azul*) is nevertheless attributed to the desire of Santo Daime's founder to establish an alternative dress code for the religion's other rituals. The blue uniform is worn at the Mass, Concentration, non-official Hymnals and other rituals such as the Cure. Uniforms are common to the three ayahuasca religions of Brazil (i.e. *A Barquinha*, Santo Daime and the Union of the Plant), derive in large part from traditional Catholic festivals, reflect the millenarian ethos of popular religious paradigms and embody esoteric notions of hierarchy (A. Dawson, 2007: 67–98; Labate and Pacheco, 2004: 331–4). The white uniform has undergone a number of revisions since its introduction and, like the blue uniform, has male and female versions.[25] Ignoring organizational variations and embellishments, the white uniform for women comprises a white pleated skirt or dress worn to below the knees, long-sleeved blouse and socks. A short green skirt signifies the forest and is worn over the top third of the white skirt. Two green ribbons criss-cross the front of the white blouse to form a 'y' shape and a sequined tiara or crown is worn on the head in reference to the Queen of the Forest. An assortment of flowers, ribbons, and pins may also be worn and are often located on different parts of the upper body to differentiate the married from the unmarried (traditionally, 'woman' and 'virgin'). Men wearing this uniform sport a jacket, shirt, trousers and socks, all of which are white. A black necktie is also worn. For women, the blue uniform consists of a white blouse (with optional short sleeves), blue bow tie, blue pleated skirt worn down to below the knee and white socks. For men, it comprises a white shirt, blue necktie and blue trousers.

Ritual dynamics

Henri Lefebvre observes that social space is something created by us and something by which we are created; it is both product and producer. As such, it is 'instrumental' (as producer) and 'ideological' (as product). In turn, these characteristics make social space a 'political' arena (1991: 27–8, 410–16). The same applies to ritual space. A form of social space, ritual space is neither passive nor neutral. As something through which individuals are ordered and regulated, ritual space actively wields influence over what cultic participants may or may not do and upon what they may or may not be. It is, then, instrumental to the extent that it impacts and shapes those upon whom its disciplinary powers fall. As Pierre Bourdieu would have it, ritual space is a 'structuring structure' (Bourdieu and Wacquant, 1992: 139). Such instrumentality, however, is neither blind nor random. As something created by human beings, ritual space bears the marks of its creators and cannot thereby be neutral. Speaking from and to the socio-cultural ethos of those responsible for its production, ritual space is consequently ideological. Neither passive nor neutral, the instrumental and ideological character of ritual space makes it unavoidably 'political'. Reflecting one set of values rather than another or favouring this mode of practice instead of that, different configurations of ritual space structure and distribute ritual power in ways which work better for some than they do for others.

The insights furnished by Foucault's treatment of modern institutional technologies of power and their attendant political anatomy go some way to elucidating the instrumental, ideological and political character of the *daimista* ritual regime. Preoccupied with understanding 'the body as object and target of power', however, Foucault overplays its 'docility' and thereby offers a rather lopsided account of the individual as an overly passive object of disciplinary regulation and control (1991: 136–7, 156, 194). The preceding framing of the *daimista* ritual repertoire as a disciplinary regime has reflected Foucault's concern to underline the manner in and extent to which institutional (here, ritual) space regulates or 'structures' those who occupy it. Given the aforementioned strictures and obligations at play within *daimista* ritual space, such an emphasis is by no means unwarranted. To stop here, though, would be misleading in two fundamental respects. First, and somewhat generically, such a one-sided emphasis would not do justice to the myriad ways in which ritual participants make and continually reconstitute ritual space by and through their cultic practice. Individuals are not simple passive objects of ritual regulation. Rather, they are active subjects whose practical and symbolic agency creates, sustains and modifies ceremonial space. Ritual space, then, is not only a 'structuring structure', but also a 'structured structure' (Bourdieu and Wacquant, 1992: 139). Second, and rather more to the point, failure to engage the active role played by ceremonial practitioners in constituting and reforming cultic space prevents a proper appreciation of the ongoing transformations to which the contemporary *daimista* ritual repertoire is being subjected. Treating the growing popularity of ritualized spirit possession in Santo Daime, Chapter 4 offers a detailed working example of the ongoing modification of the traditional *daimista* ritual repertoire. The repertorial transformations under way, Chapter 4 argues, are directly related to the now dominant position of the urban middle classes within the *daimista* movement. In effect, ritual space is being restructured to better reflect the prevailing urban-professional ethos of its principal occupants. By way of laying the ground for this treatment, while also serving as an analytical complement to the preceding Foucauldian frame, the remainder of this section uses some relevant insights from the French social theorist Pierre Bourdieu as a means of highlighting the dynamic nature of *daimista* ritual space.

The dynamic nature of *daimista* ritual space may be characterized using Bourdieu's notion of a 'field of force/power'. Although applied as a broader category of social analysis, the defining characteristics of a field of force appropriately describe a range of processes which underwrite the dynamic nature of *daimista* ritual space. For Bourdieu, a field of force comprises a 'network' or 'configuration' of different 'positions'. The individual condition and relative standing of each position is determined by the amount and kinds of 'power' or 'capital' (e.g. cultural, economic and social) to which it has access. Regulated by the 'rules of play' in operation within a field of force, the different occupants of each position 'struggle' to optimize their condition by maximizing the 'benefits' which the field makes available to them. Including 'competition' with those in other positions, the different occupants of the field of force pursue their betterment through the use or 'exchange' of the respective capital (power) at their disposal. Although the prevailing rules of play within any field of force dictate modes of competition and rates of exchange, they are not immune to change. The struggles through which individual positions are optimized are, then, also struggles by which the prevailing 'rules of the game' are reinforced and thereby 'preserved' or contested and subsequently 'transformed' (Bourdieu, 1991: 229–31; 1993: 33–4; 1998b: 34; Bourdieu and Wacquant, 1992: 76–115).

The benefits pursued by the occupants of ritual space come through the correlation of individual endeavour (underwritten by the force of Daime) and collective practice (empowered by the spiritual current). Two distinguishable, though related, kinds of benefits are implicated in Santo Daime's ritual field of force: those which are primarily private and those which are principally public. Private benefits exist most explicitly as the spiritual goods enjoyed by ritual practitioners in the form of, for example, healing, purification and self-understanding; whereas public benefits comprise relational goods manifest through notions of status, prestige and reputation. Although analytically distinct, the two kinds of benefits are related on two counts. First, an individual's position in ritual space is believed to reflect not only her standing in the community but also her level of spiritual maturity. In effect, the more spiritually advanced one is assumed to be (spiritual benefit), the nearer one's position to the central table (public benefit). Second, by being nearer or further from the central table, an individual's position in ritual space provides more or less proximity to the most concentrated part of the collective spiritual current. Consequently, the closer one is to the central table (public benefit) the more potentially efficacious one's ritual practice (spiritual benefit). On each count, then, an individual's position in ritual space embodies both private and public benefits. Private and public benefits are thereby mutually implicating.

Pursuit of the private benefits which the ceremonial field of force makes available to the occupants of its respective positions is, first and foremost, the raison d'être of *daimista* ritual practice. Upon entering and being situated in ceremonial space, ritual practitioners are expected to pursue the private benefits made available by optimizing their position to the best of their ability. Framed by the practical regulation of sacred space, positional optimization relies most upon the symbolic appropriation of ritual virtues such as discipline, firmness and vigilance. This primary explicit function, however, has never excluded a concern with acquiring the public benefits also on offer. Indeed, given the linkage between spatial location and spiritual well-being, it is axiomatic that ritual practitioners should strive to move up the ranks. Consequently, and though principally concerned with optimizing their assigned position, occupants of ritual space are by no means averse to trading up when they can. Traditionally, however, the relatively conservative and homogenous nature of the *daimista* community restricted, both symbolically and practically, the latitude enjoyed by individuals seeking to better their respective positions in the pursuit of public benefits. Closely associated with the norms and practices endemic to popular *caboclo* culture (e.g. kinship, gender and collectivism), the rules of play regulating the ritual field of force have traditionally inhibited both the desire and ability of individuals to game the system in pursuit of the benefits associated with positional advancement. Such is very much less the case among the urban middle classes now predominant across the Santo Daime movement.

Chapter 1 introduced six orchestrating principles which both exemplify the contemporary character of the *daimista* ritual repertoire and reflect the now dominant influence of its urban-professional practitioners. These characteristics are: the *subjectivized* valorization of the individual as the ultimate arbiter of religious authority and the primary agent of spiritual self-transformation; an *instrumental* (i.e. strategic and reflexive) religiosity oriented to the goal of absolute self-realization; a *holistic* world view which both grounds the individual self in an overarching cosmic Whole and relativizes religious belief systems as contingent expressions of otherwise universal truths; an *aestheticized* demeanour characterized by strong experiential preoccupations manifest through inward self-exploration and outer self-expression; a *meritocratic-egalitarianism* which is expectant of rewards for efforts expended and qualifies traditional hierarchical structures; and a *this-worldly* ethos which looks for the benefits of spiritual transformation as much in the here and now as in the there and then of any future incarnation. These characteristics are combining to transform Santo Daime's ritual field of force in a way which is both eroding its traditional rules of play and introducing both novel positional relationships and more flexible modes of capital exchange.

The precise manner in which these characteristics combine to reshape the *daimista* repertoire is discussed at length in later chapters. The key point here, though, concerns their combined transformation of received modes of practical and symbolic ritual regulation in ways which furnish occupants of cultic space with an enhanced degree of individual determination in the pursuit of both private and public benefits. While urban-professional *daimistas* continue to articulate a deep-seated respect for traditional modes of ordering and regulating ritual space, they are imbued with a range of values, expectations and aspirations not straightforwardly compatible with inherited modes of ritual regulation. Whether in respect of traditional gender distinctions, attitudes to hierarchy or disposition to self-abnegation, for example, urban middle-class *daimistas* view and occupy ritual space in a manner which is markedly different than that of their *caboclo* counterparts. Consequently, while the ritual field of force very much remains a disciplinary regime oriented to the maintenance of physical and symbolic order, the rules of play through which order is maintained are inevitably modified relative to a changing conceptualization of precisely what constitutes physical and symbolic order.

Treated as a field of force, *daimista* ritual space comprises a network of positions configured, à la Foucault, through aforementioned modes of spatio-temporal order and practical-symbolic regulation. Individual occupants of the ritual field of force obtain their respective positions through the application of an 'instrumental coding of the body' effected through aforementioned criteria such as age, experience, height, sex and status. Relative to their position within the ceremonial field of force, and in pursuit of both private and public benefits, cultic practitioners mobilize a variety resources which, following Bourdieu, may be identified as kinds of ritual capital. There are five types of ritual capital upon which occupants of *daimista* ceremonial space may draw to enhance or improve upon their respective position with the cultic field of force. The five types of ritual capital are: individual, performative, social, cultural and economic.

Individual capital includes the subject's sex, age, height, physical well-being and psychophysical capabilities. The most obvious impact of Santo Daime's instrumental coding of the body relates to its real and ideal ordering of ritual space relative to the dictates of biological sex. As well as the clear distinctions between the male and female battalions, ritual space embodies a range of divisions of ritual labour made according to individual sexual capital. Whereas traditional gendered distinctions have tended to restrict particular tasks to a specific sex, as Chapter 4 details in respect of spirit mediumship, established divisions of ritual labour are being increasingly challenged by the more liberal mindset of the urban middle classes. At the same time, for example, the often arduous demands of *daimista* ritual space require physical endurance as well as the ability to cope with the psychotropic and bodily effects of ayahuasca consumption. The inability to 'remain firm' and 'stay in your place' during ceremonial practice is not simply injurious to the continued occupation of one's ritual position but ultimately terminal to the pursuit of both private and, especially, public benefits. Consequently, ritual practitioners with a range of individual capital suited to the ideal ordering and demanding nature of ceremonial space are best placed to optimize the prevailing conditions of the ritual field of force. Those whose individual capital is not well suited to the rigours of *daimista* ritual space invariably find it a very tough environment indeed.

Performative capital comprises the gamut of ceremonial practical-knowledge upon which individual participants may draw. On the one hand, performative capital includes knowledge of traditions, lore and customs which is most commonly allied with time spent within and subsequent experience of respective *daimista* circles. The ability to reference facts about key figures and events or to quote hymns and sayings from memory is valued as a sign of personal dedication and commitment to the doctrine. Especially, but not solely, among initiates to the movement, *daimistas* will commonly spend large amounts of time and energy learning hymns and seeking out factual information about Santo Daime. Likewise, knowledge of the symbolic and practical disciplines regulating ritual space is integral to efficacious cultic performance. On the other hand, performative capital involves particular skills which range, for example, from the basic requirements of dancing, singing and Portuguese pronunciation, through instrumental proficiency and hymnic reception, to recognized expertise in healing and mediumship. As with ritual capital in general, scarcer forms of *daimista* practical-knowledge (e.g. mediumship) are highly valued and thereby much sought after (see Chapter 4).

Social capital is accrued through interpersonal relations, general utility and extra-cultic prestige such as fame or political power. More pronounced in Brazil than elsewhere, blood relations or close friendships with those in authority go some way to enhancing an individual's position within ceremonial space. As remarked earlier, individuals will often name-check *daimista* luminaries with whom they have had contact or shared ritual space and, even better, from whom the membership star or a cup of Daime has been received. Likewise, possession of technical expertise useful to the local community (e.g. construction or tailoring) or movement as a whole (e.g. IT or legal training) contributes to ritual standing. In the same vein, and like other new religions in search of organizational security, those with public profiles or broader social influence are often afforded a positional prominence and ritual status not always in keeping with their actual experience.

Cultural capital is at its most prestigious when closely associated with the spiritual cradle of Santo Daime. While Brazilians are generally esteemed across the movement on account of their cultural association with their religion's homeland, those from the Amazon region are looked upon as living embodiments of the heritage and wisdom which Santo Daime regards as its principal contribution to the world at large.[26] Whether Brazilian or not, stays at *Céu do Mapiá* and other traditional *daimista* communities (further valorized by attending a major Hymnal ritual or *feitio*) are an important source of cultural capital; as well as the social capital gained through the relationships made. A moderate or secure fluency in Portuguese is likewise a valuable source of cultural (and performative) capital. Many of those lacking the means or ability to acquire linguistic fluency, however, will take great pains to ensure that their pronunciation of Portuguese hymn-lyrics, prayers and miscellaneous terminology is as accurate as possible.

Economic capital is both important in its own right and supports the acquisition and nurturing of other forms of ritual capital (e.g. social and cultural capital acquired through travel to and across Brazil). Most fundamentally, economic capital allows access to Santo Daime rituals. The costs associated with ritual participation are a sensitive topic to *daimistas*. On the one hand, government-sponsored bodies in Brazil (e.g. Confen and Conad) stipulate that ayahuasca should not be commercialized and thereby bought and sold like any ordinary commodity (Labate, 2011). On the other, the costs involved in producing, distributing (including payment of taxes), storing and ritually accessing ayahuasca are considerable and must, therefore, be met in one way or another. *Daimistas* are, however, strident in their assertions that no one is 'charged' to attend a ritual. For members, the costs involved in staging rituals are covered by the gifting of a monthly sum which also includes contributions to both local community and the wider organization. To non-members, it is 'suggested' that a 'donation' be made of an amount commensurate with the costs involved in facilitating ritual participation. As with the monthly contribution of members, a portion of the donations received from non-members may be passed on in support of broader organizational structures and campaigns. Paralleling monthly membership costs, the amount of the donation suggested to non-members varies relative to national and local contexts as well as different ritual events. Whatever the membership status or geographical and ceremonial context, however, regular participation in *daimista* rituals requires a not inconsiderable degree of financial commitment. In addition to accessing ceremonial space, ritual economic capital may be mobilized, for example, to obtain related cultic accoutrements such as psychoactive agents other than ayahuasca.

In tandem with the correlation of individual endeavour and corporate practice, the dynamic nature of Santo Daime's ceremonial field of force resides primarily in the mobilization of ritual capital in pursuit of the private and public benefits on offer. What, how and why different aspects of ritual capital are mobilized by individual occupants of the ceremonial field of force varies relative to subjective, positional and communal factors. As with the young man at the beginning of this chapter, newcomers to the ritual field, whatever their experience in other contexts, lack the necessary capital (principally, though not solely, performative) upon which they might draw in pursuit of either private or public benefits. At the same time, and irrespective of length of membership, those lacking the individual capital to manage the psychotropic effects of Daime or meet the exacting physical demands of ritual practice are likewise fundamentally impeded in respect of properly acquiring the benefits made available by *daimista* ritual space. In the same vein, those able to mobilize significant cultural or social capital have, other things being equal, something of an advantage over those unable to call upon such resources.

Among the urban middle classes now dominant across the movement, the ritual pursuit of private and public benefits embodies a range of characteristics which are progressively modifying established rules of play and transforming traditional modes of practical and symbolic regulation. Treated by Chapter 4 in connection with ongoing shifts in spirit-oriented practices, for example, established conventions framing spirit mediumship (e.g. by whom, where, when and how it may be practised) are, through their challenge or transgression, being progressively eroded. A source of common complaint by those of a more traditional bent, the number and kinds of individuals claiming to receive hymns and the increasingly popular practice of publicly disclosing recently experienced visions are likewise indications of the ongoing transformation of inherited modes of ritual regulation. Individuals leaving the ranks for longer than they should (e.g. to lie down or 'do their own thing'), transgressing spatial boundaries, customizing their uniforms or behaving inappropriately in their positions (e.g. interacting with their neighbours) are incrementally common events which exemplify the contravention of traditional restrictions upon individual comportment during ritual practice. The rise in the numbers bringing musical instruments into ritual space (thereby getting nearer the central table than they otherwise might) or exhibiting increasingly expressive behaviour (e.g. flamboyant dance steps or melodramatic spirit mediumship) during cultic practice further attest to the ongoing transformation and inherently dynamic nature of Santo Daime's ceremonial field of force.

Conclusion

The religious efficacy which Santo Daime affords its practitioners is believed, in large part, to be constituted by the communal dynamism of its collective ceremonial practice. Corporate ritual practice generates the collective spiritual current, the power and concentration of which magnifies individual exertion through its catalysing and dynamic affect. Collective ceremonial practice thereby furnishes a return on subjective cultic action far greater than that ordinarily available to an individual working in ritual isolation. Although underwritten by collective practice, the religious efficacy of Santo Daime rests also upon individual ritual endeavour. The collective spiritual current upon which *daimista* ritual efficacy rests is ultimately grounded in the subjective exertions of individual practitioners infused by the force of Daime. The sustained and focused application of individual cultic practitioners is thereby a necessary condition for the generation and maintenance of the collective spiritual current. Founded upon their mutually implicating relationship, the ritual efficacy of Santo Daime rests squarely upon the respective management and successful coordination of individual application and collective practice. Ritual efficacy is premised upon ritual order, and ritual order requires ritual regulation.

The ordering of the *daimista* ritual sphere has been explored through the Foucauldian notion of a disciplinary regime comprising spatio-temporal means of organization and practical-symbolic modes of regulation. By way of complementing this regulatory emphasis upon ritual space as a disciplinary regime, Bourdieu's concept of the 'field of force' has been employed to explicate both the dynamic and transformative nature of the contemporary *daimista* ritual arena. The dynamic character of *daimista* ritual practice resides primarily in the pursuit of the benefits made available to occupants of the ritual field of force. Of a private and public kind, the positional hierarchization of ritual space intimately connects the respective pursuit and enjoyment of each type of benefit. An integral part of *daimista* ritual practice since its beginning, this dynamic is nevertheless undergoing a series of transformations at the hands of a now predominant urban middle-class constituency. The rules of play which have traditionally regulated Santo Daime's ritual field of force are now being progressively modified relative to aforementioned orchestrating principles embodying a range of typically late-modern, urban-professional characteristics. As a result, *daimista* ritual space is being incrementally liberalized.

In view of the above, much of Santo Daime's religious efficacy can be said to reside in the personal appropriation of private and public benefits made available to occupants of ceremonial space relative to their assigned position, individual endeavour and embroilment in collective regulation. On the one hand, the mutual implication of individual application and corporate practice requires of ritual practitioners the voluntary subjection to a disciplinary regime informed by cooperative intent and sustained by collective responsibility. While external regulation of individual participants is important, it nevertheless remains secondary to a subjective commitment to ceremonial practice exemplified by the internalization of ritual virtues such as discipline and firmness. On the other, the reciprocal relationship between positional standing and the pursuit of ritual benefits engenders a curious marriage of subjective aspiration and interpersonal rivalry. Viewed in this light, the aforementioned proliferation of hymnic reception, sharing of visions and expressive ritual behaviour, for example, constitute more than straightforward public manifestations of otherwise private benefits. They also comprise self-promotional status claims made in the interests of positional advancement and benefit maximization. Although explicitly characterized by ritual codependence, the ceremonial field of Santo Daime is no less marked by cultic competition.

3

New world – New selves: *Daimista* discourse as an apolitics of transformation

Introduction

Having some housekeeping chores to complete between bouts of fieldwork, I visited São Paulo city centre in the company of a *daimista* friend, Bernado. Prior to making our way to the shops, we dropped by the Catholic Cathedral where Bernado was keen to point out the symbolic associations between popular Catholic iconography and some of the central imagery of Santo Daime. At ground level, statues of the Holy Family and the saints were enthusiastically highlighted, as was the two-sparred Cross of Caravaca featured in the carving of a past pope. In the crypts below, Bernado drew attention to the important *daimista* symbols of the boat and star carved on the tombs of former archbishops and was particularly impressed to find the word *firmeza* (firmness) appearing in a number of prominent official crests. During our walk around the cathedral, Bernado told me how the water turned to wine by Jesus at the Marriage in Cana was actually the sacrament of Daime. He also mentioned the historical 'coincidence' that the birthplace of Master Irineu, São Vicente de Ferrar, was named after a saint who preached the second coming of Christ; subsequently achieved through the reincarnation of Jesus' spirit in the person of Irineu Serra.

When eventually arriving at the shops, my companion announced his intention to purchase a new charger for his eco-friendly, reusable batteries. Moving from shop to shop, Bernado first requested to handle the units in which he was interested before asking the price of the chargers in question and then attempting to secure a discount on the model most desired. Unwilling or unable to pay the asking price of the particular chargers on offer, Bernado moved briskly on the next shop while proclaiming volubly that experienced reality is but an 'illusion', society is 'filthy' and the world is 'passing away'. Waving generally to the merchandise on offer around us, battery chargers included, he denounced it all as 'unreal', 'illusory' and 'worthless' (*sem valor*). Over ten shops later, and with such pronouncements repeated between almost every establishment, we made our way home; my housekeeping chores completed but without a charger having been purchased.

Setting aside the idiosyncrasies of my friend Bernado, what stood out for me from these events was the range of interpretative resources which the Santo Daime religion furnishes its members in their day-to-day dealings with the world at large. Very much in keeping with the characteristically pluriform and polyvalent nature of the *daimista* world view, Bernado moved easily between reading his social environment as, in one moment, a source of symbolic significance for him and his beliefs and, at another, a place devoid of meaning in outright opposition to what he stood for. Reflecting upon the ease of Bernado's shift between affirmation and condemnation, and searching for a means to explicate the polyvalent character of the *daimista* world view, I came up (or, at least, thought I did) with the term 'dislocution'; a neologism formed by mixing dislocation with mislocution. First, the term 'dislocution' is intended to capture Santo Daime's locution of the world in a way which relativizes its contents (as illusory, unreal and passing away) without fully foreclosing on the practical and symbolic possibilities made available by the prevailing socio-cultural context. Although narrating an explicit suspicion of the world at large, the contemporary *daimista* paradigm does so by rhetorically distancing rather than actually extracting its members from the prevailing processes and constitutive dynamics of late-modern society. It is an act of dis-*locution*, not one of dis-*location*. Second, the term 'dislocution' is intended to conceptualize the polyvalent nature of *daimista* approaches to the contemporary world in a non-pathologizing way. While paradoxical in their discursive relationship, the interplay of alternate positions in respect of the world at large should not be dismissed too readily as a contradictory, hypocritical or ill-conceived misspeaking. An act of *dis*-locution rather than *mis*-locution, Santo Daime's polyvalent narration of its social environment furnishes its members with an optimal range of possible positions through which practical and symbolic returns from worldly engagement might best be maximized.

Upon further investigation, I found the term 'dislocution' to have already been coined by Fritz Senn in his writings on the Irish author James Joyce (1984). According to Senn, Joyce employs dislocution as an 'expediently blurred trope' which encompasses 'all manner of metamorphoses, switches, transfers, [and] displacements'. In so doing, Joyce's distinctive style uses dislocution to reconfigure spatial relationships (through 'dislocations', 'displacements' and 'diversions'), unsettle personal interactions (by 'heterographic dissensions' and 'switches') and disturb temporal associations (through 'disruptions', 'incongruities' and 'anachronistic checks') (1984: 199–212). By happy coincidence, Senn's description of the process of dislocution includes much of what I strove to articulate when originally (as I then thought) coming up with the term. The dislocutory character of *daimista* narrations of contemporary society does indeed reconfigure, unsettle and disturb mainstream understandings of humankind and its relationship with the world at large.

The process of dislocution at the heart of *daimista* narrations of the world might fruitfully be understood as an 'illocutionary' strategy or 'speech act'. Formulated by Austin (1962), popularized by Searle (1969) and later developed by the likes of Habermas (1984) and Butler (1997), a speech act is a mode of discourse which constitutes rather than simply describing a state of affairs. Also termed a 'performative utterance', a speech act brings something about by articulating matters in a way which impacts upon the context in question by effecting a change to prevailing conditions. By declaring a defendant guilty, for example, a judge does not simply pronounce but actively confers guilt upon the individual in question. Likewise, by informing her mother that 'I'm thirsty', a daughter is not only describing a state of affairs but also seeking a change to her current condition. Understood as a speech act or performative utterance, Santo Daime's dislocution of the world disrupts and reconfigures established hermeneutical frames by positioning *daimistas* in a relationship of constructive tension with their respective social environment. On the one hand, the narration of the world as illusory, worthless and passing away engenders a demeanour of suspicion and mistrust by which *daimista* relations with society are imbued with the constant possibility of rejection and condemnation. On the other, the tensions in worldly relations generated by *daimista* discourse serve only to relativize rather than debar the things of this world. Being *in* but not *of* the world, *daimistas* continue to make constructive use of the material and symbolic resources made available. Narrated as worthless on account of their inherently illusory and ephemeral status, the things of this world nevertheless continue to serve, when deemed appropriate, as potential sources of practical and significatory value. Albeit worthless, the things of this world are by no means useless.

The following sections develop the notion of the *daimista* world view as a dislocutory speech act, the narration of which situates believers in a relationship of constructive tension vis-à-vis their prevailing socio-cultural context. By way of doing so, two important emphases are identified and treated as narrative leitmotifs informing the *daimista* world view. Each of these leitmotifs embodies the principally apolitical character of Santo Daime, with the former reflecting a communitarian ethos while the latter involves a more individualized focus. Defined here as an 'apolitics of social transformation', the first leitmotif is typically Brazilian in its make-up and has enjoyed historical dominance as an orchestrating force within the *daimista* narrative. While no less integral to the *daimista* world view, the second leitmotif has traditionally been qualified by reference to the first. Identified as an 'apolitics of self-transformation', the second leitmotif gained relative prominence subsequent to Santo Daime's expansion beyond the Amazon region and the ensuing dominance of the urban middle classes across the movement as a whole. Consequently, whereas an apolitics of social transformation is still narrated by certain sectors of the *daimista* movement, the apolitics of self-transformation is now by far the most prevalent leitmotif of the Santo Daime world view.

An apolitics of social transformation

The apolitics of social transformation historically prominent within *daimista* narrations of the world is heavily influenced by millenarian themes drawn principally from Brazil's popular religious imaginary. The presence of millenarian beliefs within the Santo Daime world view has been somewhat under studied relative to other aspects of the *daimista* paradigm. Although acknowledged by academic treatments of the movement, little has been done to explicate the presence and influence of millenarian motifs within the *daimista* world view (e.g. Goulart, 2004: 62; Gregorim, 1991: 103; MacRae, 1992: 75; Schmidt, 2007: 107). In one of the most quoted definitions of millenarianism, Norman Cohn identifies it as a 'particular type of salvationism'. According to Cohn, the millenarian paradigm can be identified through its characterization of salvation as:

> (a) collective, in the sense that it is to be enjoyed by the faithful as a collectivity; (b) terrestrial, in the sense that it is to be realized on this earth and not in some other-worldly heaven; (c) imminent, in the sense that it is to come both soon and suddenly; (d) total, in the sense that it is utterly to transform life on earth, so that the new dispensation will be no mere improvement on the present but perfection itself; (e) miraculous, in the sense that it is to be accomplished by, or with the help of, supernatural agencies. (1970: 13)

Likewise regarding millenarianism as offering a form of 'collective salvation', Yonina Talmon fleshes out the sudden and total transformation identified by

Cohn. According to Talmon, transition to the renewed world envisaged by the millenarian world view is

accompanied by terrible tribulations which are the birth pangs of salvation. The new dispensation is born out of unprecedented cataclysms, disastrous upheavals and bloody calamities. The apocalyptic victory will be won by means of a prodigious and final struggle which will destroy the agents of corruption, purge the sinful world and prepare it for its final redemption. (1966: 167)

Building upon cross-cultural studies of millenarian belief systems by her and others, Catherine Wessinger offers a 'functional definition of *millennialism*' which complements the above by broadening the scope of where and by whom the new world is to be realized.[1] For Wessinger, while the collective salvation envisaged by the millenarian paradigm 'is often considered to be earthly . . . it can also be heavenly'. Likewise, although often believed to 'be accomplished either by a divine or superhuman agent alone', historical transition to the new world may also be achieved 'with the assistance of humans working according to the divine or superhuman will and plan' (2011: 5).

Brazilian millenarianism

Landes observes that the 'common traits' shared by millenarian belief systems manifest themselves in specific socio-cultural contexts through 'a wide variety of forms'. Precisely 'when and how' the new world will emerge, 'who' brings it about and 'what' it will 'look like', for example, receive highly varied concretizations relative to the structural dynamics, institutional processes and symbolic resources at play across a particular socio-cultural context and within a given group or movement (2006: 10). Although likewise the case for the Brazilian context within which Santo Daime emerged, messianic emphases from popular Catholic traditions tended to furnish something of a common motif for a good number of the most significant movements. As Negrão maintains, messianic millenarianism involves the 'belief in a saviour (God himself or his emissary) whose anticipated arrival will put an end to the present iniquitous or oppressive order and establish a new era of virtue and justice' (2001: 119). The history of messianic millenarianism in Brazil is a fertile one and Levine believes it 'likely that dozens or even hundreds of millenarian and messianic movements sprang up and died of their own accord over the centuries' (1992: 218). Indeed, such has been the prevalence of messianic millenarianism in Brazil that Da Matta regards it 'as a fundamental part of

Brazilian culture' (1996: 5).[2] In the same vein, Myscofski's treatment of the 'Luso-Brazilian messianic tradition' shows that Portuguese Catholicism was replete with millenarian themes and imagery which passed into the popular religious consciousness of the fledgling nation of Brazil (1988: 43–76).[3]

Established almost entirely among the rural poor, traditional millenarian movements in Brazil emerged on the back of long-standing systemic marginalization from prevailing structures of socio-economic power and political representation. Resulting from a mixture of geographical, historical and socio-cultural dynamics, the Brazilian peasantry was disenfranchised on account of its social status and isolated by its dependence upon the landowning elite (Monteiro, 1974: 13–14). Both literally and figuratively, the Brazilian peasantry lived on the periphery of things. In addition to experiencing systemic marginalization from prevailing structures of power and representation, Brazilian peasants suffered from a deep-seated strategic impotence. The strategic impotence experienced by the peasantry was characterized by a symbolic and practical inability to conceptualize and implement strategies of social transformation. Indicative of the practical implications of systemic marginalization, the strategic impotence experienced was also fed by dominant symbolic representations of prevailing social structures as God-given hierarchies not to be interfered with (Otten, 1990: 287). A direct correlate of the heavenly order, traditional society was imbued with a fixity which allowed for change only in a cyclical (i.e. seasonal) and thereby closed sense. Enlightenment notions of linear (i.e. open) progress through incremental social transformation were alien to traditional Brazilian society. Together, systemic marginalization and strategic impotence fed a world view in which prevailing structures of power and representation were regarded by peasants as neither belonging to them nor open to change. Consequently, if social transformation were to occur it would have to be achieved through an agency other than theirs and by means external to the system. On both counts, then, social transformation would be extraordinary not simply in effect but also in the manner of its arrival.

Although opinion differs as to the causal mechanisms involved, treatments of traditional millenarianism in Brazil agree that some form of practical-symbolic crisis acts as a trigger of millenarian activity. The most popular causes of the crises which triggered traditional millenarian outbreaks are identified as the ingression of modernizing capitalist dynamics within rural society (e.g. mechanization and wage labour) and the inward expansion of centralized state systems already established within Brazil's growing urban centres (e.g. Amado, 1978; Della Cava, 1970; Martins, 1981; Oliveira, 1985; Otten, 1990). Alternative readings place causal emphasis upon dynamics internal to the religious field (e.g. Myscofski, 1988) or the breakdown of established kinship structures (e.g. Queiroz, 1965). Whether socio-cultural, economic-political or religious in nature, the crises which triggered millenarian activity did so because they impacted upon both practical mechanisms of support and symbolic structures of signification. Practically speaking, for example, the transition from landed tenant to wage labourer brought on by the introduction of capitalist means of production quickly eroded established modes of socio-economic reproduction (e.g. *mutirão* and *compadrio*) which served to ameliorate the hardships associated with rural life. In the same vein, and undermined by the rapid erosion of established means of socio-economic reproduction, traditional meaning structures which likewise mitigated hardships were quickly exhausted as symbolic resources for making sense of what was going on. Crises of practical-symbolic reproduction thereby provided fertile ground into which the seeds of existing millenarian motifs could take root as the negation of a negation. Driven by practical-symbolic crisis and the resulting longing for change, systemic marginalization and strategic impotence combined to produce a world view which held that prevailing structures must end before things could change for the better, and that this end would come by means both external to the system and other than collective agitation. Although not the only possible response, the extraordinary transformational model furnished by the millenarian paradigm squared the significatory circle in that it provided the possibility of a much-desired social change when both systemic marginalization and strategic impotence dictated such a state of affairs to be an otherwise practical and symbolic impossibility.

The combination of systemic marginalization and strategic impotence foundational to Brazilian millenarianism gave it a non-political tenor in that it did not, by and large, seek to change prevailing societal structures. The kind of social transformation sought by traditional Brazilian millenarianism was principally apolitical in character.[4] The vast majority of groups which became embroiled in some form of violence, for example, did so only by way of response to or defence against armed intervention by existing political authorities.[5] Instead, millenarian groups tended to adopt an internally focused and strongly communitarian ethos which, imbued with sectarianism and orchestrated by a messianic leadership, oriented both external relations and internal organization of the newly formed community. In discursive terms, such was done by situating the practical-symbolic crisis (or crises) to which the millenarian community responded within an overarching transhistorical frame. Drawing upon the popular religious imaginary, the trials and tribulations of the millenarian community were commonly interpreted against the transhistorical backdrop of a supernatural battle between good and evil. Identifying itself and its leadership with the heavenly forces of righteousness, strict sectarian divisions were employed between the millenarian community as a gathering of the saved and those outside as beyond the pale of salvation. *Ad extra* sectarian narratives were complemented by *ad intra* collectivist concerns which organized the faithful according to strict hierarchies and demanding regimes. Just as the community of the righteous sacrificed itself to the cause of the greater transhistorical good, so too individual members were expected to subordinate their personal interests to the corporate well-being of the millenarian collective.

Daimista *millenarianism*

The fact that most recorded millenarian outbreaks in Brazil occurred in the north-east is highly relevant. The founding community of Santo Daime was almost entirely made up of economic migrants drawn to the Amazon region from north-east Brazil. Likewise, the overwhelming majority of Cefluris members prior to Santo Daime's spread to south Brazil comprised descendants of *nordestinos* ('north-easterners'). Whether exposed directly or socialized second-hand, the strength and prevalence of millenarianism throughout north-east Brazil was such that its impact upon the Santo Daime movement was no less likely than that of other aspects of popular north-east culture detailed by Labate and Pacheco (2004). Though forming only part of the nascent and already hybrid *daimista* repertoire, millenarian themes nevertheless made a significant contribution to the overarching world view of the foundational community, informing both its external relations with society at large and internal organizational arrangements as a community of the faithful.

Noted in Chapter 1, the paucity of contemporary documentation and independent historical sources limit what can be said with confidence about the early *daimista* paradigm. As with Afro-Brazilian components of the originary repertoire, for example, certain elements of the millenarian world view (not least its more apocalyptic tones) may well have been subject to later revision or removal from the historical record subsequent both to the rationalizing impact of European esotericism and the relative respectability eventually achieved by Master Irineu and the Alto Santo community within Rio Branco society. Much of relevance, however, remains in place. Detailed in Chapter 2, for example, the foundational hymnal of Santo Daime (*O Cruzeiro*) employs millenarian motifs to situate the *daimista* community within a transhistorical battle between the supernatural forces of good and evil, the denouement of which involves an historical reckoning of 'judgement' and 'purification'. As well as identifying its leader as the messianic figure of the 'Imperial Chief', *ad extra* sectarian divisions between the community of believers and the world of 'illusion' are employed. Such is complemented by a strongly defined communitarianism articulated through *ad intra* organizational hierarchies (e.g.

'battalions') and collectivist representations of individual 'obligation' and 'discipline'.

Discussed in Chapter 1, the formative period of the early *daimista* community was characterized by a number of hardships. By the beginning of the 1920s, for example, Brazil's first rubber-cycle had ended, with the economic migrants who had first made their way to the plantations from the north-east now having to move again in order to survive. Comprising such migrants, the community forged by Irineu Serra on the edge of Rio Branco endured much by way of struggle as its members strove to make a success of their precarious and demanding subsistence lifestyle (Goulart, 2004; Silva, 1983). The nature of its beliefs and ritual practices also generated hardships for the nascent community through the periodic persecutions unleashed by local ecclesiastical and political authorities. From land invasions, through house searches, to actual imprisonment, members of the early community were subjected to a variety of official actions which, combined with their everyday struggles to survive, served only to heighten individual and collective anxieties (MacRae, 1992). As well as speaking to the hardships endured by the first generations of Santo Daime, the millenarian paradigm served as a symbolic support for their emerging religious project. Appeal to its messianic motifs helped reinforce Irineu Serra's still nascent charismatic authority, just as its sectarian themes rationalized the group's progressive separation from popular cultural beliefs and practices. In the same vein, millenarian models and tropes contributed to galvanizing communal identity, in addition to underwriting both emergent organizational arrangements and ongoing ritual innovations. Oriented to the formation of a distinct and inwardly focused community, and very much in keeping with traditional Brazilian millenarianism, the social transformation sought by the earliest *daimistas* was typically apolitical in character.

The same applies to Cefluris, both before and after its initial expansion beyond the Amazon region. Indeed, millenarian discourse was central to articulating the foundational experiences of the earliest communities established beyond the Amazon region as they struggled to establish themselves and their countercultural lifestyles. Writing of the hardships endured by Padrinho Sebastião's community as it moved from Colony 5000 to Rio do Ouro and then to Mapiá, Goulart records a marked increase in the millenarian motifs appearing in the leader's hymns (2004: 85). At one point giving a date of '2014', Padrinho Sebastião claims that 'the New World is now going to happen. What I said is this: a new life, new people and new system'. The year '2000' is also identified as significant, after which 'a time will come when no one will know what is going to pass . . . the old things are finishing and the new is emerging' (Polari, 1998: 128, 178, 190). His son and current leader of Cefluris, Padrinho Alfredo, likewise maintains that 'We are in the squeeze of the end of time and the return of Christ' (Polari, 1999: 235). Elsewhere, Alfredo talks of 'the third millennium' as 'the time of the Divine Holy Spirit' in which the 'war' against 'illusion' and 'the old life' will be won as 'a new generation is going to adapt itself to the system of the new time' (Polari, 1998: 12–13). Alfredo's brother, Padrinho Valdete, says in the ninth hymn ('The Infinite') of his hymnal *The Little Book of the Apocalypse*: 'It may be in the year 2000; I don't know when it is; I know it's going to strike; As it struck; In the time of Noah.' Speaking around the time of Padrinho Sebastião's death, Padrinho Alex Polari is recording as saying that

> we believe the New Age that is coming will be a passage – it's going to be a very difficult birth for humanity. People all over the world will have to find alternative ways of life that can be sustained materially, socially, and spiritually. (Richman, 1990/1: 41)

Writing later as a fully established member of the Cefluris leadership, Padrinho Alex links the emergence of Santo Daime and its 'spiritual message of universal value' with the 'birth of the era of Pisces' and 'our current planetary crisis' (1998: 18–21, 49–50). Coming at 'the end of a great cycle', the 'difficult birth of the new era' involves a 'transition between the old and the new world' resulting in 'the transformation of the whole planet' (1999: 7, 15, 129, 215).

Exemplified by Polari's comments and illustrated further below, the millenarian discourse employed by the traditional *daimista* community was no less familiar to new members of the movement drawn from Brazil's urban middle classes. Melding traditional motifs with new-age narratives, urban millenarian movements were an established part of the alternative religious scene by the time of Santo Daime's expansion beyond the Amazon region. Founded in Rio de Janeiro in the late 1940s by the Venerable Master Yokaanam, the 'Universal Spiritualist Eclectic Fraternity' (*Fraternidade Eclética Espiritualista Universal*) is one of the earliest examples of urban Brazilian millenarianism. Having relocated his group in 1955 from Rio de Janeiro to the *planalto*, north-east of Brasília, Yokaanam announced that the third millennium would be ushered in by way of the calamitous effects of an asteroid which would crash into the Atlantic and raise sea levels to catastrophic proportions. Initially forecast to occur in 1979/80, this global catastrophe was later put back to 1990, at which point the appearance of a second sun and the outbreak of a third world war would herald the impending calamity (Negrão, 1984: 57, 96). The 'Blue Butterflies' (*Borboletas Azuis*) founded in the 1970s by Roldão Mangueira in the north-east city of Campina Grande is another example. Mangueira prophesied that 'in the month of May, 1980, there will be a great deluge as in the time of Noah and there will be 120 days of rain', after which 'no stone will remain upon another' (Consorte and Negrão, 1984: 328, 341).

In respect of modern-day non-mainstream millenarianism in Brazil, a significant number of movements continue to mobilize millenarian motifs as important elements of their religious world view. According to Master Joaquim José de Andrade Neto, leader of the Campinas-based 'Union of the Plant' (*Centro Espiritual Beneficente União do Vegetal*), for example, 'humanity is currently living through one of the most crucial moments of its history'. Characterized by, among other things, 'moral corruption', 'family disintegration' and 'growing prostitution', the present 'transitional' era is beset by 'seismic shocks, floods, nuclear accidents, incurable illnesses, and other global disasters'. Surrounded by evidence of its own disobedience, humankind nevertheless 'appears not to understand or does not wish to understand that it is fatally making its way towards its own destruction' (Milanez, 1988: 129). Similar sentiments are expressed by the First Master Sun Tumuchy, Mário Sassi, of the 'Christian Spiritualist Order of the Dawn Valley' (*Ordem Espiritualista Cristã do Vale do Amanhecer*). According to Sassi, the current 'civilizational cycle . . . is about to end and the world will pass through great transformations which are already evident to those with common sense' (1979: 4). In the same vein, José de Paiva Netto, leader of the 'Religion of God' (*A Religião de Deus*), asserts that 'people are marching towards death in the forthcoming and last Armageddon of this cycle . . . these final times of deep changes for the World' (Netto, 1988: 28). Building upon the prophecies of the Venerable Master Samael Aun Weor, the 'Gnostic Church of Brazil' (*A Igreja Gnóstica do Brasil*) claims that the world will be transformed by a forthcoming 'final catastrophe' in the year 2043. Extraterrestrial 'beings from the Pleiades' will support those deemed worthy enough to have survived this catastrophe by communicating valuable scientific and cultural information, along with genetic materials, which will aid in reconstruction. Within '50 to 100 years' of the predicted catastrophe taking place, an 'Age of Gold' of 'freedom, 'abundance' and 'universal love' will have been established (see A. Dawson, 2007: 103).

Especially in Brazil, *daimistas* offer a similar fusion of traditional motifs and new-age themes to produce a narrative structure paralleling that of the modern-day non-mainstream millenarian paradigm. Natural disasters (e.g. earthquakes, famine and floods) and environmental issues (e.g. pollution, global warming and escalating species extinction) were among the most common things expressed as critical signs of impending global catastrophe. Frequently connected with moral degeneracy, rampant materialism, egocentricity or spiritual superficiality, the impending global catastrophe was also regarded as an ineluctable historical event grounded in cyclical (à la Eastern paradigms) or evolutionary (à la Western models) transhistorical dynamics. Driven by such transhistorical dynamics, the path of human history assumes something of a roller-coaster-like trajectory, as periods of moral, philosophical and scientific distinction (e.g. Atlantis, Greece, India and Meso-America) are followed by civilizational decline, eventual destruction and subsequent socio-cultural ascent. For many *daimistas*, the periodic process of civilizational rise and fall is accompanied by the appearance of religio-spiritual repertoires tasked with guiding humankind (or sections thereof) through the particular crises associated with their respective historical decline. Santo Daime is regarded by members as one such religion; 'founded', according to a south-Brazilian community leader, for 'the new time' (*o novo tempo*).

The narration of Santo Daime's status as a religion for a 'new time' draws on a variety of discursive strands. In keeping with the millenarian paradigm, Santo Daime is commonly viewed as equipping its members with the practical-knowledge necessary both to survive the impending global catastrophe (occasioned by, for example, resource exhaustion, environmental disaster, the meltdown of the capitalist system, nuclear war and asteroid collision) and subsequently to flourish on the newly transformed earth. On the one hand, the *daimista* repertoire's concern for the higher-self is seen to furnish a spiritual regime oriented to understanding and meeting the trials and tribulations associated with the calamitous passage to the new world. On the other, the 'simple', 'basic' or 'sustainable' lifestyle and intimate relations with nature promoted by Santo Daime are perceived to equip *daimistas* with the appropriate discipline and skills to best exploit post-apocalyptic environmental conditions. Viewed as the 'new Jerusalem', the mother community of Mapiá is frequently idealized as an exemplar of post-transformational sustainability and working model of a 'Noah's Ark' within which refuge will be found during the troublesome times ahead. As one informant put it, events associated with the 'end times' will throw humanity 'back to the Stone Age', with only those knowledgeable about 'working with nature' able to survive. Though timely, Santo Daime's emergence at the close of the current civilizational cycle is no coincidence.

Daimistas also employ traditional esoteric motifs narrating the cultural migration and ensuing accumulation of specialist practical-knowledge to underwrite the 'new world' status of Santo Daime. Here, Santo Daime is presented as the culmination of a prolonged historical process in which the practical-knowledge necessary for the 'new time' has eventually made its way to the South American continent. Informant accounts generally maintain that the migratory accumulation of specialist beliefs and practices which culminated with Santo Daime in Brazil originated with the tantric and yogic traditions of pre-modern Asia before moving to the mystery religions and priestly cults of the classical Greco-Roman world. Arising from the incarnation of Christ (though incorporating elements from Asia and the classical pagan period), the birth of Christianity initiates a new chapter in the discursive migration from the far East to far West of the new world. The Christianity brought to South

America by the Conquistadors, however, is believed by some not only to be that of the church but also to have secretly included components of European nature and esoteric traditions (e.g. Druidism and Hermeticism). Terminating in South America, the migratory model of religio-spiritual accumulation affords the geographical new world an historical significance as the epicentre of the impending new time.

The migratory model traditional to the esoteric paradigm is complemented by the established Brazilian narrative of cultural confluence. Mirroring modern nationalistic readings of Brazil as born of the socio-cultural melding of American, European and African sources (Ortiz, 1985), the confluence narrative builds upon the migratory model by identifying Santo Daime as an historical nodal point combining the accumulated spiritual wisdom of the world at large. Typical of those employing the confluence model, one informant told me that the sacrament of Daime was bequeathed by the Incan civilization, subsequently preserved by the Amazonian tribes and then passed down to Master Irineu who represents the merger of African (as a 'black man') and European (as a 'Christian') cultures. Somewhat less typical, but by no means a rare sentiment, my informant also believed that the Incas received the secret of Daime from extraterrestrials originating in the constellation of the Pleiades. In tandem with the timeliness of its emergence during the current civilizational crisis, Santo Daime's status is further underlined by its identification as the terminal combination of the twin-track processes of migratory accumulation and cultural confluence. Master Irineu and his disciple Padrinho Sebastião stand as spiritual teachers at the end of a long line of distinguished yogis, sages, priests, magi and masters; while the community founded by them serves as the 'vehicle' through which the practical-knowledge necessary to founding a new world order is preserved and subsequently passed on.

Narrative functions

Like its traditional forebear and modern-day equivalents, *daimista* millenarianism posits the wholesale transformation of society but does so by ignoring the established mechanisms through which social change is customarily achieved. Instead, an *ex machina* scenario is proposed in which social transformation occurs not by way of but despite prevailing economic-political structures and socio-cultural dynamics. As an apolitics of social transformation, *daimista* millenarianism eschews both civic engagement and political activism (see Postscript). Employing typically countercultural discourse, *daimistas* espousing a millenarian world view do so by expressing dissatisfaction, distrust and indifference in respect of prevailing economic-political structures and socio-cultural processes; variously written off as materialistic, morally degenerate, egocentric and spiritually superficial. Whether articulating indifference, dissatisfaction or distrust, the discursive tension in respect of society is nevertheless a creative one in that it still generates meaning for those by whom it is narrated.

As said earlier, the apolitics of social transformation at the heart of *daimista* millenarianism comprises neither a misplacing (dislocation) nor misspeaking (mislocution) on the part of those concerned. Rather, the reconfiguration of normative spatio-temporal patterns wrought by *daimista* millenarianism is better understood as a mode of dislocution, the performative utterance of which both relativizes prevailing socio-cultural processes and situates *daimistas* in a relationship of constructive tension through which practical and symbolic affirmation is gained without a professed investment in or reliance upon the world at large. Embodying a countercultural stance in respect of society, the dislocutory utterance of millenarianism nevertheless establishes a qualified relationship with the world as a narrative foil through which individual beliefs and collective repertoires are valorized. For example, millenarian discourse valorizes *daimista* belief and practice through its articulation as a form of practical-knowledge oriented to meeting the very particular demands of the calamitous times through which the world is now passing. By placing them within an appropriate transhistorical framework, the *daimista* world view enables individuals to appreciate the overarching historical significance of the 'tempestuous events currently underway'. At the same time, the practical repertoire afforded by Santo Daime's disciplinary regime is believed to equip its members with a range of techniques suited to successfully enduring the trials and tribulations associated with the 'hard times' out of which the new world will be born. The ensuing state of emergency declared in association with the end times relativizes prevailing modes of practical and symbolic reproduction, while the sense of urgency engendered by the discourse of imminent transition further reinforces the relevance and value of *daimista* belief and practice.

The new world scenario portrayed by the millenarian paradigm also furnishes *daimistas* with a sense of vindication and pending reward for their perseverance and faithfulness in the face of popular scepticism and perceived public persecution. On the one hand, beliefs and practices currently marginal to contemporary mainstream society are soon to become central to a new world order structured around the *daimista* world view. On the other, adherents to *daimista* beliefs and practices will not only survive the calamitous transition but will also be among the righteous remnant which is to form the vanguard of the renewed world and its new civilization. The narrative association of *daimista* belief and practice with impending civilizational renewal thereby endows both organizational repertoire and individual adept with a significance of truly global proportions. Yet, it does so in a manner which preserves its countercultural ethos by linking its vindication and reward not with adoption by mainstream society of the here and now but with a new and transformed society of the there and then.

The decimation of prevailing economic-political structures and socio-cultural dynamics wrought by the millenarian narrative also furnishes *daimistas* with an external complement to their interior preoccupation with nurturing the higher-self (known also as the 'inner', 'cosmic', 'true' or 'Christic' self). Noted in Chapter 1, the higher-self is believed to be the interior aspect of the human subject most attuned to the universal Whole of which we are all a part. Only when the higher-self is developed are the latent powers residing deep within each of us able to be tapped, harnessed and manipulated to the end of obtaining absolute self-realization. Absolute self-realization, however, is conditional upon the eradication of the 'ego' (known also as the 'lower' or 'material' self). By impeding the higher-self and its development, the ego inhibits the individual pursuit of absolute self-realization. Originating through embodied interaction with the world at large, the ego is the part of the individual most affected by and attached to the external, material world. Millenarianism's rapid and far-reaching transformation of the material world to which the ego is attached thereby has significant implications for the absolute realization of the higher-self.

Functioning, in effect, as the social self, the ego serves as a cipher for the plethora of forces and dynamics perceived to stand over and against the individual *daimista*. That is, the ego signifies society at large, just as its dissolution signifies the liberation of the individual from external forces and dynamics otherwise beyond his control. By annihilating the ego, the *daimista* repertoire eradicates societal determination. In so doing, the discourse and practice of Santo Daime frees the individual from unwarranted external interference, thereby allowing the unfettered pursuit of absolute self-realization. In narrative terms, the annihilation of the ego and the emergence of the higher-self correlate directly with the dissolution of societal determination and the achievement of absolute self-realization. By completely reconfiguring the societal dynamics responsible for the birth of the ego, millenarianism's new world scenario removes all forms of external determination which might otherwise hinder the absolute realization of the higher-self. Albeit at the cost of civilization as we know it, the renewed earth of the millenarian paradigm furnishes *daimistas* with a blank canvas upon which they are unqualifiedly free to explore and express themselves within a societal context wholly conducive to the higher-self and its spiritual preoccupations.

An implicit but no less important strand of the apolitics of social transformation is the belief that people will not be able to achieve what they can and should be until the world becomes a different place; i.e. one more conducive to the nurture and absolute realization of the higher-self.

However, given the apolitical character of the *daimista* world view, the social transformation upon which self-realization is contingent has to come about through extraordinary means beyond those customarily used (e.g. civic engagement, social agitation and political activism). For those espousing an apolitics of social transformation, the millenarian scenario thereby furnishes the extraordinary means necessary for the world and its inhabitants to become something other than they presently are. In parallel with aforementioned traditional modes of millenarianism, this approach included for the early *daimista* movement a pronounced collectivism involving, among other things, the valorization of alternative communities as concrete anticipations of the new earth to come. Separate from the world at large, structured appropriately and oriented by a disciplinary ritual regime, such communities would furnish a social environment conducive to the nurture, if not full realization, of the higher-self. While providing a refuge and ark through which the turbulent times of transition to the new world could be survived, these communities would also allow their members to pursue the lifestyles and spiritual regimes of the impending new order. Taking the community of Mapiá as their template, nearly all of the early communities founded beyond the Amazon embodied a strongly communitarian ideal which, infused with millenarian beliefs, idealized their alternative lifestyles as concrete anticipations of both the new world and new self to come. Whereas the growth and spread of Santo Daime is resulting in the progressive modification of the foundational narrative of self-sustaining, alternative communes, the ideals embodied by the original communities continue to shape contemporary *daimista* discourse; especially in Brazil where the majority of these communities (albeit in modified form) still exist.

Upon reading an early piece I had written upon millenarian beliefs within Santo Daime (2008), a North American community leader said that 'I don't recognize myself there'. He, like most *daimistas* I encountered outside of Brazil subsequent to writing the chapter, does not employ millenarian language as a staple part of his countercultural world view. As committed members of the movement, however, most of these individuals are aware of the millenarian motifs employed by the founding figures of Santo Daime and their continuing resonance with many of their Brazilian counterparts. Likewise, as typical countercultural religionists, they are not averse to using a variety of new-age tropes imbued with millenarian overtones (see Landes, 2004: 333–58; Lucas, 2011: 567–86). Unlike their Brazilian counterparts, however, *daimistas* in other parts of the world are much less familiar with the millenarian imagery which has been so influential and, indeed, continues as a popular component of non-mainstream religious discourse in Brazil. Also, the alternative communities in which Santo Daime first spread beyond the Amazon, and for which millenarian discourse played an important role, have not traditionally been part of the diaspora model. Rather, non-Brazilian *daimistas* have customarily (at least, to date) engaged with Santo Daime through gathered forms of participation more in keeping with congregational than communal modes of membership. Consequently, and while happily describing Santo Daime as a new spirituality for a new time, non-Brazilian *daimistas* are less inclined to use the explicit millenarian terminology reproduced above and, even more so, much less likely to articulate an imminent transformational scenario involving the catastrophic reconfiguration of the world at large. Espousing an apolitics of self- rather than social transformation, these *daimistas* are much more likely to assert that the world will not become a better place until individuals become what they can and should be. Inverting the implicit linkage of self and society within the apolitics of social transformation, the apolitics of self-transformation makes societal improvement contingent upon the betterment of the individual. In keeping with the apolitics of social transformation, however, it does so while neglecting to identify any specific mechanisms whereby the betterment of the self begets the thoroughgoing transformation of the world at large.

An apolitics of self-transformation

Without employing the catastrophic millenarian themes which have traditionally formed an important part of the *daimista* world view, those espousing an apolitics of self-transformation nevertheless continue to articulate a narrative of dislocution through which a relationship of constructive tension is constituted with the world at large. Although foregoing the catastrophic reconfiguration of the world as we know it, a countercultural discourse of crisis, dissatisfaction, mistrust and indifference regarding prevailing societal dynamics remains very much in place. As part of a wide-ranging conversation involving much by way of disparagement of contemporary 'materialist' and 'selfish' society, for example, an Australian *daimista* asserted that 'it's not our job to worry about social transformation. It's our responsibility to transform ourselves and social transformation will follow'. Likewise, and speaking of her former involvement in the Brazilian labour movement, another informant told me how

> As soon as I took the Daime, I gave it all up. From being heavily involved in regional and national union campaigns, I stopped it overnight. I realized when I took the Daime that there is only one power; power in Heaven. There's no power here on earth, none whatsoever. So, from then on: no politics, no union business. You see, the world is an illusion, a complete illusion. The only real thing is the Father in Heaven [*o Pai no Céu*]; the rest is illusion. Since taking the Daime, I've left the illusion completely.

Associating the current 'planetary crisis' with the sheer 'quantity of suffering, depression and existential emptiness', Padrinho Alex Polari also maintains that 'the struggle for social transformation gets us nowhere without a personal, interior transformation'. It is for this reason, the former political prisoner says, 'that when I left jail I did not reinsert myself into society' (Nogueira, 2012).[6] As with the apolitics of social transformation, those articulating an apolitics of self-transformation do so against the backdrop of a world in crisis and a social environment ultimately viewed as injurious to the spiritual well-being of its members. Likewise in common with an apolitics of social transformation, the apolitics of self-transformation furnishes little by way of substance to underwrite any meaningful association between the religious regime advocated and the changes to the prevailing societal context which purportedly flow from it.

What traditional millenarianism gives an apolitics of social transformation, European esotericism provides the apolitics of self-transformation. Noted in Chapter 1, European esotericism impacted significantly upon the *daimista* repertoire through Master Irineu's association with the Esoteric Circle of the Communion of Thought and the Brazilian Rosicrucian Order. Also a member of the Esoteric Circle and influenced by the mystical-esotericism of Jorge Adoum, Padrinho Sebastião was likewise taken with the esoteric paradigm, with its practical and symbolic concerns forming a major part of the Cefluris world view. A characteristically 'modern' religious repertoire, the adoption and continued employment of European esotericism placed the self and its transformation at the very heart of *daimista* belief and practice. Such repertorial concerns would be further cemented within Santo Daime subsequent to the ingression of an urban middle-class constituency imbued with typically alternative, countercultural preoccupations in which the valorization of the self and its absolute realization take centre stage.

Subjectivizing modernity

The 'turn to the self' or 'subjective turn' has been identified and well treated as a fundamental marker of both modernity in general and the modern esoteric paradigm in particular. The rise of modernity and its valorization of the modern self is customarily charted by moving from the socio-cultural transformations of the Renaissance, through the religious and political changes of the Reformation and, then, the philosophical and scientific developments of the Enlightenment, to the rapid and widespread societal upheavals unleashed by the Urban-Industrial Revolution. Each in their own way, for example, Protestantism, Rationalism, Romanticism and Liberalism are identified as contributing to modern estimations of the self as characterized by, among other things, free will, rational reflection and creative expression (e.g. Seigel, 2005; Taylor, 1992). Grounded in the complementary dynamics of urban industrialization, the established constraints of corporate determination (e.g. family, class and religion) are said to be incrementally weakened and, as a result, the modern self is progressively empowered to engage an increasingly diversified socio-cultural environment on subjective rather than collective terms (e.g. Beck and Beck-Gernsheim, 2002; Giddens, 1991). The importance of the socio-cultural processes of individualization and pluralization are further discussed in Chapter 5 when set alongside other constitutive dynamics of the late-modern societal context of the urban middle classes now dominant within Santo Daime.

Embodying the symbolic valorization and practical empowerment of the modern self, the European esoteric repertoire which emerged in the mid-nineteenth century is a quintessentially modern phenomenon. Typified by movements such as Anthroposophy, Rosicrucianism and Theosophy, the esoteric paradigm instantiates a range of characteristically modern tropes, not least of which are progress, merit and self-determination (Faivre and Needleman, 1992; Hammer, 2001; Hanegraaff, 1996). Esotericism offers an ameliorative view of the universe in which its inhabitants evolve from lower to higher spiritual forms through successive incarnations. Evolutionary progress is managed by scientifically modelled universal laws (e.g. karma) which administer justice according to the application and probity of spirits during periods of incarnation. Constituting a modern work ethic of equality and justice, every spirit receives what is merited, with those in credit moving up the evolutionary chain (to be reincarnated in less material climes) and those in debit making no such advance. In contrast to the deferred supernatural rewards of traditional religious paradigms (e.g. heaven), esotericism allows for the immanent, this-worldly impact (e.g. health, wealth and happiness) of karmic credit earned in prior incarnations. Modern liberalizing tendencies are also reflected in the replacement of tradition-oriented beliefs (e.g. miracles) and authorities (e.g. scripture) by a non-religious morality orchestrated by universal values such as love, forgiveness, patience and charity. Above all, the modern provenance of the esoteric world view is exemplified by its representation of the individual as a sacralized subject (i.e. spirit) endowed with free will and responsible for its own self-determination.

The typically modern tenor of many of these features was not lost on contemporary commentators of the classic modern period (e.g. Durkheim, 1961; Simmel, 1997; Troeltsch, 1931; Weber, 1992). Like Kardecist Spiritism before it, however, the reception of esotericism in Brazil commonly involved its incorporation within explicitly religious and therapeutically oriented repertoires which, though maintaining the majority of its typically modern preoccupations, mitigated both its anti-religious rhetoric and overtly rationalistic tenor. In so being, esotericism spread easily across Brazil and had played a major role in shaping the non-mainstream religious sector by the time of Santo Daime's move beyond the Amazon region (Amaral, 2000; A. Dawson, 2007; Magnani, 2000). Indeed, the neo-esotericism at the heart of the alternative scene populated by Brazil's urban middle classes was highly influential in aiding their reception of Santo Daime and its particular rendering of the traditional European esoteric paradigm. The same can also be said of Santo Daime's internationalization. While a good number of Santo Daime's features appeal on account of their exoticism, the indebtedness of Western non-mainstream religiosity to European esotericism furnishes many shared elements, similarities and correlations which facilitate its international expansion. Among all of the features which Santo Daime has in common with alternative Western repertoires, the valorization of the self and the ritual facilitation of its absolute realization are, without doubt, the most important.

Working in tandem, the sociologists Peter Berger and Thomas Luckmann were among the first to focus upon the progressively subjectivized character of a growing number of twentieth-century religious repertoires. Developing earlier reflections upon the modern processes of individualization and pluralization, Berger and Luckmann argue that individuals are being increasingly required to formulate their own, subjectively oriented meaning systems in the face of the rapid and far-reaching relativization of traditional collective modes of signification ('plausibility structures' or 'symbolic universes') (1966). According to Luckmann, modernity is responsible for 'the emergence of a new social form of religion', as society and its inhabitants shift from collective and socially defined symbolic universes to privately formulated 'individual systems of "ultimate" significance' (1967: 91, 104–5). Arising from modernity's particular characteristics (e.g. individualization and pluralization), says Luckmann, individuals are progressively freed from social constraints in respect of what they should believe and how they might render their worlds meaningful. Relying now upon an 'autonomous' sense of self and the 'private' resources (e.g. family and friends) which support it, individuals are increasingly formulating 'highly subjective' meaning systems directly tailored to a range of idiosyncratic criteria (e.g. 'self-expression' and 'self-realization'). Orchestrated by personal predilection and chosen from a growing range of socio-cultural ingredients, individual meaning systems are characterized by 'heterogeneity', highly 'flexible' and 'ad hoc' in nature, and 'relatively unstable'. Oriented 'to discovering the "inner self"', emotionally expressive and expectant of 'this-worldly' rewards, the kind of transcendence celebrated by this 'new social form of religion' differs markedly from that articulated by traditional systems of meaning informed by institutionalized religion (1967: 104–5; 1990).

Berger likewise links an increasing reliance upon individualized meaning systems with the 'widespread collapse of the plausibility of traditional religious definitions of reality' (1967: 127). As religious world views work best in stable, undifferentiated and homogeneous social contexts, he argues, the rapidly changing and increasingly plural character of modern society undermines their ability to function (i.e. render existence meaningful) and reproduce themselves (i.e. gain new adherents). The destabilization and relativization of traditional religious meaning systems wrought by modern society result in modern individuals increasingly seeing themselves as sources of the certainty and stability essential to their existential well-being. Because subjectivity rather than sociality is the modern author of signification, individuals turn inwards and religion is progressively subjectivized. As a consequence,

religious 'realities' are increasingly 'translated' from a frame of reference of facticities external to the individual consciousness to a frame of reference that locates them *within* consciousness. Put differently, the *realissimum* to which religion refers is transposed from the cosmos or from history to individual consciousness. Cosmology becomes psychology. History becomes biography. (1967: 167)

Echoing earlier sociological commentators interested by the rise of the esoteric paradigm (e.g. Durkheim and Simmel), Berger sees the subjectivization of religion as resulting in an interiorized, humanistic and immanentist preoccupation with physical and psychological well-being. In effect, religion becomes one among a range of therapeutic regimes oriented to bettering the self in every aspect of its existence. Whereas Berger's reading of subjectivization as an expression of socio-cultural crisis is somewhat problematic, his identification of the preoccupation of 'modern Western culture' with 'subjectivity' and the assertion that 'modernization and subjectivization are cognate processes' are very much nearer the mark (Berger, 1979: 20–1).

The subjectivization narrative is now a staple component of modern academic treatments of both alternative and mainstream religious repertoires of the urban-industrialized world (e.g. Bellah et al., 1985; D'Andrea, 2000; Heelas and Woodhead, 2005; Roof, 1993). It should not, though, be taken to signal the wholesale individualization of the religious sphere. Rather than eradicating individual participation in collective forms of religion, the subjectivization of contemporary religiosity involves the recalibration of individual – communal dynamics in a manner which shifts the balance of power (e.g. authority, commitment, determination and priority) from the latter towards the former. As Heelas notes, the 'traditional self' of communally oriented repertoires is understood to be 'embedded' within an 'established order of things' (e.g. tradition, hierarchy and gender stereotypes). Operating 'in terms of "external" (supra-individual) voices of authority, control and destiny', the traditional self lives and finds meaning by 'heeding social, cultural or religious duties and obligations' rather than using 'incentive' and exercising 'autonomy or freedom of expression'. 'By definition', claims Heelas, the traditional self inhabits a 'collectivistic' order and is thereby 'primarily other-informed or sociocentric rather than self-informed or individualistic' (1996a: 78). The modern, subjectivized self is, however, primarily self-oriented such that established orders and external voices of authority are no longer automatically heeded. In contrast to its traditional manifestation, the modern self lives and finds meaning by using its incentive, exercising autonomy and expressing itself freely according to subjectively oriented more than objectively determined criteria. While collective duties and obligations neither disappear nor go unacknowledged, they are relativized by constant reference to the perceived needs and desires of the modern, subjectivized self. In terms of its contemporary religious manifestation, argues Heelas, this is nowhere more categorically expressed than in the practical and symbolic 'Selfism' of the alternative, non-mainstream milieu (1996b: 82); the very same milieu into which Santo Daime has progressively entered since its expansion beyond the Amazon region and ensuing dominance of the urban middle classes.

Prior chapters have successively identified the spiritual efficacy of Santo Daime as residing in its ritualized interface of individual endeavour and collective practice. Such is the importance of this interface that it is closely managed and monitored through a strict regime comprising the spatio-temporal ordering and practical-symbolic regulation of ritual participants. More traditional than modern, the ritual management of individual – collective dynamics furnished the template through which the practices and beliefs of European esotericism were originally appropriated and subsequently modified. As such, the individual pursuit of absolute realization achieved through nurturing the higher-self was inextricably bound with the dynamics and demands of collective ritual activity. Though progressively informed by esotericism's characteristically modern conceptualization of the self, ritual participants in the established *daimista* repertoire nevertheless continued to remain subject to a range of corporate obligations and communal expectations. Likewise identified in preceding chapters, the ingression of the urban middle classes is progressively modifying the established interface of individual behaviour and its collective framing. Imbued with a highly subjectivized sense of self, urban middle-class *daimistas* are incrementally transforming traditional modes of spatio-temporal order and practical-symbolic discipline. While the sincerity of the respect for and adherence to the traditional ritual repertoire espoused by urban middle-class *daimistas* is beyond doubt, the gradual modification of established modes of cultic regulation is an unintended consequence of the ongoing, if not unrelenting, assertion of the late-modern, subjectivized self.

Exemplary characteristics of the contemporary daimista *repertoire*

Relating it to the 'new middle class' spawned by late-modern society, much more is said in Chapter 5 about the socio-cultural character of urban-professional *daimistas*. Some of these details are, though, briefly anticipated here by way of contextualizing the following engagement of Santo Daime's contemporary repertoire of self-transformation. Part of the new middle class which arose in the second part of the twentieth century, urban-professional *daimistas* are thoroughgoingly late-modern subjects in respect of their expansive aspirations and meritocratic preoccupations. Their environment (material and immaterial) is perceived as both pliant to individual endeavour and furnishing due return upon the subjective energies expended. Familiar with socio-cultural plurality and rapid societal change, urban middle-class *daimistas* are comfortable with value relativity and enjoy relatively fluid and decentred identities. They are highly reflexive in character, demonstrating a strategic and self-conscious instrumentality preoccupied with advancement (spiritual and mundane) and careful as to image and impression management. Urban-professional *daimistas* are endowed with an individualized subjectivity which is mobile, expressive and self-oriented in pursuit of aesthetic satisfaction, intellectual gratification and psychophysical stimulation.

The typical characteristics of the new middle class from which urban-professional *daimistas* are overwhelmingly drawn are further developed in Chapter 5. In respect of their impact upon the religious repertoire of Santo Daime, however, six components are now treated which, in combination, exemplify the contemporary *daimista* paradigm as an apolitics of identity orchestrated by the leitmotif of self-transformation. Particularly since the integration of European esotericism from the mid-1900s, an apolitics of self-transformation has served as a complementary strand of the *daimista* world view to that of the aforementioned apolitics of social transformation. Attuned more to valorizing the individual than galvanizing the community, the apolitics of self-transformation has since superseded its older counterpart to furnish the principal orientation of Santo Daime's contemporary dislocutory narrative. Whereas the movement's expansion beyond Brazil and progressive adoption of a congregational rather than communal model have played something of a role in this, the preponderance of an urban middle-class membership imbued with a highly subjectivized sense of self is primarily responsible for the shift in emphasis. The following six characteristics of the contemporary *daimista* repertoire very much reflect the now established dominance of the urban middle classes and their highly subjectivized preoccupations.

First, and perhaps foremost, the contemporary *daimista* repertoire is characterized by a highly valorized sense of subjectivity in which the individual is viewed as both the primary agent of self-transformation and ultimate arbiter of spiritual authority. In many ways, each of the other characteristics identified below flows from and speaks to Santo Daime's valorization of the self. The agency and judgement by and under which the transformed self is wrought are underwritten by asserting the subject's connaturality with an overarching, all-pervasive cosmic Whole. In keeping with its pluriform character, the *daimista* repertoire affords its members a wide range of themes and tropes by which the sacralization of the self can be articulated. Esoteric notions of the self as a 'miniature replica' of the universe or 'divine spark' are frequently employed, as are Judeo-Christian portrayals of the subject as an 'image of God'. Spiritist conceptions of the self as an otherwise disincarnate spiritual entity imprinted with cosmic knowledge are likewise common, with extraterrestrial derivation narratives also beginning to emerge. Used in a south-Brazilian community, my favourite trope describes the self as being 'joined' both 'to the centre of the galaxy' and each of its occupants by a giant 'umbilical cord' which passes 'from the heart, through the sternum' and on to the universal Whole. Irrespective of the source and motif mobilized, the status and trustworthiness of the self are assured by ontological and epistemological claims which both guarantee and valorize subjective agency and judgement. Nowhere is this more apparent than in the matter of health and well-being.

According to the *daimista* world view, much of what any individual enjoys or suffers in this life results from karmic credit or demerit earned in prior incarnations, with most of the remaining pleasures or hardships generated by the contemporary religio-moral disposition of the incarnate self. Speaking of someone dying of cancer and seeking help in her community, for example, an American *daimista* told me how part of the individual's treatment involved him being asked to 'find out when it was that you decided to die'. Although the patient subsequently died from his illness, my informant believed some form of healing to have occurred thanks to the individual tracing his decision to die back to an accident when he was five years old in which his actions resulted in the death of a playmate. By no means a 'punishment' for his actions, the cancer which killed the patient was nevertheless caused by him. Whether inherited from prior lives or engendered in this life, issues and events which impact upon subjective well-being are ultimately grounded in the thoughts and deeds of the self. While the self is affected by them, the self is also their actual cause. And, as the originator of nearly everything that affects the self, the self is thereby the ultimate solution. The cyclical reasoning which defines the self as self-caused and self-solving is exemplified by the *daimista* notion of 'self-cure' (*curar-se*). According to an informant who believed sickness to be something which each self 'manufactures' by virtue of misplaced thoughts and erroneous actions: 'I mean, yes, Masters, Padrinhos and Jesuses have their place. Ultimately, though, because it's you who causes the sickness, it's up to you to cure it.'

Part and parcel of the pursuit of absolute self-realization, the notion of self-cure is typical of the instrumentalized nature of the *daimista* repertoire. The second characteristic explored here, the instrumentally oriented focus of ritual practice furnishes a clear rationale in which cultic activity is viewed as a means to the end of absolute self-realization; variously conceived as including, for example, 'self-perfection', 'self-transformation' and 'self-understanding'. Indicative of its subjectivized ethos, ritual activity exists to support the self in its inwardly focused endeavours through which self-scrutiny occurs, faults are identified and self-correction ensues. Above all, such endeavours are undertaken to the end of nurturing the higher-self through the incremental eradication of the ego and its stultifying effects. Cultic activity including the consumption of Daime is said to 'burn off' karma at a faster rate than ordinary ritual practice, just as the practical-symbolic demands of *daimista* cultic activity are believed to earn cosmic merit for ceremonial participants. Fundamentally, however, the benefits engendered by ritual activity are generated by the self, working on the self, for the benefit of the self.

The sacralization of the self as connatural with the cosmic Whole furnishes the practical and symbolic means by which self-realization is pursued. Anchored to the cosmos and pervaded by universal forces, the spiritual connaturality of the self endows it with the powers necessary for its own transformation. Supernaturally resourced by its sacral nature, the self pursues its absolute realization by learning to identify, harness and focus the astral energies inherent to it. Equipped with the fundamental powers underwriting its agency and judgement, the self nevertheless requires guidance as to the most efficacious ways of manipulating them in the cause of self-transformation. Although the sacral (connatural) character of the self provides much by way of (super)natural resourcing, the disorienting or stultifying impact of bodily incarnation is such that the self needs some form of instruction as to the best ways of optimizing its inherent resources. Commonly referred to as 'the doctrine', Santo Daime is one such purveyor of this requisite practical-knowledge.

The self's relationship with the practical-knowledge necessary for its appropriate guidance is shaped by a meritocratic-egalitarianism which constitutes the third characteristic of the contemporary *daimista* repertoire. On the one hand, the meritocratic aspirations of the late-modern self inform a ritual work ethic in which cultic participants expect due returns commensurate with the efforts expended. As noted below, these returns are both material and immaterial in nature. On the other, ritual exertions are underwritten by the law of reciprocity ('what one gives up, one gets back') and thereby guaranteed to elicit a favourable return when undertaken appropriately.

Reflecting a deep-seated respect for established practices, adherence to the requirements of practical-symbolic regulation is also motivated by a concern to ensure the spiritual efficacy associated with their appropriate execution. Obedience to prescribed modes of behaviour thereby embodies a typically procedural preoccupation to obtain sought-after results (i.e. self-realization) through appropriately executed measures.

The egalitarian aspect of this characteristic is similarly grounded in a mixture of esteem for given authorities and commitment to procedural efficacy. Held to be steeped in the ancient wisdom of miscellaneous religio-cultural traditions, *daimista* authorities are venerated as tried and tested sources of the practical-knowledge necessary to guiding the self on its path to absolute realization. The duties and constraints through which traditional authority asserts itself and by which individual freedoms are restricted are thereby offset against the subjective benefits enabled by them. In the same vein, and as long as they can be climbed, corporate hierarchies are tolerated as structured indicators of individual spiritual maturity which, as such, serve as way-markers for the aspirational self. At the same time, the authority enjoyed by high-status members of Santo Daime (including its founders) is always exemplary rather than exceptional. Even in cases of ascribed status, the authority borne by leadership is portrayed as something achieved by virtue of long-standing engagement 'with the Daime'. Serving to guide by example, leadership exists to show the way along which all *daimistas*, by virtue of their sacral nature, have the innate ability to travel. As Padrinho Alex Polari remarks, what was once 'thought to be a faculty of a few specially predestined and prepared people, Sebastião Mota guarantees to be accessible to each one of us as long as we correctly follow the Doctrine' (1998: 32). While some of the feats of Master Irineu and Padrinho Sebastião may well have been extraordinary, they were by no means exceptional. Serving to underwrite their status, such extraordinary feats nevertheless stand as examples of what every *daimista* is capable when the practical-knowledge of the doctrine is learned and employed appropriately. Ultimately, the authority of leadership resides not in its exceptionality as something beyond the ordinary individual but in its exemplification of what every self can become.

The nature and operational scope of established authority is further qualified by the fourth characteristic of the *daimista* repertoire, that of its holism. The holistic perspective posits a universal force, principle or dynamic, the ubiquitous presence of which underlies every aspect of cosmic existence. The unmitigated nature of this ubiquity ensures that every individual component of the universe, no matter how small or seemingly insignificant, is joined to it and, by virtue of cosmic mediation, to every other unit of existence. The ontological avowal of universal holism, in which every aspect of reality is connected to every other aspect of reality, underwrites the aforementioned connaturality of the self with the cosmos. This, in turn, furnishes the individual with the requisite universal energies to be harnessed and manipulated in the service of self-realization. The ontological aspect of holism which equips the self with the necessary means of its absolute realization is accompanied by an epistemological assertion that individual, unitary or differentiated existence is only ever apparent. As every individual component of existence is in reality part of an all-embracing whole (ontological avowal), no specific unit can be properly understood without reference to the overarching whole of which it is but a particular expression (epistemological assertion). Articulated by the *daimista* world view, the holistic narrative lends itself to the relativization of all forms of practical-knowledge as metaphorical, and thereby contingent, expressions of one and the same all-encompassing, universal reality.

The overwhelming majority of *daimistas* espouse a relativizing holism in which Santo Daime is viewed as one spiritual path among many others. By and large, however, *daimistas* differentiate between 'spiritual' repertoires such as theirs and traditional paradigms generally dismissed as 'religion'. As an informant put it, 'religion and spirituality are two different things, two different ways'. Most frequently associated with Christianity, 'religion' is variously rejected on account of its preoccupation with 'doctrines', 'traditions' and 'rules'. As a 'spiritual way', however, Santo Daime is believed to facilitate and empower rather than hinder or obstruct self-realization. A 'catalyst' or 'short cut' to self-realization, Daime stands alongside other 'power plants' (entheogens) believed to furnish access to the astral plane. Indeed, among those using or having used other kinds of entheogen (e.g. cannabis, fungi, iboga and peyote), informants commonly spoke of encountering different spiritual realms or supernatural agents than those engaged through the sacrament of Daime (see Chapter 4). Nevertheless, alternative and non-mainstream repertoires which do not employ entheogens but are regarded as 'spiritual' rather than 'religious' are likewise viewed as legitimate (albeit, according to some, less efficient) means of engaging the astral plane and nurturing the higher-self.

The relativization of rituals and beliefs as contingent socio-cultural expressions of an overarching universal Whole renders all forms of practical-knowledge amenable to appropriation and inclusion within the *daimista* repertoire. Whereas repertorial insertion inevitably involves some form of modification both to the beliefs and practices appropriated and the context into which they are fitted, such adaptation is frequently rationalized as allowing previously unappreciated aspects of transcendent reality to be comprehended in a new light. Underwritten by its relativizing holism, Santo Daime's conspicuous appropriation and ongoing revision of practical-knowledge from a wide range of sources and contexts results in a religious world view which is both hybrid and rapidly evolving. Perhaps more importantly, however, the range and mutability of the beliefs and practices at hand furnishes the individual *daimista* with an enhanced degree of choice and expression through which the pursuit of absolute self-realization can be undertaken. Even more so, of course, as the relativization of practical-knowledge applies just as much to Santo Daime as it does to other world views and repertoires. In combination with aforementioned characteristics, holism's relativization of belief and practice endows the self with a versatile and mobile demeanour which empowers individuals to pursue their absolute self-realization by whatever means and in whatever context they judge to be most suitable for them, for now. Indeed, the vast majority of *daimistas* I have met have established histories of participation (consecutive and concurrent) with various non-mainstream spiritualities and alternative repertoires. As an informant explained by way of referencing Santo Daime's traditional mode of dress, 'the heart has no uniform'.

The final two elements of the contemporary *daimista* repertoire most worthy of note are its aestheticized and this-worldly character. The aestheticized character of the contemporary *daimista* repertoire involves an experiential preoccupation which manifests most explicitly in the exploratory bent and expressive demeanour of its ritual participants. The experiential preoccupation of contemporary *daimistas* is grounded in the valorization of inner states informed, among other things, by aforementioned processes of individualization and subjectivization. In the first instance, the self's connaturality with transcendent reality underwrites the belief that inner, subjective states (e.g. thoughts and emotions) are actually reflective of outer, external realities. What the self thinks and feels is thereby of potential cosmic significance. In the second, modern recalibrations of the individual – collective relationship result in the growing estimation of and provision for personal concerns and opinions relative to those of corporate bodies such as family, community and religion. The subjective preoccupations of the I/me thereby take increasing precedence over the objective concerns of the you/them. In tandem, these two emphases contribute to reordering established dynamics by which inner – outer and private – public boundaries are managed. As a result, traditional estimations of modesty, reservation and self-deprecation, for example, are downgraded in favour of more overt, less restrained and self-assertive displays of personality.

Of a principally inward nature, the exploratory bent of the aestheticized self is mediated by a preoccupation with subjective experiences and emotions. Above all, this involves the stimulation and nurturing of new and familiar affective states through ritual regimes designed to elicit, sustain or heighten particular feelings and subjective conditions. The intensification of inner states associated with psychoactives and novel experiences helps explain the importance of power plants such as Daime and Santa Maria as well as the inveterate openness to, if not perennial pursuit of, the avant-garde and exotic. The inward focus of mystical self-exploration is complemented by an outwardly expressive dynamic. On the one hand, the expressivity of contemporary *daimistas* reflects the relative esteem with which late-modern culture regards the externalization of otherwise subjective experiences. So much so, that the expression of one's inner emotions is now viewed as an integral component of a well-rounded personality. On the other, the outward expression of inner states constitutes an important element of self-presentation and subjective-assertion. Noted in Chapter 2, Santo Daime's cultic field of force is a dynamic environment in which participants strive to optimize and, where possible, better their respective positions through various strategies; chief among which are self-promotional status claims which call upon ritual capital and exploit traditional associations of spiritual accomplishment and public standing. Because subjective states reflect objective realities, the outer expression of inner conditions communicates far more than simple individual experience. It is, then, not just a case of 'look what I'm experiencing' but also that of 'look what I'm capable of experiencing'. Exemplified by the growing popularity of spirit-oriented practice, the aestheticized character of the *daimista* repertoire furnishes ritual participants with a self-affirming combination of mystical exploration and assertive expression.

Comprising the sixth characteristic of the contemporary *daimista* repertoire, the term 'this-worldly' is taken from Luckmann's notion of the 'this-worldly' emphasis of the 'intermediate transcendences' mediated by modern religiosity (1990). Treated at greater length in Chapter 5, the this-worldly character of the *daimista* world view includes an expectation that the benefits accrued by ritual practitioners have a tangible, immanent quality which manifests as much in the here and now of earthly existence as in any future incarnation. The link between spiritual practice and the rewards it merits was mentioned in the preceding chapter in connection with the intimate association of private and public benefits operative within Santo Daime's ritual field of force. The self's sacralization and concomitant embroilment within supernatural dynamics does much to underwrite the relationship between private, spiritual advance and its outward manifestation through such things as public recognition (e.g. status) and psychophysical well-being (e.g. health).[7] The narrative framing of the mundane sphere as regulated by and ultimately reflective of underlying supernatural dynamics likewise collapses material – immaterial boundaries in a way which both sacralizes the material and materializes the sacred. The resulting fusion of material and immaterial horizons thereby relativizes traditional readings of worldly goods as material impediments to spiritual development (A. Dawson, 2011a). Indeed, for some *daimistas* this de-problematization of material goods is combined with aforementioned ameliorative preoccupations and their work ethic of just deserts to furnish an explicit relationship between religio-moral advance and material well-being. As the current leader of Cefluris, Padrinho Alfredo, remarks:

> The dangers of the illusion, of the old life, are in the mind and heart of humankind. It is not by fearing progress, money and our own prosperity that we are going to combat the illusion. What generates fear is confusion and not knowing how to use all these things in a way which allows [spiritual] growth to bring better health . . . and improved standards of living. Those who know wealth should feel happier and nurture that which transcends necessity. (Polari, 1998: 13)

Although not every member espouses the *daimista* version of a 'health and wealth' gospel, there is nonetheless a widespread expectation that subjective developments of a spiritual nature have immediate implications for the psychophysical well-being of the individual concerned. For most, such well-being at the very least includes the enjoyment of good physical and mental health; for many, it may also involve interpersonal or contextual elements such as satisfying relationships and secure employment; and for some, it comprises additional benefits like wealth and status.

These six exemplary characteristics combine to make the contemporary *daimista* repertoire a typically late-modern form of religious practical-knowledge. As an apolitics of self-transformation, the contemporary repertoire not only facilitates the autopoietic (self-making) preoccupations of the late-modern subject but actively underwrites them. It is a mode of belief and practice oriented to the transformation of the self, undertaken by the self, with resulting benefits accruing to the self. The theme of self-making (autopoiesis) is further explored in Chapter 5 in relation to late-modern notions of commoditization and their impact upon the new middle class from which Santo Daime draws the overwhelming majority of its members.

Conclusion

Freely acknowledging the impact of modern processes of individualization and the ensuing subjectivization of contemporary religiosity does not necessarily entail declaring the terminal decline of collective modes of belonging. Rather than eradicating religious modes of collective association, the impact of subjectivization involves the recalibration of individual – community dynamics such that traditional forms of corporate determination are reconfigured and modern modes of self-expression progressively prioritized (see Ammerman, 1997; Flory and Miller, 2000; Roof, 1999; Wuthnow, 1994).[8] According to Wade Roof, for example, the assumption that individualism and community 'are antagonistic to each other' and thereby 'locked into a zero-sum relationship . . . is far too simple a way of posing the problem' (1993: 256). Flory and Miller also reject overly 'individualistic' portrayals of contemporary religiosity, instead arguing that individualized forms of spiritual questing may still be 'mediated through' collective modes of 'membership and belonging' (2008: 185–9). Calling for 'a better way of conceptualizing individual religion, in all its complexity', Meredith McGuire likewise argues that more understanding is needed of 'how personal religious experience and expression is linked with collective experience and expression – especially in the late-modern context where people participate in multiple and often contradictory communities or impersonal collectivities' (2008: 229). Working along the same lines, Danièle Hervieu-Léger links modern processes of individualization with the 'deinstitutionalization' of religious authority. Treating religious world views as 'regimes of validation', she defines deinstitutionalization as 'the erosion of institutional regimes of the validation of religious faith'. Likewise dismissing either/or construals of 'the individualization of faith and religious communalization', Hervieu-Léger nevertheless regards the deinstitutionalization of traditional modes of authority as a 'tendency that shapes religious institutions and profoundly transforms them while also provoking a global reorganization of the religious landscape' (2001: 173).

By way of describing modernity's deinstitutionalizing tendency, Hervieu-Léger offers a fourfold typology which moves from the most traditional (i.e. 'institutional') mode of religious validation, through its 'communal' and 'mutual' expressions, to the most individualized form of self-validating faith. The 'institutional' regime of validation focuses religious authority in constituted hierarchies 'with the power to proclaim the truth of faith'. Individual members of the institution are thereby validated (i.e. affirmed, authenticated, commended) to the extent that their subjective beliefs and practices are in 'conformity' with the corporate 'norm' dictated by institutional authorities. 'Communal' regimes of validation invest 'the group' as a whole with the authority to determine collective 'norms', 'objectives' and 'truths'. Whereas official modes of leadership exist, their power is qualified by an 'egalitarianism' which entails that 'leaders are always supposed to express themselves in the name of the whole group: they are the voice of the group'. The beliefs and practices of community members are thereby validated relative to their 'coherence' with 'the homogeneity of truths' embodied in a corporate 'code of communal faith'. The regime of 'mutual' validation relies upon the processes of 'intersubjective interaction' to affirm the individual beliefs and practices of group members. Preoccupations with the subjective spiritual 'search', 'personal appropriation of meaning' and 'accepted acknowledgment of differences' stand to the fore, while notions of hierarchical authority, 'norms of belief' and communal determination are relativized. Here, personal concerns and experiences find validation through their 'convergence' with collective beliefs and practices to the extent that 'there is no "true faith" but that which is personally appropriated'. The most individualized of Hervieu-Léger's four types is the 'regime of self-validation' in which all other forms of affirmation and authentication 'vanish'. Within self-validating regimes, 'it is in individuals themselves, in the subjective certitude of possessing the truth, that the confirmation of the truth of faith is found'. Such is the certainty invested in individual beliefs and practices, that all other modes of validation (i.e. institutional authority, communal identity and mutual affirmation) are deemed surplus to requirements (2001: 165–74).

In relation to Santo Daime, Hervieu-Léger's typology is helpful if viewed not as a spectrum (moving from the institutional, through the communal and mutual, to the individualized) on which any one religious organization, group or community is situated relative to its particular regime of validation. Rather, Hervieu-Léger's typology may fruitfully be employed as an idealized delineation of certain aspects or emphases, more than one of which may be more or less present in any single institution, community or group. In addition to helping engage the contemporary *daimista* repertoire, such usage might offer a constructive response to McGuire's aforementioned call for a better conceptualization of late-modern religiosity and the complex nature of its individualized character (2008: 229). As an idealized emphasis rather than discrete typological spectrum, the institutional regime of validation identified by Hervieu-Léger lends itself to describing much of the traditional *daimista* repertoire. Treated at length in Chapter 2, Santo Daime's hierarchical authority structures, tradition-oriented ethos and practical-symbolic modes of regulation collectively constitute a religious repertoire oriented to validating its members relative to their conformity with established preoccupations with spatio-temporal order and ritual discipline. These established institutional features were reinforced by the traditional socio-cultural context of Amazonian *caboclo* society and its strongly collectivistic ethos. Consequently, while the founding community's aforementioned appropriation of European esotericism was accompanied by a characteristically modern discourse of the self, its repertorial framing ensured that an institutionally oriented regime of validation remained significantly undiminished.

To a certain extent, the different personality and leadership style of Padrinho Sebastião went some way to modifying the institutional validatory regime inherited from the Alto Santo community. Individual members of Cefluris thereby enjoyed a greater degree of practical and symbolic determination than that available in Santo Daime's mother community. Yet, the modifications made to the foundational regime of validation were relatively minimal, not least in view of the continuing presence of conservative socio-cultural dynamics of *caboclo* society and the hierarchical authority structures, tradition-oriented ethos and disciplinary modes of regulation implicated in them. Somewhat modified in their discursive and practical expressions, individual conformity with collective beliefs and practices nevertheless continued as the overwhelmingly dominant regime of validation. The overwhelming dominance of an institutional mode of validation, however, was incrementally altered by the gradual influx of urban middle-class 'backpackers' from beyond the Amazon region. Although highly respectful, if not in awe of established forms of corporate organization, a combination of the countercultural values and middle-class ethos of the new arrivals unavoidably expressed itself through an explicit preoccupation with communally oriented modes of validation. As a result, the long-established dominance of an institutional validatory regime was gradually qualified through the discursive valorization of 'the group' as a locus of practical and symbolic authority.

The charismatic authority invested in Padrinho Sebastião and esteem for the traditional ways of the *caboclo* remained strong in the earliest urban-professional converts who made their way to the Amazon region. Over time, however, the momentum generated by the sheer number of middle-class incomers and their rapid rise to prominence within the movement ensured that the initial demeanour of deference was complemented by an increasingly confident assertion of communal egalitarian ideals, not least as the first wave of alternative *daimista* communities was established beyond the Amazon region. By no means replacing traditional structures and dynamics, a communally oriented commitment to more egalitarian modes of governance and participant representation progressively made itself felt as a complement to the established institutional regime of validation. Whereas many of the practices and processes connected with inherited forms of leadership remained in place, articulation of their authority and significance was now explicitly qualified by reference to communitarian ideals and their relative valorization of the group as a whole. Likewise, the validation of individual belief and experience came increasingly to rest on a dual combination involving both their correspondence with institutional hierarchies and their coherence with communal codes and concerns.

The institutional-communal regime of validation remains predominant across the now internationalized contemporary *daimista* movement. As such, the continuing combination of hierarchical authority structures, tradition-oriented ethos and corporate modes of practical-symbolic regulation furnishes Santo Daime with a relatively conservative profile in comparison with certain other non-mainstream religious paradigms. Exemplified by the aforementioned six characteristics of the contemporary *daimista* repertoire, the prevailing institutional-communal regime is, however, undergoing incremental transformation through its subjection to a range of processes and practices embodying the kind of validatory dynamics which Hervieu-Léger identifies as 'mutual' and 'self-validating'. While the institutional-communal regime of validation continues to dominate, it certainly does not hold a monopoly upon the means of practical-symbolic signification through which individual belief and experience are affirmed and authenticated (see Chapter 4). Although appearing relatively conservative, the combination of aforementioned characteristics imbues the contemporary *daimista* repertoire with much that is typically late-modern in respect of its valorization of subjective determination and its concomitantly instrumental, meritocratic-egalitarian, relativizing, aestheticized and this-worldly preoccupations. Albeit chiefly unintended, these preoccupations refract individual engagement with received authorities and collective demands in a manner which both qualifies their established foundations and modifies their contemporary format along increasingly mutual and self-validating lines.

The qualification of received authorities and collective demands does not undermine the esteem in which they are held, but does involve their reconfiguration as helpful guides more than dictates and fruitful means of structuring subjective experience rather than objective determinations of it. Yes, inherited traditions continue to be viewed as important means of linking the belief and practice of contemporary *daimistas* with that of former generations. Yet, the same inherited traditions also serve as subjectively appropriated sources of self-authentication, the countercultural character of which is reinforced by the exotic provenance of the practical-knowledge appropriated. At the same time, traditional modes of practical-symbolic regulation and the psychophysical exertions demanded by them are believed to reinforce and magnify individual application in a manner which guarantees efficient, if not advantageous, rates of return. The esoteric maxim 'what one gives up one gets back' finds a contemporary parallel in 'no pain, no gain'. Yes, established hierarchies continue to be regarded as significant forms of corporate structuration embodying legitimate differentiations of rank and status. Yet, these same hierarchies are relativized by their exemplarization and, as external manifestations of inner spiritual standing, serve as climbable pecking orders, the ascent of which affirms the late-modern self in both its public ambitions and private aspirations. In the same vein, the attendant demands associated with corporate ritual practice are balanced against the aesthetic and confirmatory experiences furnished by a collective forum populated by expressive and like-minded individuals oriented to self-exploration.

Characteristic of its palimpsestic and evolving repertoire, Santo Daime's contemporary regime of validation is both variegated and changing. Informed by the foundational years of the Amazonian communities and early experiences of its first middle-class converts, institutional and communal aspects of the *daimista* validatory regime remain important emphases for the movement as a whole. The continuing vitality of hierarchical authority structures, tradition-oriented ethos and corporate modes of practical-symbolic regulation attest not only to the enduring influence of established forms of belief and behaviour but also to their ongoing importance to the contemporary membership. The overwhelming majority of contemporary members are, however, drawn from an urban middle-class constituency with a highly subjectivized sense of self. Exemplified by the aforementioned six characteristics of the contemporary *daimista* repertoire, the urban-professional membership embodies typically mutual and self-oriented validatory concerns which combine both to relativize and progressively reconfigure received authority structures, established forms of practical-knowledge and traditional modes of disciplinary order. The relative decline of the narrative leitmotif of an apolitics of social transformation and subsequent ascendency of an apolitics of self-transformation further attests to the self-oriented mutualization to which the contemporary *daimista* repertoire is progressively subjected.

Both of the narrative leitmotifs treated here constitute dislocutory speech acts which relativize relations with the world at large without fully foreclosing on the practical and symbolic possibilities made available by the prevailing socio-cultural context. In contrast to the apolitics of social transformation, however, the contemporary narration of an apolitics of self-transformation comprises a double dislocution which complements the qualification of *ad extra* relations in respect of society in general with the implicit relativization of *ad intra* relations between the individual self and its overarching corporate context. The external relativization of the world effected through its narration as, for example, illusory and materialistic is thereby joined by the internal relativization of collective modes of practical-symbolic regulation through their framing along mutual and self-validating lines. In so being, Santo Daime's corporate disciplinary regime is qualified by the valorization of the late-modern self and its instrumental, meritocratic-egalitarian, relativizing, aestheticized and this-worldly predilections. Through their dislocutory narration as ancillary aides to the subjectivized pursuit of absolute self-realization, received authority structures are disturbed, established forms of practical-knowledge unsettled and traditional modes of disciplinary order disrupted. As with the *ad extra* relativization of society in general, the *ad intra* qualification of corporate dynamics does not foreclose on the practical and symbolic opportunities furnished by prevailing environmental conditions. Typical of dislocutory narratives in general, the now dominant apolitics of self-transformation articulates a *both/and* rather than *either/or* scenario. By no means capturing it entirely, the *both/and* character of the contemporary *daimista* repertoire goes some way to exemplifying the aforementioned complexity of late-modern relations between the subjectivized self and collective contexts of religious practice. As the next chapter argues, the late-modern relativization of traditional repertorial dynamics is exemplified by the growing popularity of particular forms of spirit-oriented practice across the contemporary *daimista* movement.

4

Ritual reinvention: Shifting profiles of spirit-oriented practice

Three exchanges

1 In conversation about reincarnation and 'incorporation' (a *daimista* term for spirit mediumship) with Ricardo, he reminded me that Master Irineu and Padrinho Sebastião were the respective reincarnations of Jesus and John the Baptist. When Ricardo added that Padrinho Alfredo 'incorporates' the spirit of King Solomon, one of our companions, Claúdio, took issue with the use of the term 'incorporates'. A member of a different community than Ricardo, Claúdio interjected that Padrinho Alfredo 'does not incorporate' but is, rather, 'the reincarnation' of the spirit of King Solomon. Ricardo disagreed and reasserted his position which, in turn, elicited from Claúdio a further rejection of his fellow *daimista*'s opinion. No agreement was reached.

2 Norma had experienced the spirits of the dead (including her grandfather) since she was a child. Indeed, she first learned of a neighbour's recent death by encountering her now disincarnate spirit in her bedroom. Norma told me that she was raised within the Spiritist tradition but now practises 'mediumship' (*mediunidade*) only within Santo Daime. Employing a distinction I had learned from *daimistas* elsewhere in Brazil, I asked Norma whether she incorporated spirits from the 'right line' (i.e. Spiritism) or those from the 'left line' (i.e. Umbanda). Norma, however, rejected these categories, arguing instead that Santo Daime does not use the terms 'right line' (*linha direita*) and 'left line' (*linha esquerda*) to distinguish between different kinds of spirits.

3 Chatting after an evening's work with mapacho ('sacred tobacco'), conversation turned to the danced Hymnal ritual we had attended a few days prior. A practising medium within her North American community, Diane remarked that she could still not fully control when and how she incorporated during rituals as she often gets 'taken by surprise' by the spirits while she is 'connected with the astral'. A fellow medium, Hank, responded that when the ritual context does not permit it, he thinks it 'much cooler' to work with the spirits in a way that does not involve the 'full-on' gestures and sounds usually associated with incorporation. In cases like this, you do not allow the spirits to enter your body but only permit them to occupy its surrounding 'energy field'. 'If you stay in your body', Hank said, 'then it's already full and nothing else can get in.' From among those, like myself, watching this exchange, a young woman commented that she wished 'every work could be a mediumship work'.

Evidenced by preceding chapters, the palimpsestic repertoire and rapidly evolving character of Santo Daime makes for a variegated religious terrain. Different communities across the movement increasingly employ, mobilize and articulate *daimista* belief and practice in ways which reflect local dynamics as much as, if not sometimes more than, they adhere to wider organizational conventions and established traditions. Santo Daime belief and practice is both pluriform in the diversity of its outward manifestation and polysemic by way of the breadth of subjective experience it allows. In respect of the spirit-oriented practices treated here, these three exchanges go some way to expressing both the objective and personal variegation inherent to the *daimista* world view.

More than a divergence of personal opinion, the disagreement between Ricardo and Cláudio reflects the, then, contrasting approaches to spirit-oriented activity of their two respective communities. Although a now integral component of its ritual repertoire, at the time of this conversation in 2008, mediumistic possession had yet to establish itself securely among the communal rites of Cláudio's community in the south of Brazil. Cláudio's discomfort with the 'spirit idiom' (Crapanzano, 1977) of incorporation (*incorporação*) was wholly in keeping with the, so far *unspiritized*, communal repertoire through which his personal experience of Santo Daime had chiefly been refracted. In contrast, however, Ricardo's community in São Paulo had long since accepted the incorporation of spirits as a standard repertorial component. While not disavowing the traditional esoteric discourse of reincarnation, Ricardo was equally as comfortable employing the spirit idiom of mediumistic possession. To be discussed in the next section, *daimista* portrayals of the human subject as porous and thereby open to the spiritual realm plays a fundamental part in underwriting the repertorial idiom of spirit possession.

Norma's rejection of the classificatory distinction between spirits of the 'right' and 'left' lines further reflects the palimpsestic and evolutionary character of the *daimista* repertoire. Originally employed within Spiritism, the distinction between spirits of the 'right' and 'left' lines was used by *daimistas* subsequent to the growing appearance of Umbandist influences within the traditional cultic practices of Cefluris. Whereas for some, this distinction was implicitly pejorative in respect of Umbanda spirits (the 'left' being associated with the 'sinister'), for others it represented no more than a straightforward difference of category. This distinction is now rarely employed, however, as a result of the spirit idiom of Umbanda subsequently outstripping its older Spiritist counterpart (see below) and the *daimista* movement spreading to parts of the world unfamiliar with the mode of differentiation it employs. Norma's refusal to distinguish between spirits of the left and right not only separated her from her traditional Spiritist upbringing but also embodied a typical *daimista* commitment to working, for the good, with spirits of all kinds. Detailed below in a section treating the principal spiritual agents of the *daimista* paradigm, the categories employed in their differentiation are neither universally applied nor unchanging in their conceptualization of the spirit-world.

Occurring in the United States, the exchange between Diane and Hank concerns a dual-natured dynamic which is nevertheless influencing communities in every region where Santo Daime is present. First, ritualized spirit possession is becoming so popular across the movement that its ongoing adoption is reshaping not only the overall balance of the established *daimista* repertoire (as more mediumship rituals are staged) but also the particular character of individual rites not traditionally open to public displays of spirit-oriented practice. Second, and on account of its progressive divergence from established practices, the kind of spirit mediumship (viz. 'expressive possession') growing in popularity is incrementally transforming the *daimista* ritual field through its challenge to and transgression of inherited modes of practical-symbolic regulation. Whereas Diane's relative lack of control would debar her from practising mediumship in Santo Daime's more traditional communities, the growing incidence of expressive possession across the movement as a whole reflects not only the increasing acceptance of such practice but also an actual preference for publicly demonstrative modes of spirit-oriented activity. Subsequent to engaging Santo Daime's respective conceptualizations of the self and the spiritual agents it works with, some of the issues captured by Diane and Hank's exchange are treated in a section detailing the ritual context in which spirit mediumship occurs. A following section then develops the themes embodied in this exchange by relating the growth of expressive modes of spirit possession across the *daimista* movement to the now preponderant position of the urban middle classes.

In her overview of spirit possession studies in the late twentieth century, Janet Boddy maintains that spirit possession

> commonly refers to the hold over a human being by external forces or entities more powerful than she. These forces may be ancestors or divinities, ghosts of foreign origin, or entities both ontologically and ethnically alien . . . [It] is a broad term referring to an integration of spirit and matter, force or power and corporeal reality, in a cosmos where the boundaries between an individual and her environment are acknowledged to be permeable, flexibly drawn, or at least negotiable . . . Taking the givenness of spirits as a matter of salience, three parties of variable inclusiveness are implicated in any possession episode: a self, other humans, and external powers. (1994: 407, 422; see also Behrend and Luig, 1999: xv)

Using Boddy's comments as a guide to framing spirit-oriented activity within Santo Daime, the bulk of what follows comprises four sections in which each of the constitutive components identified by this quote are respectively treated. Prior to a concluding section, the remainder of this chapter thereby engages: (i) *daimista* conceptualizations of the self as open to but not determined by the spirits; (ii) the kinds of spirits with whom the self interacts; (iii) the cultic context (re. 'other humans') in which ritualized spirit possession occurs; and, by way of treating relevant 'external powers', (iv) the impact of certain socio-cultural dynamics upon practical and symbolic aspects of spirit-oriented practice.

The possessable self

As Boddy remarks, the discourse of spirit possession articulates a permeable boundary between the human self and its supernatural environment. The permeability of this boundary is, though, predicated on a self who is not just orchestrated by spiritual agencies but actually disposed to being penetrated by them. By definition, the possessable self is both 'porous' and 'dividual' (Smith, 2006; Strathern and Lambek, 1998). Upon asking a *daimista* how many mediums her community had, I received the polite but impassioned reply, 'But Andy, we're all mediums!' On reflection, I should have enquired as to how many *practising* mediums were present in the community at which I was then conducting fieldwork. As with Kardecist Spiritism in general, Santo Daime regards all humans, by virtue of being incarnate spirits, as having mediumistic tendencies. Indeed, the term *aparelho* ('apparatus' or 'utensil') is often employed in traditional contexts to connote the human body as something oriented or prone to being used by the spirits. Consequently, and irrespective of age, spiritual maturity and formal training, every human being is prone to some form of interaction with the spirit-world. For many, however, this interaction is so subtle and our experience of the spiritual world so dulled by our embodied condition that it goes unnoticed at a conscious level. This is unfortunate because a lack of awareness of the manner in and extent to which the spirit-world impacts upon the material sphere at best undermines human freedom (here, self-determination) and at worst leaves the unwary self open to spiritual assault. Even for those without the aptitude or desire to become a practising medium, some degree of training in respect of managing spirit interaction is highly recommended. For those with a greater receptivity to and desire of interacting with the spirit-world, formal training is something of a necessity. To this end, and with the growing popularity of spirit possession practices, communities affiliated to Santo Daime are expected to offer regular mediumistic training.

The dominant representations of the possessable self at play across Santo Daime are informed by both the various sources making up its palimpsestic repertoire and the contemporary orchestrating principles (subjectivization, relativizing holism, etc.) identified in prior chapters. In combination, these elements engender a self both predisposed to interacting with supernatural others and reflexively preoccupied with its own subjective condition. To best appreciate *daimista* understandings of the possessable self, five aspects of this conceptualization are now sketched. These aspects comprise representations of the self as: project; primary principle; cosmically grounded; associational; and multifaceted. As the *daimista* conceptualization of the self is treated at length in other chapters, the following comments refer only to those aspects immediately relevant to Santo Daime's narration of the possessable self as both oriented to and penetrable by spiritual agents.

Daimista understandings of the self as *project* embody both the ameliorative aspirations of modern religious paradigms and late-modern concerns with individual subjectivity as something strategically managed and reflexively nurtured. Shared by Spiritist, esoteric and miscellaneous non-mainstream world views, the ameliorative preoccupation with self-improvement is underwritten by a combination of universal metaphysical processes (e.g. reincarnation and karma) and human psychophysical capabilities (e.g. morality and discipline). Although it may indeed take millennia, the perfectibility of the self is enshrined in a cosmic equation within which individual endeavour (of the incarnate subject) correlates precisely with evolutionary ascent (of the disincarnate spirit). The perfectible-self of the modern religious paradigms upon which Santo Daime draws is echoed by what some have described as the typically late-modern trait of the urban middle classes to regard individual subjectivity as something strategically managed (Featherstone, 2007; Lash, 1994). As with the perfectible-self of modern religiosity, the managed-self of the urban middle classes is in constant need of attention and thereby permanently under construction; there is always more to do and what can be done can always be improved upon. Likewise in tandem with the perfectible-self, the late-modern managed-self is perennially in pursuit of its own self-betterment. Paralleling the universal laws guaranteeing metaphysical returns on subjective endeavour, the betterment pursued by the managed-self is informed by a meritocratic work ethic imbued with characteristically modern aspirations; not least the expectation of just rewards for labours expended. The possessable self of Santo Daime is thereby a project on the way to completion, the incremental pursuit of which manifests through both spiritual and material dimensions.

The possessable self conceptualized by Santo Daime is the *primary principle* by and through which the project of self-betterment is pursued. Santo Daime's estimation of the self reflects modern valorizations of the individual permeating both esoteric and Spiritist influences and the now dominant constituency of the urban middle classes. The *daimista* self is the primary arbiter of religio-moral authority and principal agent of self-transformation. It is, in Bourdieu's terms, the 'principle of hierarchization' by which all else is judged and relative to which everything else is ordered (1991: 168). Although framed by corporate ritual dynamics and their disciplinary processes, the spiritual efficacy of the *daimista* repertoire rests ultimately upon the will and application of the individual subject. And while mitigated by the spiritual agents engaged, the possessable self of Santo Daime nevertheless remains the final arbiter and principal agent of the encounter taking place.

The *cosmic grounding* of the possessable self underwrites its openness to the spiritual other. It is perhaps in this respect that *daimista* understandings of the individual diverge most radically from modern conceptualizations of the 'buffered subject' as a self-sufficient agent 'closed' to the supernatural sphere (Taylor, 2007: 300). Variously portrayed as an 'image of God', 'divine spark', 'miniature cosmos' or 'spirit receptacle', the *daimista* self is grounded in otherwise universal forces and dynamics. *Daimista* renderings of the possessable self thereby invoke a continuum of being underwritten by a connatural relationship between the self and its cosmos. By virtue of its connaturality, the self is metaphysically anchored to the universe at large and, as such, both oriented to and suffused by its most fundamental energies. Although cosmically grounded, and again variously conceived relative to the motifs employed, the self lacks the practical-knowledge by which to harness, manipulate and apply the universal forces to which its connaturality with the spiritual domain guarantees access. Reliant upon instruction, the individual pursuit of self-betterment depends upon engagement with like-minded others.

Unable to develop fully in isolation, and likewise at variance with modern representations of the 'atomic' subject (Taylor, 1992), the possessable self is ineluctably *associational*. As discussed in prior chapters, the instrumental character of contemporary *daimista* religiosity qualifies associational ties by making them conditional upon their continued contribution to the individual project of self-betterment. Although reliant upon the generic instruction and support of like-minded others, the actual forms of association undertaken by the possessable self are those qualifiedly deemed most appropriate *for me, for now*.

The *multifaceted* nature of the possessable self manifests clearly in the variegated benefits accrued through the incremental advance of self-betterment. On the one hand, self-betterment involves the development of various religio-moral dimensions which include, for example, greater self-understanding (of this life and prior incarnations), superior self-control, enhanced extrasensory perception and rapid accumulation of cosmic credit (i.e. karma). On the other, self-betterment also comprises improvement in sundry aspects of psychophysical well-being such as better health, enduring contentment and more secure, if not raised, standards of living. As detailed in Chapter 5, Santo Daime's negation of traditional distinctions between sacred and profane aspects of personal existence is, in large part, founded on the cosmic framing of the self and its narrative fusion of natural and supernatural horizons. Informed by the permeability of physical and spiritual domains, the multifaceted nature of the possessable self embodies a dual dynamic in which the materialization of the sacred is complemented by the sacralization of matter. As a result, the benefits accrued by self-betterment are neither wholly deferred to any future existence nor solely 'spiritual' in conventional terms.

Exemplified by its representation of the human subject as cosmically grounded, associational and multifaceted, the possessable self of Santo Daime corresponds to a significant extent with a good many portrayals by traditional possession paradigms of the individual as porous, oriented to others (of a natural and supernatural kind) and subjectively multidimensional (e.g. Kenyon, 2011; Smith, 2006). At the same time, Santo Daime's emphasis upon the self as project and primary principle is shared with a wide range of typically modern repertoires involving ritualized interaction with supernatural entities and other cosmic forces (e.g. M. Brown, 1997; Ezzy, 2011). Of both a traditional and modern bent, these characteristics collectively constitute a subjectivity marked by the twin dynamics of self-centredness and alterity (here, openness to something other than oneself). Embodied in the possessable self, these dynamics combine an experiential preoccupation with prevailing subjective states with an exploratory inclination to pursue new and heightened experiences through engagement with human and non-human others.

Alternate states of consciousness

Although the possessable self is connaturally oriented to engagement with the supernatural realm, *daimistas* nevertheless regard the act of incorporation to impact upon the human host in a manner involving some kind of alteration to the normal functioning of everyday subjectivity. Noted in Chapter 1, the occupation of the body or its vibrational field by more than one spirit is, to borrow Crapanzano's term, an 'exceptional state' of affairs (2006: 201). Following Spiritist beliefs, this alteration has not customarily been held to involve the possessed individual entering a full-blown trance and thereby losing self-conscious control or subsequent recollection of the possession event. Due to ongoing modifications of the traditional ritual repertoire, however, the established valorization of self-conscious control is increasingly being complemented, if not at points replaced, by modes of incorporation involving the temporary suppression of the host's self-awareness (see below).

Alterations to individual consciousness implicated in a possession event have traditionally been defined by medicalized approaches as 'dissociation' or 'displacement' (see A. Dawson, 2011b: 5), but also labelled 'trance' by a number of important studies (e.g. Bourguignon, 1976). Transformations in subjectivity connected with spirit-oriented practice tend now to be treated within the broader category of 'altered states of consciousness'. Exploring altered states of consciousness related with spirit possession practices, Crapanzano lists the following characteristics:

> Alterations in thinking such as disturbances in concentration, attention, memory, and judgment as well as an impairment in reality testing and a marked tendency toward archaic modes of thought, a disturbed time sense, loss of control, changes in emotional expression (ecstatic and orgiastic feelings, detachment, etc.), changes in body image, perceptual distortions, changes in meaning or significance such as an increased evaluation of subjective experiences, ideas, and perceptions, a sense of the ineffable, feelings of rejuvenation, and hypersuggestability. (1977: 8)

As much in this list equally applies to the altered state of consciousness engendered by the consumption of Daime, the alterations to consciousness associated with *daimista* possession practices may justifiably be regarded as variations on an already established theme.

In respect of the *daimista* world view, however, it may be more apt to refer not to an 'altered state of consciousness' but to *alternate states* of consciousness. Already noted, Santo Daime regards the self as a multifaceted phenomenon with various (e.g. higher and lower) aspects of a more or less developed nature. In the same vein, human subjectivity is held to play out against a variegated backdrop in which the supposedly real (i.e. materiality) is actually illusory while the purportedly unreal (i.e. immateriality) is the most real of all. By way of inverting everyday understandings of the ordinary and the normal, this perspective not only valorizes alternative experiences of 'reality' gained, for example, through dreams, introspection, power plants and spirit-oriented practice, but also actively ranks them above those conventionally available to the uninspired self. The notion of a single, uniform and fixed state of consciousness which is altered from an otherwise default position of 'normality' thereby sits uncomfortably with *daimista* readings of both the multidimensional self and the pluriform world(s) it inhabits. Consequently, the prefix 'alternate states' rather than 'altered state' of consciousness better renders the multifarious experiences implicated in *daimista* ritual practice.

In combination with aforementioned characteristics of the possessable self, the spirit-oriented practice undertaken by *daimistas* may fruitfully be treated as involving one or more alternate states of consciousness. Engendered through the ritualized engagement with the spirit-world, the alternate states associated with incorporation are not only manifestations of a supernatural other but also means by which the strategically minded and multifaceted self experiences, explores and expresses aspects of subjectivity generally hidden, suppressed or unavailable to the uninspired individual. Informed by the hermeneutical turn, numerous studies of possession have done much to underline the place and strategic character of subjective agency within spirit-oriented activity. Concerned with explicating the possessable self as both an active maker of meaning and purposive subject forging her own identity, agential interpretations regard spirit possession not as something which happens to a passive individual but rather as a process which he plays a fundamental part in initiating, directing and concluding (e.g. Kramer, 1993; Wafer, 1991). Undertaken within a given ritual context and ostensibly determined by the spiritual entities engaged, spirit-oriented activity nevertheless affords ample scope for the strategic assertion of the individual subject involved. The possessable self remains no less an expressible self.

The spirits

Striving to articulate the deep-seated variegation of its religious repertoire, I have elsewhere adapted Besnier's use of Bakhtin (1996) to describe the spirit idiom of Cefluris as 'hyper-heteroglossic' in character (2011d: 149). The evolution of spirit-oriented practices within Santo Daime is characterized by the appropriation of successive spirit discourses of a variegated and often contrasting kind. Occurring within the relatively short period of 80 years, Santo Daime has evolved from the Afro-Amazonian cult of a small community of impoverished, mixed-race peasants to become a globally diffused, late-modern religion practised by a predominantly white urban-professional constituency. Throughout this time, a wide variety of discourse and practice has been appropriated from an array of religious paradigms, not least of which are Amazonian *caboclo* religiosity, traditional European esotericism, Kardecist Spiritism, new-age spirituality and Umbanda. Catalysed by rapid geographic and demographic shifts in membership, the character of its spirit idiom has been further diversified by Santo Daime's progressive insertion within the alternative cultic milieu populated by the urban middle classes and suffused by the increasingly vertiginous dynamics of late-modern spirituality. In keeping with its rapidly evolving and palimpsestic character, the *daimista* repertoire continues to grow through the ongoing appropriation of discourse and practice from a diversity of sources such as the Afro-Brazilian religion of Candomblé, Japanese new religious paradigms (e.g. Perfect Liberty), Eastern traditions (e.g. Hinduism and Buddhism) and miscellaneous autochthonous spiritualities indigenous to geographical regions new to Santo Daime (e.g. North American native religiosity, Australasian aboriginal spirituality and European nature religions). The spirit idioms appropriated by *daimistas* are further complemented by the progressive addition of contemporary extraterrestrial narratives and their attendant motifs of 'channelling' and 'walk-ins'.

The spectrum of spiritual entities engaged by *daimistas* is as hybrid and fluid as the religious repertoire through which they work. Santo Daime's highest and most powerful supernatural agents are inherited principally from popular Catholic and traditional esoteric paradigms. As with many other spirit-oriented religions, Santo Daime acknowledges the existence of a creator deity whose originary status and generative cosmological activity sets the metaphysical backdrop against which cultic practice plays out. Likewise in keeping with other religious paradigms, the creator god of Santo Daime (traditionally, though decreasingly, termed 'Father') is a remote divinity who, though lauded in hymns and prayers, remains otherwise disengaged from ritual activity. In addition to the popular Catholic trinity of Jesus, Mary and Joseph, archangels (e.g. Michael, Gabriel and George) feature prominently in the *daimista* liturgy. The spirits of saints and important biblical characters (e.g. John the Baptist, Solomon and David) are also praised. In tandem with the growth and spread of Santo Daime, the higher heavenly beings of traditional Catholic and esoteric paradigms are progressively complemented by gods and deities appropriated from other religious world views. The gods of Candomblé (e.g. Xangô and Oxum), deities of Hinduism (e.g. Brahma and Shiva) and eminent spiritual agents from other religious traditions and belief systems (e.g. Buddha and Tlaloc) are increasingly appearing in hymns alongside or instead of Santo Daime's more traditional supernatural referents.

Though called upon and referenced at regular intervals within cultic practice, supernatural entities from the higher echelons of the *daimista* pantheon have not traditionally been engaged through embodied (i.e. incorporated) modes of mediumistic activity. Following established motifs employed in relation to Master Irineu and Padrinho Sebastião (respectively held to incarnate the spirits of Jesus and John the Baptist), the language of reincarnation is customarily used on the relatively rare events when higher spiritual agents are believed to assume bodily form. The current head of Santo Daime (Padrinho Alfredo) is, for example, believed to be the reincarnation of King Solomon, while his fellow leadership member, Padrinho Alex Polari, is held to reincarnate King David. Whereas I have met many *daimistas* believing themselves to have lived former lives as prominent figures or during historically significant periods and events, those professing to be the reincarnation of a senior supernatural agent are relatively few. As discussed below, however, the ongoing popularization of ritualized spirit possession across the *daimista* movement is accompanied by increasing accounts of individuals claiming to incorporate higher spiritual entities not customarily engaged through mediumistic practice.

In contrast to aforementioned higher supernatural agencies, the spirits of Brazilian Kardecism and Umbanda have traditionally borne the ritual workload of mediumistic activity; although the growth and spread of Santo Daime is progressively populating cultic space with spiritual entities not customarily associated with its traditional ritual repertoire. Two classes of spirit tend to bear the ritual workload. Variably expressed across the movement, these two classes are most commonly referred to as 'spirit-guides' and 'suffering spirits'. Spirit-guides are spiritual entities whose nature or evolutionary status places them beyond the normal cycle of reincarnation. As such, these spirits reside permanently in the astral plane where they may be called upon to assist human beings through a variety of means, not least mediumistic possession. The most famous guides of Brazilian Kardecism regularly called upon during rituals of incorporation are the now disincarnate spirits of the historical figures Prof. Antônio Jorge and Dr José Bezerra de Menezes. The spirit of the mythical Dr Fritz is also popular (see Santos, 2004). Appropriated from the multitudinous Umbanda spectrum, the spirit-guides of deceased indigenes (*caboclos*), black slaves (*pretos velhos*) and children (*erês*) appear most frequently, with representatives of other 'lines' (e.g. 'oriental') also making an appearance. Likewise acting as guides, spirits and entities populating the new-era paradigm or originating from regional traditions and indigenous world views are increasingly engaged in *daimista* ritual practice. Along with extraterrestrial beings, fairies and elves, former occupants of Atlantis, Avalon and King Arthur's court, for example, are among the wide variety of spiritual agencies appropriated from the alternative religious scene. The spirits of Native American warriors, aboriginal leaders, Celtic kings and

Druidic priests have also been identified to me as spirit-guides. Animal spirits are also popular, with the eagle, hummingbird and jaguar featuring among those regularly cited.[1] Whereas interaction with the spirits of or through plants other than Daime or Santa Maria (e.g. cactus, iboga, mushroom and tobacco) also occurs, such tends to happen during private or non-official ritual practice.

Commonly termed 'suffering spirits', the third class of entities is believed to exist at the lower end of the spiritual hierarchy. These spiritual entities are commonly held to be the disincarnate spirits of human beings, although other kinds of 'low' spirit may also be encountered. Reflecting an unwarranted attachment to the material plane or disorientation arising from the sudden demise of its physical body, for example, a spirit may remain present within the earthly sphere rather than moving on to the astral realm whence it will subsequently be reincarnated. Such entities often make their presence felt by attaching themselves to the energy fields of spiritually unwary, ill-prepared or careless human beings. They may also enter the body of their physical hosts whereupon their impact is more serious. Either way, the presence of a suffering spirit impacts deleteriously upon the physical and general well-being of its victim. In addition to working with those involuntarily affected by a suffering or low spirit, cultic engagement with these entities may involve their voluntary admission into a medium's body or surrounding aura whereby they are ritually treated and subsequently sent on their way back to the astral plane (see below).

Although by no means formally codified, *daimista* communities practising mediumistic possession work broadly with the three classes of spirits just identified. Different communities, though, work with varying kinds of spiritual entities within each of these classes and, as discussed in the next section, do so in a variety of ways. While in some communities the spirits of Kardecism remain important, within others they are virtually inoperative, having been superseded by the supernatural entities of Umbanda. Some communities working with the supernatural agents of Umbanda, however, only incorporate aforementioned spirit-guides and suffering spirits, while others also incorporate the powerful *orixás* or lower spirits traditionally regarded within Umbanda as morally dubious (e.g. Exu). Whereas the spirits of Umbanda remain significant for most communities practising ritualized possession, spiritual entities from the alternative scene, other religious traditions and local (i.e. non-Brazilian) contexts are rapidly gaining in popularity. In the same vein, and increasingly so, *daimistas* are recounting experiences with higher spiritual beings such as angels and archangels not customarily engaged through mediumistic practice. In short, and in keeping with the ritual repertoire in which they sit, the spirits engaged across the *daimista* movement are both highly variable and rapidly evolving.

Ritual context

Since the hermeneutical/cultural turn of the mid- to late twentieth century (see Geertz, 1973), the communal context of spirit-oriented activity has been of central interest to possession studies by way of its focus upon the collective processes of signification; not least, the interpersonal dynamics of communication, performance and interpretation. The most influential of such approaches use textual, idiomatic and dramaturgical models to explicate the corporate dimensions of spirit possession. For example, Lambek explores the 'social basis' of spirit possession by viewing it 'as a system of communication' whereby 'possession operates to transmit messages (verbal, material, etc.) between senders and receivers along particular channels' (1981: 70). In the same vein, Crapanzano explicates the corporate framing of spirit possession by treating it as a kind of 'idiom' embodying 'traditional values, interpretational vectors, patterns of association, ontological presuppositions, spatiotemporal orientations, and etymological horizons'. 'Polysemic' in nature, the 'language of spirit possession' must be mastered in both its 'technical' and 'symbolic' dimensions if the one possessed is to achieve anything approaching success (1977: 11, 15).

In addition to stressing the communicative and idiomatic dimensions of spirit possession, those underlining its communal context have also emphasized its performative character. Levy, Mageo and Howard, for example, maintain that the 'highly skillful' performance of spirit possession 'requires mastery of role playing and of subtle kinds of communally significant communication' which 'implies an audience' (1996: 18–19). Characteristically late-modern in their preoccupation with the interpersonal dynamics of hermeneutical exchange, performative approaches to spirit possession appropriate a range of dramaturgical concepts and theories which underscore its theatrical ethos and intent (see Laderman and Roseman, 1995; Stoller, 1989). As with an actor in a play, the possessed individual assumes a role which plays to its respective audience (along with its expectations, tastes and desires), requires competence and skill to achieve, is directed by a given script and enacted relative to the props and staging furnished by its respective communal context. In light of the hermeneutical turn, spirit-oriented activity is understood as inextricably woven within a complex web of symbolic processes and material practices of a collective kind. Paralleling a good many other religious repertoires, Santo Daime's ritual framing of spirit-oriented practice furnishes practical and symbolic conditions of possibility which determine where, when, how and by whom mediumistic activity is undertaken.

Types and modes of spirit-oriented activity

The hybrid and self-consciously eclectic character of the *daimista* repertoire allows for a wide variety of spirit-oriented experience and its outward ritual expression. Santo Daime exhibits aspects of many of the classic types (e.g. possession, mediumship and shamanism) and modes (e.g. involuntary/ voluntary and conscious/unconscious) associated with spirit engagement (see A. Dawson, 2011b). Among the types most referenced by academic studies of spirit-oriented activity are those of 'possession', 'mediumship' and 'shamanism' (e.g. Bourguignon, 1976; Firth, 1967; Lewis, 2003; Smith, 2006). The type of spirit-oriented activity termed 'possession' is chiefly associated with non-specialist (i.e. untrained) individuals who are involuntarily overcome by a spirit or spirits, often losing consciousness during and subsequent recollection of the possession event. Given the inexperience of the individual concerned and the impact of the spirit's occupation of its bodily host, possession tends to exhibit a relative lack of control on the part of the possessed person. Understood as an unsolicited but explicable, if not sometimes deserved, spiritual assault, possession both lacks an explicit ritual function and is generally pathologized as an undesirable state of affairs. In contrast to spirit possession, mediumship and shamanism are most closely associated with ritual specialists whose training equips them with the knowledge and techniques necessary to handling the spirits appropriately. Although subsequently characterized by an educated control of the spirits, the earliest experiences of those who become mediums or shamans often involve some kind of involuntary or uncontrolled interaction with the spirit-world. Undertaken by trained specialists, mediumship and shamanism are voluntary modes of spirit engagement, comprising a varying measure of self-control and clarity of ritual purpose. Sometimes involving the practitioner's bodily occupation by a spirit, the manageability and ritual utility of mediumship and shamanism nevertheless contribute to their positive connotation.

While sharing a number of characteristics, mediumship and shamanism are also contrasted. The ritual function of mediumship is typologically confined to a delimited cultic context and, though sometimes involved in healing, revolves principally around the oracular or written communication of information gleaned from interaction with the spirits. Shamanism, however, classically furnishes an extensive range of ceremonial and otherwise mundane services which combine the explicitly religious with socio-cultural, economic and political matters. By extension, this typically requires of the shaman a broader skill-set than that of the medium, including greater versatility in handling a more varied array of spiritual forces. Unlike mediumship, in which the self remains situated within the body, shamanism is also predicated on the ecstatic practice of soul-flight through which the shaman's spirit is believed to become temporarily disembodied in order to make a journey to the supernatural realm. In contrast with enstatic (from *enstasis* – 'staying within') forms of mediumship comprising bodily occupation by a spirit, shamanic ecstasy characteristically involves a greater degree of self-awareness on the part of the shaman.

In keeping with the palimpsestic and rapidly evolving nature of the *daimista* repertoire, the articulation of spirit-oriented practice is highly varied both across the movement as a whole and within individual communities. Whereas some make a distinction between possession and mediumship or mediumship and shamanism, others do not. At the same time, while two typologically distinct kinds of spirit engagement may be described using the same terminology, what is characteristically the same type of event may be expressed through different terms. Nevertheless, and despite the polyvalent use of relevant vocabulary, many of the practical and symbolic experiences expressed contain aspects which correlate with one or more of the classic types identified above. The same can also be said of the different modes implicated in spirit-oriented practice. Although the emic terminology rarely matches that of conventional academic discourse, the most common modes articulated by *daimistas* broadly correspond with established etic categories of involuntary/voluntary, negative/positive, unconscious/conscious, enstatic/ecstatic and gnoseological/therapeutic forms of spirit-oriented activity.

Possession

As with the classic type of spirit possession, involuntary modes of encounter with spiritual entities are generally pathologized by *daimistas* as negative events in need of ritual resolution. The terms *atuação* (literally, 'activation') and *obsessão* ('obsession') are used by some Brazilian communities to designate involuntary and negatively connoted forms of spirit assault (though others employ the word activation in a non-pathologizing way as a synonym for incorporation or mediumship). Communities beyond Brazil commonly use their respective linguistic equivalent of 'possession' to describe the unwarranted attentions of a spirit. In tandem with other modes, pathologized forms of spirit engagement may be graded by degrees. A disoriented or malign spirit may attach itself to the vibrational field (also termed 'aura', 'energy field' or 'matrix') which surrounds an individual, or the spirit may actually gain entry into the body of its host. Whereas the former kind of spirit attachment tends to be less serious than full-blown possession, its manifestation is also less obvious. Consequently, it is often harder to spot and can thereby take an extended amount of time to diagnose and subsequently treat. At the same time, some spirits are harder to deal with than others. As a trained medium of long-standing told me:

> Some people have spirits on them and don't know it. What shows is sickness, bad feelings and bad things. I had one recently which was the spirit of a young man who died in an accident . . . and in his confusion attached himself to me. It was not until I was in the work [i.e. ritual] that someone else identified what was going on and we were able to send him on his way. Others have forms attached to their energy fields which also need dealing with. Some can be dealt with easily, straight away, while others are much tougher and need longer.

The most serious cases of spirit possession are treated in the 'Cross Ritual' (*Trabalho de Cruzes*) formulated by Master Irineu as a 'work of exorcism and disobsession' (www.santodaime.org). Complementing the consumption of Daime, singing of specified hymns and an assortment of typically esoteric arrangements, the 'Prayer to Dispel the Curses of Evil Spirits and Infernal Demons' is collectively recited. During Master Irineu's time, less serious cases in need of a cure were dealt with in the Concentration ritual. Subsequent to the formation of Cefluris, however, Padrinho Sebastião and others devised a number of works (e.g. the rituals of Cure and Saint Michael) explicitly designed for the pursuit of healing through ritual engagement with the spirits involving, where necessary, their voluntary incorporation.

Mediumship

The terms 'incorporation' and 'mediumship' are most commonly used synonymously to designate voluntary, and thereby positively connoted, engagement with a spirit in a formal ritual context. For some, incorporation refers only to enstatic forms of mediumship involving the bodily occupation of the medium by a spirit. Others, though, make no categorical distinction between the actual embodiment of a spirit and work with an entity occurring only in the medium's surrounding energy field. Describing their experiences of incorporation, many *daimistas* adopt a typically Kardecist perspective to describe themselves as remaining conscious throughout the possession event. Whereas some regard their subjective presence as integral to directing the possessing spirit, others talk of the self as an interested but passive third party looking on to what the spirit is doing through their body. One practitioner described her experience of incorporation as being 'pushed to the side' by the occupying spirit. In common with a good number of informants, another talked of feeling like 'someone else is looking through my eyes'. A North

American medium, Katherine, articulates her experience of incorporating one of her guides in this way:

> It's like Katherine gets out of the way because she has no clue what's going on and the doctor does the work . . . Katherine is back here, she's always there. She can take charge if somebody needs help. But she's at the back and the doctor's forward. She's just being a channel, just open.

Paralleling the growing influence of non-Spiritist motifs, however, incorporation is progressively being described as involving suppression of consciousness and a resulting inability to remember certain aspects of the spirit's bodily occupation. In conversation with a *daimista* leader, he initially talked of 'three degrees of incorporation', each involving different levels of 'control' in respect of the spirit engaged. The greatest level of control enjoyed by a medium occurs when the spirit is 'not inside' the body, he said, but occupies its surrounding aura. The medium's control decreases somewhat when parts, but not all, of the body come under the sway of the spirit. Such partial influence is most commonly manifest through the hands and arms making 'gestures and signs' (sometimes called 'mudras') that are not of the medium's doing 'but come from the spiritual force controlling these limbs'. The least control a medium has is when 'he is completely occupied' by a spirit which is 'like looking through someone else's eyes. He's still present, but back there' (said while pointing to the rear of the head). When he denied ever being fully unconscious while practising mediumship, I asked my informant what he thought about *daimistas* claiming to lose self-awareness when incorporating higher deities such as the *orixás*. 'Ah', he said, 'of course, the *orixás* are gods; so if you're incorporating an *orixá* the power is going to overwhelm you.' On a related note, and while chatting to a young Brazilian the day after a *gira* ritual (see below) in which we had participated, I asked her why she swirled round the room when incorporating the spirit of the *orixá* Oxum. She responded by saying, 'I really don't know. I've no idea whatsoever. I just do.'

Spirit mediumship in Santo Daime has three explicit ritual functions which respectively comprise gnoseological, therapeutic and illuminatory emphases. The gnoseological function involves the oral or, less commonly, written communication of information from the astral plane. Here, the spirits engaged may be wholly incorporated within the medium's body or 'channelled' in a way which stops short of full bodily occupation. Reflecting its Kardecist provenance, gnoseological mediumship usually involves engagement with entities from the Spiritist tradition such as the aforementioned Dr Bezerra de Menezes and Prof. Antônio Jorge. Senior members of Cefluris, not least those with kinship ties to the founding family, may also communicate messages from key figures of the movement who have since 'passed over'.

Padrinho Sebastião, for example, is regularly mediated by his daughter who co-leads the Rio de Janeiro community of *Céu do Mar*. Except for instances such as local crisis or organizational challenge (when the incorporating spirit offers sometimes quite specific guidance), the information communicated through gnoseological mediumship tends to more general exhortatory and pedagogical concerns.

As the term suggests, therapeutic mediumship is oriented to the healing and general psychophysical well-being of those being tended. Under the sway of a relevant spiritual entity (often called 'doctors'), the medium undertakes a range of diagnostic, prescriptive and curative measures. Subsequent to the spirit-assisted diagnosis of the issue in question, the medium may prescribe any number of treatments including, for example, homeopathic remedies or dietary and lifestyle changes. Instances where more robust forms of intervention are deemed necessary may involve the medium acting directly upon the patient by way of recalibrating the surrounding energy field through the 'pass' or, in more serious cases, by performing 'spiritual surgery' in the astral plane (see Chapter 1). Noted prior, illness, malaise or general hardships may also be attributed to the presence of a malign or disoriented spirit, the removal of which often requires more concerted ritual action. It is here that illuminatory mediumship comes to the fore.

Illuminatory mediumship has customarily been the most common form of spirit-oriented activity within Santo Daime and is oriented to 'low', 'suffering' or 'disoriented' spirits whom the medium engages through full-blown incorporation or by way of their presence in her surrounding energy field. Whereas gnoseological and therapeutic modes of mediumship are traditionally restricted to a relatively small number of practitioners, the process of instructing, and thereby 'illuminating', spirits in need of guidance is something which all *daimistas* are, at least in theory, able to practise. According to informants, illuminatory mediumship has, from its beginnings in Santo Daime, assumed two distinct forms; one of which is interactive and the other private. The interactive form of illuminatory mediumship involves designated practitioners working with or assuming control of disoriented or troublesome spirits. Like its therapeutic counterpart, the interactive practice of illuminatory mediumship was traditionally restricted to particular rituals and trained personnel. In contrast, the private form of illuminatory mediumship was theoretically open to everyone and could be practised in various ritual contexts *as long as* its undertaking did not draw attention to the practitioner, distract others or detract from individual contributions to the collective spiritual current. In effect, the private illumination of spirits should involve no other ritual practitioner but the individual concerned.

The spirits engaged by illuminatory mediumship may be sensed by the medium, appear suddenly to or within him or be identified as occupying the body or aura of another person. As one medium put it, 'I invite. I say "okay, I'm open. Do you want to drink Daime and go to the light? I'm open for you" . . . What happens [then] is I get up to drink a service of Daime . . . and as I'm getting into line it's like all of a sudden I'm not the only one there.' Another practitioner, Tina, recounted how she was suddenly 'occupied' by the spirit of a woman who died in a car crash. Describing the occupying spirit as 'using my body', Tina 'began sobbing for 45 minutes' as the woman's spirit cried in despair at her violent and premature death. Upon presenting herself for a dose of Daime, Tina recounted how the first cup was drunk by the spirit in control of her body. Tina then requested a second serving which, she said, was for her (i.e. Tina's) benefit rather than the spirit's.

Not always accompanied by the additional consumption of Daime over and above that ordinarily consumed, illuminatory mediumship nevertheless requires the medium working with the spirit in a disciplined and concentrated manner to the end of directing it on its way to the astral plane. Sometimes technically described as an act of religious 'instruction' or 'indoctrination', interaction may also be explained using more pastoral terms such as 'calming' or 'reassuring' the spirit in question. In cases where a medium is unable to manage and ultimately 'despatch' a spirit incorporated voluntarily, or in instances of involuntary possession, more experienced mediums 'transport' the troublesome spirit into their own body and thereby take control of the situation. The more recalcitrant the spirit, the more likely it is that an additional dose of Daime will need to be taken by the medium for the spirit. Although decreasingly in force (see below), it has traditionally been expected that mediums of greater experience should exhibit higher levels of self-conscious control than that demonstrated by mediums with less competence or those involuntarily possessed.

Reflecting their Kardecist origins and befitting their established status, these three mediumistic modes have a clear ritual rationale which centres upon the earning of cosmic merit through ritualized charitable practice. On the one hand, the spirit-guides implicated in mediumistic practice are said to hasten their evolutionary ascent by accumulating cosmic merit through the charitable service they provide to humankind and their lower spiritual counterparts. On the other, practitioners of incorporation likewise earn cosmic merit by way of the guidance and instruction which their mediumship affords both disoriented or suffering spirits and their fellow human beings. Furthermore, and in keeping with the generic ritual virtues of firmness and discipline, the demands associated with incorporating spirits also earn merit for those able to meet their charitable obligations by maintaining self-control in the face of the additional trials involved. Nuanced relative to the particular mode of mediumship concerned, traditional readings of incorporation closely associate the merit earned through its practice with an act of charity undertaken on behalf of others.

Shamanism

A number of studies of Santo Daime have identified 'shamanism' as an important component of its ritual repertoire (e.g. Couto, 2004; Groisman, 1996; MacRae, 1992; T. K. Schmidt, 2007). Employing Couto's description of Santo Daime as a form of 'collective shamanism' (2004: 404), MacRae also identifies Master Irineu as a kind of modern, 'urbanized' shaman (1992: 127). Schmidt, though, is at pains to distance *daimista* practices from the 'neo-shamanism found in New Age circles' and its 'individualistic "psychologising" of the religious realm'; instead rooting Santo Daime 'within a unique regional form of shamanism' (2007: 108–9). The terms 'shaman' and 'shamanism' were also frequently used by practitioners in each of the three continents in which fieldwork was conducted. Although incorporating the *orixás* Xangô and Ogum, as well as working regularly with 'suffering spirits', the 'commander' of a Dutch community identified himself as a 'shaman' and Santo Daime as a 'shamanic religion'. In the same vein, and while reluctant to talk about other aspects of Santo Daime's spirit-oriented activity, the leader of one of São Paulo's most important churches self-designated as a 'shaman' and spoke at length about the shamanic practice of 'soul-flight' as an 'ecstatic' (i.e. out of body) experience in which the human spirit is temporarily decoupled from its physical moorings. Referencing both Amazonian and Native American shamanic traditions, ecstatic modes of spirit engagement were likewise commonly employed by North American *daimistas* to describe disincarnate journeys to supernatural realms populated by spiritual beings of human and non-human origin.[2]

Academic treatments of Santo Daime which argue for its identity as a shamanic religion do so by citing parallels between the *daimista* repertoire and various indigenous and mixed-race world views in which shamanism occurs. In addition to ecstatic representations of spirit-oriented practice, such parallels include, for example, use of psychoactives, ritual-related dietary restrictions, notions of initiation and apprenticeship and employment of song, instrumentation and dance. Delineated in Chapter 1, the presence of these features in the religious repertoire of Santo Daime does indeed reflect indebtedness to indigenous and mixed-race religio-cultural paradigms exhibiting, at least in part, shamanic preoccupations. At the same time, many of the defining characteristics of shamanism listed by Langdon resonate with key components of the *daimista* world view. These characteristics are

> the idea of a universe of multiple levels in which visible reality always presupposes an invisible one; a general principle of energy that unifies the universe . . .; a native concept of shamanic power which is tied to the system of global energy . . . through which extra-human forces

exercise their powers in the human sphere and through which humanity, mediated by the shaman, in turn exercises its powers in the extra-human world; a principle of transformation . . . [by which] spirits adopt concrete human or animal form, and shamans become animals or assume invisible forms such as those of the spirits . . .; the shaman as mediator who acts principally for the benefit of his people; and ecstatic experiences which are the basis of shamanic power and make the mediatory role possible. (1996: 27–8)

Many of these parallels and characteristics, however, are generic features of other religious world views which have impacted and continue to influence Santo Daime's ritual repertoire; not least esotericism, Spiritism, new-age and Afro-Brazilian traditions. Consequently, their presence in Santo Daime cannot automatically be attributed to the influence of indigenous or mixed-race shamanism. Furthermore, the only characteristic which appears to sit definitively within the shamanic paradigm ('the shaman as mediator') involves a broadened social and extra-cultic remit not exhibited by the spirit-oriented practice of the contemporary *daimista* medium. Whereas the formation of Santo Daime was, in part, influenced by components derived from a religio-cultural world view in which shamanism played a role, the extent and enduring character of this originary influence is highly attenuated and extremely limited across the movement as a whole. Indeed, the overwhelming majority of *daimistas* who reference shamanism to describe their spirit-oriented activity do so by appropriating stereotypical characterizations and stylistic tropes furnished by typically new-age (i.e. neo-shamanic) refractions of indigenous beliefs and practices (see also Polari, 1996). Of course, this does not make these experiences any less valid or authentic. It does, though, undermine the case for shamanism being anything more than one among a number of experiential frames and performative motifs through which individual encounters with the supernatural realm are both shaped and expressed. To baldly describe Santo Daime as a shamanic religion is, then, both overly reductionist and potentially misleading.

The idiomatic spectrum

Manifest in variegated ways and to varying degrees, the classic types of possession, mediumship and shamanism structure much of Santo Daime's spirit-oriented activity. Likewise, involuntary/voluntary, negative/positive, unconscious/conscious, gnoseological/therapeutic and enstatic/ecstatic modes of spirit engagement are refracted through the *daimista* ritual repertoire. The spectrum of ritual interface with the spiritual realm is, though, a very broad one within Santo Daime and encompasses more than that allowed for by these classic types and modes. As said prior, the *daimista* spirit idiom is hyper-heteroglossic. Indeed, not every member believes the incorporation of spiritual agents to be integral to the expression of *daimista* religiosity. While the regularity of possession rituals and the incidence of individual possession events have increased markedly in recent years (see below), there remain a significant, though dwindling number, who neither incorporate nor engage spiritual entities. The majority of these individuals do, though, acknowledge spirit possession as a licit component of the Santo Daime repertoire. For others, however, this is not the case. 'Inauthentic', 'contrived', 'imagination', 'psychic stuff', 'a show' and 'counterproductive' were among the terms used by some informants to describe ritualized engagement with the spirits. Preferring the esoteric and introspective emphases of the *daimista* paradigm, for example, Jeff informed me that 'being allowed to play in the lower astral fields can be detrimental'. Speaking about the growing incidence of ritualized possession within his community, Jeff regarded those being 'possessed' by the spirits as undergoing what he describes as an 'exorcism of their own subconscious'. He went on to say that 'I think it's valuable to see them [i.e. possession events] as subconscious projections. To anthropomorphize subconscious projections is to some degree beneficial, but ultimately anthropomorphization is an amusing pastime.'

By and large, those who do not 'work with the spirits' express themselves religiously by employing *non-spiritized* (usually esoteric and new-age) components from the Santo Daime repertoire which, though not necessarily rejecting the existence of spirits, do not rely upon their engagement. Here, notions of the higher-self, past-life regression, astral projection or expanded consciousness are commonly employed to articulate interaction with the supernatural plane. As one informant put it, 'the most important thing is the encounter with your true self'; while someone else argued that 'the journey inward is all that's needed – there's no need to go anyplace else'. As well as expressing discomfort at the growth of spirit possession across Santo Daime, another *daimista* described his use of Daime 'as a vehicle for my own exploration . . . to take the radical change in myself inward and meditate and contemplate and allow that energy to elevate me'. In similar vein, others describe the spiritual forces engaged by Santo Daime not as independently existing entities but rather as astral counterparts or psychical manifestations of an embodied and multifaceted self. Yvonne, for example, portrayed mediumship as representing 'psychic fragments . . . complexes in a Jungian sense, which is a really interesting explanation for me, given I've seen different types of people incorporate beings which really seem to express an aspect of the complexes those people have'. Interestingly, however, the same informant did recount 'an experience of channelling' which occurred during ritual participation. According to Yvonne,

> I got into touch with something that was going on with my mother . . . I felt it in the depths of my being and I purged [i.e. vomited] with her. I processed her sorrow and her grief and all this stuff and purged for her. And I actually had a conversation with her the following day about how she was and she validated my experience.

Whereas some *daimistas* differentiate between 'incorporation' or 'mediumship' as a means of engaging disincarnate spirits and 'channelling' as an encounter with otherwise embodied beings (such as Yvonne's mother), others make no such distinction. Those mediating 'stellar' beings from other parts of the universe (most popularly Orion, the Pleiades and the Milky Way), for example, may or may not employ notions of channelling or 'walk-in' to differentiate encounter with extraterrestrial life forms from their incorporation of the disembodied occupants of the spirit-world. Likewise, articulations of working with otherwise embodied beings from this or any other world or dimension involve varying degrees of bodily occupation and consciousness which differ from community to community, person to person and entity to entity.

Oriented by the various idioms used to articulate the experiences involved, Figure 4.1 represents the spectrum of contemporary *daimista* engagement with the spiritual realm. Conceptualized as a typology of idiomatic expressions relating to voluntary modes of spirit-oriented practice, the categories employed by the spectrum each encompass a particular, though idealized, means of describing the perceived relationship between the individual self and the supernatural forces encountered. Whereas these ideal types are analytically distinct from each other, they are not mutually exclusive. For example, a *daimista* who claims to be the reincarnation of a particular spiritual entity may also engage other spirits by way of occupational (e.g. mediumship) or interfacial (e.g. soul-flight) means. The reincarnated spirit of the same individual may also manifest itself during ritual practice in very similar ways to those employed by entities temporarily occupying the bodies of their mediumistic hosts. Likewise, a cultic participant may use introspective means

	Idiomatic Spectrum			
Spirit	Convergent	Occupational	Interfacial	Introspective	Self
	Reincarnation	Suppressed | Marginal | Cooperative	Locomotive | Hybird | Static	Psycho-spirituality	

FIGURE 4.1 *Spectrum of contemporary daimista engagement with the spiritual realm.*

to describe one form of spiritual engagement (e.g. in a Concentration ritual) while employing interfacial or occupational modes to express other kinds of spirit encounter experienced in different cultic contexts (e.g. Saint Michael) or, indeed, separate points within the same ceremony. Furthermore, some *daimistas* describe a single event using a mixture of terminology to identify the various phases or experiences involved.

The types of self – spirit relationship towards the left-hand side of the idiomatic spectrum are characterized by their discursive emphasis upon the spiritual agent involved. Furthest to the left of the spectrum, the *convergent* idiom eschews punctual or episodic narratives of spirit engagement, instead identifying the individual subject wholly and uninterruptedly with a particular spiritual entity. By describing herself to me as the reincarnation of the 'Archangel Michael', for example, Barbara saw herself not as an independently existing agent but as the literal and ongoing manifestation of an angelic being. In effect, the earthly self of Barbara is but a contingent, secondary identity to that of the eternal, heavenly entity by which it has been assumed and to which it is ultimately subordinate. Barbara's identity may well be merged with that of the Archangel Michael, but the Archangel's persona is far more than that manifest through the single life cycle of the woman Barbara.

The *occupational* idiom involves the presence of a spirit or spirits within the body or its surrounding energy field. Detailed above, this presence comprises different levels of self-consciousness and control on the part of the human host. Although customarily rarer in Santo Daime, 'suppressed' modes of occupational encounter are becoming increasingly common across the movement (see below) and involve the wholesale loss of self-awareness on the part of the individual occupied. 'Marginal' and 'cooperative' forms of occupation remain the most popular means of describing spirit engagement, with each manifesting through relatively greater degrees of consciousness and directive agency. Whereas 'marginal' experiences of occupation describe the human host as an aware but passive onlooker to what the spirit is doing through its bodily medium, 'cooperative' expressions frame the self – spirit interaction as a partnership to which each contributes more or less equally relative to the experience and skills of the host, type of spirit involved and specific task being undertaken.

In contrast to occupational idioms, *interfacial* representations of self – spirit relations describe them as occurring beyond the psychophysical confines of the human body. As the kinds of spirit engagement involved require significant degrees of self-management, subjective agency is valorized as an important means of directing events. 'Locomotive' descriptions of interfacial encounter involve a 'journey' enabled by the psychical dislocation of human subjectivity or aspects thereof (e.g. spirit, astral body, higher-self) to dimensions, places or times other than the here and now of the material plane. Traditionally narrated through the esoteric motif of astral projection, *daimista* expressions of 'locomotive' interface with the spiritual realm increasingly employ neo-shamanic notions of soul-flight. 'Static' expressions of interfacial engagement eschew psychical dislocation, instead emphasizing modes of spiritual encounter which do not rely upon the subject propelling himself anyplace else. Involving some kind of remote connection with or telescopic view of the spiritual realm, descriptions of 'static' interface include terms such as 'vision', 'telepathic communication', 'mental mediumship' and 'channelling'. 'Hybrid' modes of spiritual interface merge both locomotive and static tropes and are most commonly expressed as an 'expansion of consciousness'. Using both traditional *vegetalista* and new-age concepts, for example, Padrinho Alex Polari maintains that 'when the Daime expands our consciousness, allowing our minds to melt into the universal, the professor [i.e. Daime] helps us understand this totality' (Richman, 1990/1: 38). On the one hand, the connection established with the spiritual sphere results from the expansion of human consciousness towards something existing beyond the psychophysical boundaries of the self. Unlike static modes of interface, however, expansion of consciousness involves subjectivity moving outwards towards something which is not ordinarily part of it. On the other hand, and in contrast to locomotive forms of interface, the spiritual encounter established by expanded consciousness does not require actual psychical dislocation on the part of the self or aspects of it. Merging locomotion and stasis, expanded consciousness articulates a mixture of both immediate and remote interface between the self and a supernatural other.

Not necessarily gainsaying the actual existence of spiritual entities, *introspective* emphases nevertheless prefer *non-spiritized*, psycho-spiritual modes of interpretation (e.g. ego or self-complexes and Jungian archetypes) to those furnished by spirit-oriented frames. Most commonly combining elements from traditional esotericism and contemporary non-mainstream spiritualities, 'introspective' idioms describe cultic activity as a processing of human subjectivity intending the annihilation of the ego and the concomitant emancipation of the inner, true or higher-self. Although many of those employing introspective motifs freely participate in spirit-oriented rituals, the experiences provoked are regarded more as psychophysical expressions of inner and previously suppressed dimensions of the self than as arising from contact with independently existing spirits.

Mediumship in ritual context

Treated at length in Chapter 2, the *daimista* cultic context in which mediumship occurs is constituted by the dual dynamics of collective regulation and individual pursuit of the private and public goods made available through the ritual field of force. In keeping with its elevated status (as a public good) and assumed spiritual maturity (as a private good), mediumship is both highly valorized as a ritual practice and much sought after as a designated role. In common with many other ritual contexts in which spirit possession takes place, the requisites of successful mediumship in Santo Daime are varied in nature. By and large, though, the successful performance of spirit mediumship customarily relies upon the possessable self meeting three sets of challenges. Pertaining chiefly to the spiritual agents involved, the possessable self must first manage the incorporation event by way of inducing it, identifying the entity concerned and controlling the side effects of such an intimate connection with a supernatural other. Relating principally to her cultic counterparts (both human and non-human), the possessable self must then execute her ritual responsibilities by way of accurately communicating, portraying or engaging the particular spiritual agency at the centre of the mediumistic performance. Finally, and in view of prevailing disciplinary demands and regulatory strictures, the medium must manage and execute his tasks in an orderly fashion respectful of the ritual regime by which his behaviour is framed.

Among the various issues dealt with in the mediumistic training offered across the *daimista* movement, most relevant are those related to the management, performance and orderliness of spirit-oriented practice. Above all, the would-be medium must first learn to induce and manage the possession event. Among other things, this involves trainee mediums learning to distinguish the signature of spirit energies from amidst the welter of other impressions, experiences and sensations associated with the psychotropic effects of Daime. As such, the would-be medium progresses by learning to differentiate between the thoughts, feelings and perceptions provoked by the Daime *for her* and those connected with someone or something *other than* the self. Most commonly, this process of differentiation develops by the student gradually identifying the particular kinds of spirit encountered (relative to typological characteristics) and subsequently acquiring a more detailed appreciation of the individual profile of the entity or entities concerned. There is much by way of trial and error involved in mediumistic training, with early classifications often proving subsequently to be erroneous. A recurring theme I noticed among trainee mediums was the identification of the first spirit-guides they worked with as a kind traditionally attributed with playful, impulsive or mischievous characteristics (e.g. child or forest spirit). Although this identification would often be altered as the medium gained in both experience and confidence, it went some way to rationalizing the sometimes haphazard and transgressive behaviour associated with learning to incorporate. Managing the possession event also requires learning to control the psychophysical side effects (e.g. shaking, gesticulating and expostulating) of incorporating an otherwise disincarnate spirit. Describing her earliest experiences to me, for example, a North American medium said that 'I started noticing shaking in my hands . . . my hands would start doing things that Katherine was not doing, and each ceremony it would become more advanced'. The same medium also related how her earlier experiences of 'telepathic communication', involving only 'thoughts and feelings', gradually evolved into a 'more visual' approach in which she learnt to keep her eyes open and thereby interact with what was going on around her. Graduating from the first inchoate impressions of other ill-defined presences on the periphery of her vibrational field, Katherine now works with a number of spiritual entities from a variety of lines (i.e. a *preto velho*, a *caboclo*, a 'spirit doctor' and some angels).

Subsequent to identifying the respective entity involved, the medium must learn to express appropriately the particular type of spirit with which she is working. Treated by academic studies as a form of imitation or mimicry ('mimesis'), a medium's ability to portray unambiguously the respective characteristics of the entity being incorporated is a vital part of his performative repertoire (see Stoller, 1995; Taussig, 1987). The calm and measured demeanour of a spirit-guide from the Kardecist paradigm or Druidic tradition, for example, contrasts sharply with the forceful and impulsive behaviour of an Umbandist *caboclo* warrior which, in turn, differs markedly from both the imperious gracefulness of an *orixá* from the Candomblé tradition and the anguished and disoriented character of a suffering spirit. Given that more experienced mediums in Santo Daime tend to work with a greater number and range of spirits, the mimetic challenges faced by practitioners likewise increase relative to status and collective expectation. In addition to the countless suffering spirits engaged in ritual activity, for example, a medium interviewed in Mapiá told me that she worked regularly with seven spirits. Importantly, and in keeping with standard mediumistic practice, these spirits come from a variety of lines and perform a range of different services. Alongside demonstrating the experience and prowess of any medium, a broad spectrum of spirits furnishes greater opportunity for cultic participation which, in turn, optimizes pursuit of the private and public benefits made available by the ritual field of force. As different rituals perform varied functions and different spirits usually execute distinct tasks at often varying points in the ritual, it is likewise important for those incorporating spirits to learn in what contexts and at what juncture a particular type of mediumship may be performed.

In view of the real and ideal ordering of ritual space, the medium must learn not only to incorporate the right kind of spirit in the correct way and at the appropriate moment, but also to ensure that incorporation occurs in an orderly manner and thereby avoids transgressing established spatio-temporal and hierarchized boundaries. In addition to influencing the number and cosmological status of the spirits incorporated, for example, ritual standing may also determine the pecking order in which individuals practise their mediumship. While traditional restrictions upon incorporation are being progressively modified, communities continue to regulate where, when, how and by whom particular kinds of spirit-oriented activity are permitted. Held to interrupt the collective spiritual current, the incorporation of the wrong kind of spirit at an inappropriate moment or by an unlicensed practitioner risks public censure from those in authority, especially for those who should know better. On occasion, I have seen both those charged with overseeing ritual space and members of the senior battalion intervene in events deemed to be in violation of one or a number of regulatory strictures. Among these ritual violations, most tended to result from the inexperience of acolytes, the over-exuberant behaviour of aspirational members and visiting *daimistas* unaware of or failing to respect the different regulatory ethos of their host community.

The relationship between the individual *daimista* and the universal force of Daime has customarily furnished a ritual template by which the medium's interaction with the spirit-world has traditionally been managed, performed and regulated. Spirit-oriented practice has thereby traditionally been hedged by the same concerns with spatio-temporal order and practical-symbolic regulation treated in Chapter 2. Daime remains the sacramental bedrock of the movement as a whole; while the alternate states of consciousness associated with both Daime consumption and spirit mediumship continue to be viewed as variations on the same theme. Within urban middle-class communities, however, established parallels between Daime consumption and the incorporation of spirits are being progressively eroded as practitioners increasingly differentiate the practices and experiences associated respectively with each. Discussed below, the progressive differentiation of mediumistic activity from the traditional practice and signification of Daime consumption is, in part, effected through narratives of alterity which articulate the ritualized encounter between the individual practitioner and a supernatural other. Informed by its narrative differentiation, the spirit-oriented practice of the urban middle classes is gradually assuming a different profile than that traditionally framed by the established *daimista* repertoire. Linking contemporary developments to the now dominant position of the urban middle classes, the remainder of this chapter explicates the changing profile of spirit mediumship within Santo Daime.

External forces

Evans-Pritchard describes the spirits manifest through the north-African Nuer possession rituals as 'refractions of social realities' (1956: 106), while others treat spiritual entities as 'metonyms' symbolizing socio-cultural influences which both frame and are mediated by respective possession repertoires (e.g. Howard and Mageo, 1996: 4). The classic treatments of Lewis (2003) and Camargo (1961) use functionalist analyses to explicate ritualized spirit possession as a conservative phenomenon oriented to the preservation of social systems, whereas others regard it as furnishing opportunity to oppose, transform or undermine prevailing structures and dynamics (e.g. Comaroff, 1985; Ong, 1987; Owen, 1989; Shaw, 2002). As well as rejecting functionalist understandings of ritualized possession as an inherently conservative phenomenon, scholars have also problematized its traditional association with peripheral status and powerlessness. While not denying the relevance of prevailing systems of inequality and exclusion, modern treatments question the almost default identification of particular possession practices as straightforward expressions of marginalization and existential despair. Rather than reflecting or compensating for some form of crisis or socio-cultural privation, it is argued, spirit possession might be regarded as, for example, a means of celebrating collective identity (e.g. D. Brown, 1994; Sered, 1994) or, as noted earlier, exploring and asserting the individual self (e.g. Kramer, 1993; Wafer, 1991). Without reducing the spirits to simple reflections of prevailing socio-cultural dynamics, such approaches exemplify the fact that a rounded appreciation of spirit-oriented practice includes reference to the varied range of overarching structures and social processes (Boddy's 'external powers') which impinge upon community and individual alike.

The remainder of this chapter develops these insights by relating the ongoing changes in Santo Daime's spirit-oriented practice to the combined impact of the now dominant urban-professional constituency and aforementioned orchestrating principles (subjectivization, instrumentalism, etc.) by which the contemporary ritual repertoire is increasingly directed. Despite a deep-seated respect for and vocal allegiance to the traditional *daimista* repertoire, the needs and aspirations of urban-professional practitioners unavoidably chafe at the restrictions imposed by established modes of spatio-temporal order and practical-symbolic regulation. Effected through their pursuit of the private and public benefits made available by Santo Daime's cultic field, the now dominant urban middle classes resolve existing tensions by incrementally modifying the content, structure and regulatory ethos of the traditional *daimista* repertoire; ultimately refashioning ritual space in a manner conducive to meeting their characteristically late-modern needs and aspirations.

The changing profile of spirit mediumship

During the first leg of my three-day homeward journey from Mapiá, I spoke at length with a prominent member of Santo Daime who, among other things, expressed concern that the growth of 'the doctrine' (a *doutrina*) was having unwelcome consequences for the practice of incorporation. Self-designating as a 'medium' (*aparelho*), he bemoaned the fact that incorporation is now taking place 'in every ritual, no matter its kind'. Although hyperbolic in nature, this statement reflects a general unease among long-standing members of Santo Daime in respect of relatively recent tendencies to practise incorporation in ritual contexts not traditionally open to spirit-oriented activity and to do so in an increasingly unconventional fashion. Whereas the formation of Cefluris under Padrinho Sebastião established spirit-oriented activity as an important component of the *daimista* repertoire, mediumship remained restricted in respect of where, when, how and by whom it was practised. The Kardecist paradigm enjoyed initial dominance within Cefluris, with aforementioned gnoseological, therapeutic and illuminatory modes of mediumship each in operation. Gnoseological mediumship, though, was restricted solely to the highest echelons of the movement (and remains so), while therapeutic and interactive-illuminatory mediumship were undertaken only by a very small band of authorized practitioners in rituals explicitly oriented to the incorporation of spirits. Theoretically open for every member to practise, private illuminatory mediumship was nevertheless an interiorized undertaking which was in no way to disrupt others or interfere with the collective spiritual current.

Indicative of the increased importance of mediumship to Cefluris, the rituals of Cure and Saint Michael were formulated by the time of Padrinho Sebastião's death in 1990. Although technically not of the same status as Santo Daime's more traditional ceremonies, aforementioned concerns with spatio-temporal order and practical-symbolic regulation are equally in force in the rites of the Cure and Saint Michael. In contrast to their contemporary versions, however, in their earliest years, these rituals were not regularly practised or as widespread across the movement. At the same time, they engaged only the traditional entities and spirits of the Kardecist and esoteric paradigms (e.g. guides, doctors, angels and disincarnate spirits) and, excluding more serious cases in need of exorcism, served as the sole official contexts in which non-private modes of incorporation should occur.

Detailed in Chapter 1, and mediated by the growing constituency of urban-professionals entering the movement, the impact of Umbandist belief and practice upon Santo Daime further reinforced the place of mediumship within its ritual repertoire. Given the formative influence of Kardecist Spiritism upon the Umbanda paradigm, there was already a degree of overlap with the *daimista* repertoire in respect of the ritualized practice of therapeutic and illuminatory mediumship. Importantly, though, the Afro-Brazilian roots of Umbanda entailed a very different spiritual pantheon than that engaged by Kardecism and, up until this point, Santo Daime itself. Whereas the disoriented and suffering spirits of Kardecism also feature in Umbandist mediumship, the spirit-guides of deceased indigenes, black slaves, oriental princesses,

Romany gypsies and Candomblé deities, to name but a few, were a wholly new repertorial component. In contrast to the Cure and Saint Michael works, the earliest *daimista* rituals involving the incorporation of Umbanda spirits were not subject to the same modes of disciplinary regimentation in force across Santo Daime's established repertoire. As if further to reinforce their difference from traditional ceremonies, and again in contrast to the Cure and Saint Michael works, 'Umbandaime' rituals were not permitted within the same cultic space as that reserved for established rites (Guimarães, 1992; Junior, 2007). Reflecting this differentiation of ritual space, and noted in Chapter 1, the Star House originally constructed in Rio do Ouro and later rebuilt at Mapiá was specifically built for the staging of mediumistic ceremonies (star works) involving the incorporation of Umbanda spirits. Likewise noted in Chapter 1, the second church building erected at Mapiá was subsequently called the Star House, with the much smaller original building being rechristened the Little Star House. The mainstreaming of Umbanda influences exemplified by the new star-shaped church at Mapiá (along with its star-shaped central table) was further reinforced by the formulation of the White Table ritual. Modelled on the Saint Michael work, the White Table ritual was designed with the express purpose of normalizing the incorporation of Umbanda spirits by framing it with the same disciplinary order and practical-symbolic regulations in force within established ceremonial practice. By doing so, the White Table ritual brought the incorporation of Umbanda spirits within sanctified ceremonial space.

The White Table ceremony, however, was intended not only to normalize the incorporation of Umbanda spirits within Santo Daime but also to bring it under the disciplinary control of its established ritual regime. Subsequent to the death of Padrinho Sebastião, and some years after the first Umbandaime works took place, disputes broke out regarding the manner and extent of mediumistic practice involving Umbanda spirits. While the fault lines were by no means clear cut, those unhappy with the spread and impact of Umbandist-inspired practices were of a more traditionalist bent, with those championing the Umbanda cause overwhelmingly from the urban middle classes. The impasse and temporary cessation of Umbandaime works provoked by the dispute was eventually resolved by the formulation of the White Table ritual which, inspired by the Saint Michael work, was designed with the twin-track aspirations of normalizing and containing the ritual incorporation of Umbanda spirits. Like the ritual on which it was modelled, however, the White Table ceremony ultimately failed in its purported attempt to restrict spirit-oriented activity to a designated portion of the *daimista* cultic repertoire.

The years of fieldwork conducted subsequent to the journey back from Mapiá confirmed the basic tenor of my informant's concerns. In each of three continents where research occurred, informant response and first-hand experience combine to indicate a twofold change in the ritual profile of mediumistic practice. First, the ritual incorporation of spirits is growing in popularity and thereby gaining practical (i.e. incidence) and symbolic (i.e. meaning) significance relative to established components of the *daimista* repertoire. Second, the increase in mediumistic activity is of a non-traditional kind. For example, community leaders and senior practitioners across the movement tell of the increasing need to open rituals with instructions concerning the unacceptability of incorporation within certain cultic contexts (e.g. Concentration, Hymnal and Mass) or the need for individual discipline in respect of when or how incorporation should take place. As well as hearing such instructions first-hand, I have also seen them regularly ignored and, at times, backed up with the removal or public sanction of offending practitioners. In the same vein, informants report the growing demand for the increased staging of rituals explicitly oriented to mediumistic practice, with some leaders reluctantly giving way to communal pressure or through fear of losing members to other communities where incorporation is regularly practised. Demand for formal mediumistic instruction is also on the rise, with members eager to gain official recognition as trained practitioners and thereby enjoy greater scope to pursue the private and public benefits associated with licensed mediumship.

Other leaders and their communities, however, are much more comfortable with spirit-oriented activity occurring both in cultic contexts not traditionally open to incorporation and as a favoured component of the *daimista* ritual repertoire. Unacceptable to traditionalists, I have participated in Concentrations, Hymnals and even a Mass where the incorporation of spirits was either actively encouraged or allowed to occur. Comparing his community to the stricter regulation of mediumship operated by his nearest neighbour, for example, a European leader spoke of being 'very open' to the incorporation of spirits whatever the ritual context. In the same vein, and speaking of visits made to an established church in a neighbouring state, a North American informant related how 'we would go to a work there and we would end up holding the centre of the work for them while all their church members were incorporating'. The ritual incorporation of spirits across the *daimista* movement is thereby not only increasing but doing so in an unconventional manner. Unevenly expressed across the movement as a whole, this twofold change in the ritual profile of incorporation nevertheless manifests in three significant ways: (i) the growing provision of cultic contexts explicitly oriented to mediumistic practice; (ii) the modification of established ritual formats to allow for spirit-oriented activity; and (iii) the appropriation of non-traditional discourse and practice through which new or modified forms of mediumship are expressed.

In combination, these three dynamics exemplify ongoing modifications of traditional restrictions within Santo Daime as to where, when, why, how and by whom spirit mediumship may be practised. In the first instance, rituals explicitly oriented to the incorporation of spirits (e.g. Cure, Saint Michael and White Table) are being increasingly staged across the *daimista* movement. While most forms of mediumship are practised at these rituals, those comprising public elements of interaction with ceremonial participants (i.e. therapeutic and non-private illumination) are most highly valorized. Not interfering with the meeting of calendrical obligations by the vast majority of *daimista* communities, the increased staging of these rituals nevertheless impacts upon the number of non-official Hymnals being performed across the movement as a whole. Rituals of incorporation are thereby displacing traditional *hinários*. Not only are these rituals being staged more frequently, however, but their specific identities and internal structures are also being modified. Contemporary celebrations of the Cure, Saint Michael and White Table works, for example, pay increasingly less attention to technical differences originally intended to frame varying modes of ritual practice involving different forms of mediumship and distinct kinds of spiritual agencies. As a result, traditional distinctions between these rituals are progressively blurred through modifications designed to accommodate prolonged periods of mediumistic activity including growing numbers of practitioners engaging a broadening range of spirits through increasingly diverse forms of incorporation. Orchestrated to facilitate more mediumship by more people incorporating more spirits in more ways, these modifications inevitably involve the transformation of aforementioned modes of spatio-temporal order and practical-symbolic discipline by which ritual space and behaviour have traditionally been regulated.

The incorporation of spirits is also occurring more frequently in cultic contexts traditionally closed to non-private forms of mediumship. Very much enjoying the latitude furnished to mediumistic practice by other ritual formats, practitioners are increasingly seeking similar experiences in ceremonies such as the Concentration, Hymnal and Mass. Unlike aforementioned rituals, however, these rites are structured in ways which traditionally make no provision for the incorporation of spirits in anything but a private and still extremely limited way. Consequently, when faced with public displays of incorporation in these rituals, leaders and senior members who happily practise incorporation in other cultic contexts may demonstrate little or no tolerance of such behaviour. Within a growing number of communities, however, these traditional limitations are overcome by transferring interactive forms of mediumship from central ritual space to its liminal surroundings. Therapeutic and non-private illuminatory mediumship are thereby accommodated by moving both mediums and those in need of healing or attention (i.e. incorporating a suffering spirit requiring intervention) away from or at least to the side of core ritual space (commonly designated the 'divine hospital' or 'spiritual first-aid centre'). Even allowing for the noises, gesticulations and movements associated with incorporation, the core business of the Concentration or Hymnal ritual is thereby allowed to continue relatively unaffected.

Despite the proliferation or modification of ritual space to accommodate increasing and varied kinds of incorporation, all of these rituals retain many of the disciplinary aspects and regulatory restrictions delineated in Chapter 2. Though now explicitly oriented to the incorporation of spirits, the rituals of Cure, Saint Michael and the White Table still include much by way of content (e.g. hymns and prayers), liturgical structure and regimentation (e.g. battalions and ranks) which limit what, where, how and by whom mediumship may be publicly performed. The same applies to the rituals of Concentration, Hymnal and Mass but only more so. As a consequence, the real and ideal ordering of the *daimista* ritual context not only restricts the time and space available for non-private incorporation but also actively rations access to it by way of selection, training and official authorization. Because the modification of inherited ritual restrictions to accommodate spirit-oriented practice can only go so far so fast without transgressing official expectations in respect of minimal orthodoxy (see Chapter 1), other strategies and developments are employed as complements to the ongoing transformation of the established ritual repertoire.

Among the most common complementary dynamics is what I have elsewhere described as the 'expressivization' of the traditional form of private illuminatory mediumship (A. Dawson, 2012b: 78). Noted above, the private incorporation of spirits has customarily been hedged by requirements that its undertaking should neither distract others from their ritual practices nor inhibit the individual's contribution to the collective spiritual current. Such is the importance of privacy to this form of incorporation that the cosmic merit earned by its undertaking is said to be vitiated by external manifestations likely to attract attention to the individual practitioner. Although still honoured in many traditional contexts, the interiorized and illuminatory ethos of private mediumship has largely given way in urban middle-class communities to an outwardly oriented and highly expressive demeanour. According to one informant,

I'm in my place and this energy is so strong that I have to get up and literally stand there . . . The force, the power is so strong that I'm having to stand feet apart, grounded. It's like, the strength, the power, and these wings [said stretching arms out wide], these amazing huge wings open . . . these huge Angel's [wings], they're just there . . . my body literally becomes these beings . . . and I'm so way back that I don't always know what or where's the hymn. And I can feel the energy starting to fade . . . and when the hymn ends, it's like they fade out and I fade in.

Always involving a higher spiritual entity or guide, expressive manifestations like this generally occur with the practitioner remaining in the allocated position but standing up (even when everyone else is seated) with arms outstretched (and sometimes waving) to the side or above the head. The individual will sometimes shake or sway, make any number of facial expressions and occasionally utter sounds. Thanks to the overwhelming power and often sudden appearance of the spiritual presence incorporated, practitioners frequently describe the event as including a meaningful reduction in self-awareness. According to an Australasian informant, 'when I'm in it, I'm in it . . . my face will screw up and my mouth assume shapes that are not mine, and short or long breaths of air will emerge, sometimes accompanied by sound that has nothing to do with the words' [of the hymn being sung].

In contrast to private illuminatory mediumship, and no doubt reflective of its novel status, the expressive performance of individual mediumship lacks a coherent ritual rationale. When asked to explain why such episodes occur, informants make no mention of charity, illumination or discipline. Rather, a relatively wide variety of explanations are offered, including entities appearing, for example, both to praise (other higher spirits) and be praised (by *daimistas*), to consume Daime, edify their individual host, distribute blessings and astral energy or demonstrate respect and support for the doctrine. Importantly, however, the expressivization of the traditional framing of individual incorporation squares a very important circle. On the one hand, expressive mediumship broadens the established profile of incorporation by increasing opportunity for its public performance by those otherwise lacking sufficient ritual capital to access traditionally restricted (and thereby highly valorized) therapeutic and interactive illuminatory modes. On the other, and albeit at the cost of modifying traditional expectations and participatory strictures, expressive mediumship broadens access to public performance by stretching rather than unduly transgressing established concerns with spatio-temporal order and practical-symbolic regulation.

For a growing number of communities, such partial modifications do not go far enough. Consequently, the staging of rites free from many of the regulations and restrictions ordinarily in force across the *daimista* repertoire is an increasingly popular means of enabling both more incorporation of a varied kind and greater participation in public forms of mediumship. As the vast majority of these rituals still involve the consumption of Daime, a degree of disciplinary order and individual obligation remains both unavoidable and, for many participants, expected. On the whole, though, the regulatory framing of these non-traditional rituals is significantly less than aforementioned ceremonies and thereby permits much greater latitude in the extent, manner and employment of spirit-oriented practices. By virtue of its long-standing influence upon mediumship in Santo Daime, the Afro-Brazilian paradigm provides many of the key motifs, interactive modes and spiritual entities which appear in these rituals. Although the term 'Umbandaime' is used in various parts to describe such rituals, the Afro-Brazilian word *gira* (from *girar* – to spin or swirl) is also employed. Over time, however, communities across the world are augmenting their formative Brazilian templates with beliefs, practices and spirits appropriated from regional contexts and local traditions along with elements drawn from generic non-mainstream sources. Freed from traditional obligations in respect of position, behaviour and dress, for example, ritual participants exploit a much expanded performative remit; from dancing and spinning, through chanting and howling, to wearing, smoking or playing the associated paraphernalia of the respective spiritual agent with whom they are engaging.

The desire within some communities to practise mediumship unimpeded by traditional restrictions has been sufficiently strong to result in local schism or the wholesale withdrawal from Cefluris membership and the calendrical obligations associated with it. For those remaining part of Cefluris, however, the growth of spirit-oriented practice occurs through the complementary processes of ritual proliferation (e.g. White Table), cultic modification (e.g. expressivization) and ceremonial augmentation (e.g. *gira*). Exemplified by this threefold dynamic, the practical expansion and symbolic valorization of spirit-oriented activity is part of the ongoing transformation of the traditional *daimista* ritual repertoire at the hands of the urban middle classes. The increase in spirit-oriented practice across Santo Daime is, though, not simply a symptom of the movement's ongoing transformation but an important means through which the modification of the traditional repertoire is being achieved. Such is the case because the contemporary practice of spirit mediumship comprises a high-utility platform which both caters for the subjectivized needs and aesthetic expectations of urban-professional practitioners and serves as an ideal vehicle for effecting the repertorial changes conducive to meeting these needs and aspirations. By way of concluding this discussion, the high-utility character of spirit mediumship is explored through the notion of *performative alterity*.

Conclusion

Noted earlier, the relationship between medium and spirit has traditionally been held to parallel that between the ordinary ritual participant and the universal force of Daime. In so being, the quadrangular relationship between the medium, spiritual others, human co-participants and prevailing cultic context is framed by the same template as that regulating the ritual consumption of Daime. Infused with the cultic virtues (e.g. firmness and discipline) and oriented by the ritual rationales of charity and trial, the incorporation of spirits thereby remains predominantly orchestrated by the spatio-temporal order and practical-symbolic regulation at the heart of the traditional *daimista* repertoire. Commitment to the cultic virtues and the obligations to the spiritual current implicated by them also involve the traditional valorization of self-conscious modes of incorporation. Whether incorporating or not, cultic responsibility in respect of individual self-scrutiny and corporate ritual practice remains; hence, the need for self-awareness and control. Likewise, the notions of charity and trial which inform the established framing of mediumship define its practice as first and foremost a means of serving the needs and meeting the demands of others. Consequently, mediumistic performance is collectively determined through its subordination to the service of humans in want of instruction and healing or spirits in need of illumination and direction. The alterity (otherness) implicated in traditional mediumistic practice is thereby of a chiefly *inter*-subjective nature.

Accompanying aforementioned changes to the ritual profile of mediumship, the traditional correlation between Daime consumption and incorporation is being progressively eroded through narratives of alterity offering alternative articulations of the ritualized encounter between the individual practitioner and a spiritual being. Describing a much greater reduction of self-awareness than that traditionally exhibited in established modes of mediumship, narratives of alterity shift the balance of agential control away from the human host and towards the supernatural other. Much discussed in academic studies of spirit-oriented practice (e.g. Lambek, 1981; Stoller, 1995), the recalibration of agential control effected by narratives of alterity is important in two key respects. First, by identifying the words or actions employed during spirit-oriented practice with a spiritual rather than human agent, alterity indemnifies the medium against what is said and done while under the influence of the spirit. Protected by a cloak of impunity, the medium is liberated from established convention and expectation and thereby empowered to say or do things beyond the normal remit of the ordinary, uninspired individual. The inculpability of the medium thereby facilitates behaviour customarily considered unacceptable, unfavourable or even beyond the pale. Second, attribution of agency to a supernatural rather than human source bestows authenticity upon the acts and experiences associated with spirit-oriented practice. This, in turn, legitimates the medium's behaviour for those being acted upon, represented or addressed by the spirit, while also endorsing the subjective experiences of the medium himself. The bestowal of authenticity thereby authorizes the external manifestations of an otherwise interior process and validates the internal conditions associated with the experiential impact of a spiritual agent. In combination, the indemnifying and authenticating ramifications of alterity furnish spirit-oriented practice with the transgressive potential to relativize prevailing regimes by subordinating them to the mediated experience of a supernatural other.

It is no coincidence that the non-traditional modes of spirit-oriented activity appropriated and performed by urban middle-class members assume a greater loss of self-awareness than that allowed by the established *daimista* repertoire. Such is the case because the narratives of alterity associated with non-traditional modes of spirit engagement help rationalize ongoing changes both to the ritual performance of mediumship and the corporate context which frames it. Downplaying self-awareness by emphasizing the spiritual force of the entities engaged, narratives of alterity actualize the transgressive potential of spirit-oriented activity by shifting agential responsibility onto a supernatural other. In some communities, for example, women mediums under the influence of their spirit-guides occasionally cross over to the male battalion. While the mediums' passage through the male battalion and back to their own side is relatively fleeting, the transgression of ritual space is highly symbolic of progressive challenges to inherited modes of gender differentiation. A cause of consternation to some, such a flagrant transgression of ideal (here, gendered) spatial distinctions would nevertheless be impossible without the indemnifying cloak of mediumistic alterity. By decoupling mediumistic performance from traditional templates of ritual behaviour, narratives of alterity relativize customary modes of spatio-temporal order and practical-symbolic regulation. In effect, narratives of alterity serve as dislocutory speech acts which, without fully dismissing them, nevertheless unsettle, disturb and ultimately reconfigure established modes of ritual regulation.

Narratives of performative alterity also broaden both the practical breadth and experiential scope of mediumistic practice. Stated prior, the established framing of spirit-oriented activity requires of the medium a meaningful degree of self-awareness and control throughout the incorporation event. Such is the case because traditional emphases upon self-scrutiny, charitable practice towards others (human and non-human) and ritual as trial demand a level of attention and application which the individual can only achieve by retaining a significant level of self-consciousness. Whereas these demands inevitably limit the range of subjective experiences available during incorporation, the ritual capital accrued through the high status profile of therapeutic and interactive-illuminatory modes of mediumship sufficiently compensates for their attendant experiential restrictions. However, and in common with private illumination, novel modes of incorporation lack the kind of ritual responsibilities associated with established, high status forms of interactive mediumship. Eschewing traditional demands in respect of the ritual synchronization of individual – collective dynamics, for example, a female practitioner of expressive possession informed me that 'One way to lose myself and be totally focussed on the spirit is to shut my eyes, then other people and their opinions cease to exist'. Not as constrained as their high profile counterparts, novel forms of incorporation can thereby include a much broader range of subjective experiences; not least, those involving heightened levels of alterity and their corresponding reduction in self-awareness and control. In contrast to traditional modes of incorporation, the alterity implicated in novel forms of mediumship is of a characteristically *intra*-subjective bent.

Although the experiential enhancement furnished by new forms of mediumship may well compensate for their lesser cultic status, their practitioners are by no means indifferent to the pursuit of ritual capital. Whether practised in established ritual contexts as expressive possession or performed in non-traditional ceremonies such as *giras*, novel modes of incorporation continue to embody the aspirations and status claims of individual *daimistas*. The kinds of spirit incorporated and the manner of their performance matter no less than in traditional mediumistic practices. Noted above, as different spirits tend to perform varying kinds of functions in different cultic contexts or periods thereof, practitioners with a broad range of spirits are better placed to pursue the gamut of private and public goods made available through ritualized engagement with supernatural others. The pursuit of goods relating to high status modes of incorporation such as therapeutic mediumship, for example, requires engagement with spirits renowned for or associatable with healing. Likewise, the subjective experiences and aspirational claims inherent to expressive modes of incorporation require the existential validation and demonstrable legitimation of spirits of admirable pedigree with prominent and robust profiles. The ritual utility and broadened experiential opportunities implicated in engaging or incorporating a wide variety of spirits has engendered something of a performative arms race in which new spiritual entities are increasingly appropriated or existing supernatural agents (e.g. angels) put to new and more varied uses. As a result, more and more *daimistas* are laying claim to a growing and progressively diverse range of spiritual entities commandeered from an expanding array of already extensive religious repertoires and cultural contexts.

Indemnified and authenticated by narratives of performative alterity, the variegation of mediumistic practice implicated in these developments further contributes to the ongoing transformation of established means of spatio-temporal order and practical-symbolic regulation. Certainly, the continuing authority of corporate modes of discipline and the deep-seated respect for received traditions combine to ensure the persistence of countervailing tendencies and ongoing resistance to the progressive modification of established repertorial practice wrought through spirit-oriented activity. Within many communities across the movement, perceived transgressions, infringements and omissions relating to spirit mediumship continue to be censured and corrected. Nevertheless, such is the transformative momentum of the urban-professional world view, and so authentic are the mediumistic experiences refracted by it, that interpretations of what precisely constitutes a transgression, infringement or omission are progressively changing to accommodate, if not promote, the incremental modification of the established *daimista* repertoire. Whatever resistance is offered, then, will serve only to slow or steer, rather than stop or reverse, the changes taking place.

5

Santo Daime in late-modern context

Introduction

Focusing upon its orientation to the world at large, the contemporary character of Santo Daime is here explored through a sustained engagement with the urban middle-class constituency which now forms the overwhelming majority of the movement. Noted in prior chapters, the contemporary dominance of its urban-professional membership is impacting upon Santo Daime through the incremental transformation of, for example, established organizational dynamics, traditional ritual practices and received religious world view. Remarked upon by various studies of contemporary non-mainstream and alternative religiosity, the prevalence of an urban middle-class demographic profile has nevertheless remained relatively undeveloped (e.g. A. Dawson, 2005; L. Dawson, 1998; Heelas, 1996b; Magnani, 2000). The following discussion goes some way to rectifying this oversight by linking Santo Daime's worldly orientation with the typically late-modern traits of its urban-professional membership. It does so by initially identifying urban middle-class *daimistas* as part of a 'new middle class' which emerged in the late-modern, urban-industrial landscape in the second half of the twentieth century. Employing the notion of 'entangled modernity', the chapter goes on to describe both the prevailing dynamics and practical-symbolic implications of the societal context which, as members of the new middle-class, urban-professional *daimistas* hold in common. By way of contributing to ongoing discussions about the relationship between religion and the market, a subsequent section employs the notion of 'mystified consumption' as a means of exploring the manner and extent to which the commoditized subjectivity of the new middle class can be said to impact upon the contemporary *daimista* repertoire. The chapter then reflects upon some relevant classificatory characteristics of Santo Daime and, citing Weber's classic typology of religious orientations to the world, concludes by identifying the *daimista* repertoire as a form of 'world-rejecting aestheticism'.

The new middle class

Beyond the Amazon region, the vast majority of adult *daimistas* are college or university educated and, when not self-employed, generally engaged by state institutions or private firms as professionals responsible for, among other things, health and social care, information technology, education, culture industry and service sector provision. These urban-professional *daimistas* are overwhelmingly drawn from the new middle class forged in the latter part of the twentieth century. The term 'new middle class' dates from the early part of the 1900s and has traditionally been used to designate the administrative occupational groups, technical professions and service sector employees engendered by the post-nineteenth-century growth of private industry and the various institutions of the state apparatus (Burris, 1995; Lederer and Marschak, 1995). Neither belonging to the established working classes nor owning capital, land or the means of production, the emergence and growth of 'new middle class, white-collar people on salary' is credited by C. Wright Mills' famous study (published in 1951) as signalling a redrawing of the economic-political and socio-cultural landscape of urban-industrial capitalism (2002: 63). Over recent decades, the notion of a 'new middle class' has been most closely associated with the transformations wrought in the latter part of the twentieth century by the advent of what has variously been termed 'advanced-', 'commodity-', 'late-' or 'neo-' capitalism (e.g. Betz, 1992; Featherstone, 2007; Giddens, 1973; A. Guerra et al., 2006; Lee, 1993; O'Dougherty, 2002; Vidich and Bensman, 1995). Allied to the post-1950s' expansion of the state apparatus, technologization of private commerce, spread of commodity capitalism, growth of the culture industry and rise of the service sector, the new middle class is chiefly employed in administrative bureaucracy and management, communications and information technology, education, health and research, and sundry provision of cultural goods, capital services and immaterial commodities. Scions of Western late-modernity, members of the new middle class have also been variously labelled the 'expressive professions' (Martin, 1981), 'new professions', 'new petite bourgeoisie' and 'new cultural intermediaries' (e.g. Bourdieu, 1984), 'new class' (e.g. Gouldner, 1979; Inglehart, 1990), 'knowledge class' (D. Bell, 1999; Berger, 1988), 'emergent' and 'service class' (e.g. Lash and Urry, 1987) and '(new) new middle', 'transformed' and 'post-industrial middle class' (Lash,

1994). Its various designations having been noted, the mid-sector grouping from which Santo Daime draws the overwhelming majority of its contemporary membership is here referred to using the most popular rendering of 'new middle class'.[1]

The new middle class as an analytical category is important to understanding Santo Daime in two major respects. First, it allows the beliefs and practices of the overwhelming majority of contemporary *daimistas* to be situated and subsequently understood relative to their place within late-modern society. As should be apparent by now, the modern-day profile and ongoing transformations of the *daimista* repertoire are here claimed to reflect the now dominant position of an urban middle-class constituency. The contemporary shape and direction of Santo Daime's profile and its incremental modification are thereby not randomly achieved but rather outcomes of a particular range of practical-symbolic forces to which the movement has been progressively subjected since its initial spread from the Amazon region in the mid-1980s. By understanding the new middle class from which the overwhelming majority of *daimistas* now hail, we understand more about the contemporary *daimista* repertoire and its respective developmental trajectory.

Second, the analytical category of the new middle class provides a theoretical lens through which the otherwise varied life-experiences of Santo Daime's urban-professional membership may be focused and treated in both a manageable and conceptually meaningful way. Hailing from various parts of the modern industrialized world, the urban middle-class membership of Santo Daime is internally variegated and thereby embodies a range of socio-cultural experience which should not be unduly homogenized. Employing the notion of 'multiple modernities', Shmuel Eisenstadt has done much to problematize the theoretical homogenization of otherwise variegated life-experiences wrought by the uncritical application of a unitary model of modernity. Eisenstadt's 'multiple modernities' thesis rejects the argument for 'the convergence of industrial societies' implicit within 'classical theories of modernization' and 'sociological analysis'. According to Eisenstadt, classical sociological approaches mistakenly assumed 'that the cultural program of modernity as it developed in modern Europe and the basic institutional constellation that emerged there would ultimately take over in all modernizing and modern societies' (2000: 1). As a result, Western understandings of modernity were unduly imposed upon emerging modern societies in other parts of the world.

Rejecting the uncritical universalization of the Western modern paradigm, Eisenstadt grounds his thesis in the socio-cultural variegation generated by 'the ongoing dialogue' between the globalizing forces of 'modern reconstruction' and local 'cultural resources' embodied by 'respective civilizational traditions'. As a consequence of this ongoing interaction, 'not only do multiple modernities continue to emerge . . . but within all societies, new questionings and reinterpretations of different dimensions of modernity are emerging'. Eisenstadt thereby regards the contemporary 'trends of globalization' as 'a story of continual constitution and reconstitution of a multiplicity of cultural programs' born of the interface of the 'cultural program of modernity' and the 'specific cultural patterns, traditions, and historical experiences' of any given locale (2000: 1–29).

> The undeniable trend . . . is the growing diversification of the understanding of modernity, of the basic cultural agendas of different modern societies . . . [G]oing far beyond the very homogenizing aspects of the original [i.e. Western] version . . . these developments do indeed attest to the continual development of multiple modernities, or of multiple interpretations of modernity. (2000: 24)

The perils of uncritical homogenization embodied by Eisenstadt's thesis have become something of a *cause celebre* among certain sections of the academic community engaged in the study of religion. Debates about the universal applicability of contemporary theories of secularization have proved a particularly popular battleground in this regard (e.g. Berger et al., 2008; Casanova, 2006; Passos, 2006). Other aspects of modern existence pertaining to the religious sphere are likewise increasingly scrutinized in respect of their variegated manifestation in different parts of the world (e.g. Blancarte, 2000; Mardin, 2006; Roca, 2007; Spohn, 2003).

Irrespective of the subject matter treated, and whether referencing Eisenstadt or not, the basic line of argument maintains that the socio-cultural diversity engendered by modern multiplicity negates the uncritical use in any particular context of concepts and theories formulated in another region. By highlighting the theoretical implications of the inherent variegation of modern social formations for academic understandings of religion, the intentions of those articulating this approach are unqualifiedly laudable. While the emphasis upon socio-cultural diversity has successfully hit its mark, an unintended consequence has nevertheless been the progressively common failure to pay serious attention to the practical-symbolic implications of the structural processes, institutional dynamics and socio-cultural characteristics which modern societies, by virtue of being 'modern', hold in common. Although correctly problematizing the uncritical and universalizing application of otherwise exogenous concepts and theories, the overemphasis upon regional difference has engendered something of a theoretical provincialism within a growing number of academic approaches to the interface of religion and modern society. As a consequence, there has been too much emphasis upon the differences implied by the 'multiple' and insufficient attention to the shared features implicated in the 'modern'.

Both its historical transnational trajectory and contemporary globalizing character make modernity a pluriform phenomenon which manifests, among other things, through a multiplicity of socio-cultural dynamics and variegated regional subjectivities. The new middle class from which Santo Daime now draws the majority of its membership is thereby not a singular, homogenous entity. It is, rather, a variegated collection of members whose subjectivities embody a range of respectively regional socio-cultural dynamics. Impacting upon the local appropriation of *daimista* belief and practice, these regional socio-cultural dynamics inform the ongoing spread and diversification of Santo Daime as it is refracted through and melded with a variety of endogenous life-experiences. Nevertheless, acknowledgement of the variegation at play across the urban-professional membership of Santo Daime should not detract from the many practical and symbolic aspects which their modern, urban middle-class existence holds in common. Local by way of their appropriation of *daimista* belief and practice, the regional variations wrought by Santo Daime's variegated urban-professional membership remain at all times variations on a modern theme. Consequently, while unavoidably involving a degree of conceptual reductionism of an otherwise globally dispersed and socio-culturally diverse cohort, the analytical category of the new middle class provides a valuable theoretical inroad to understanding the modern thematic from which these regional variations arise (e.g. Lange and Meier, 2009). Mediated through their membership of the new middle class, the common characteristics embodied by the modern thematic furnish the overwhelming majority of *daimistas* with a sufficiently shared life-experience to permit a meaningful degree of collective theorization which applies to the group as a whole (i.e. as a single unit of analysis). As the following section argues, this shared life-experience and the common theorization arising from it are rooted in the 'entangled' modern context to which the bulk of *daimistas* belong by virtue of their new middle-class membership.

Entangled modernity

A number of approaches have emerged in recent years which strive to avoid the respective pitfalls of uncritical universalization (to which the multiple modernities thesis so trenchantly responds) and theoretical provincialism (of which the multiple modernities thesis is commonly accused). In so doing, each of these approaches seeks to do analytical justice to both the pluriform character and inherent continuities of modern social existence. Among the various and potentially constructive contributions to framing the continuities and variations of the modern theme, the 'alternative modernities' (e.g. Gaonkar, 2001), 'hybrid' or 'mixed' modernity (e.g. Canclini, 1995; Ortiz, 1994) and 'varieties of modernity' (e.g. V. Schmidt, 2006) approaches are worthy of note.

The current treatment, however, uses the notion of 'entangled modernity' to engage the new middle class from which the majority of *daimistas* are now drawn. The notion of entangled modernity was formulated within the overarching project of the 'cosmopolitan modernities' paradigm (e.g. Beck and Grande, 2010; Beck and Sznaider, 2006). Entangled modernity offers the most fruitful way of explicating the late-modern character of Santo Daime's new middle-class profile for four primary reasons.

First, the cosmopolitan modernities approach avoids the dual dangers of methodological 'provincialism' and 'universalism'. It does so by distinguishing between the 'basic principles' and 'basic institutions' of modernity. The 'basic principles' of modernity refer to the range of 'structural and organizational' dynamics (e.g. differentiation, pluralization and individualization) which, by virtue of its definition, are foundational characteristics of modern society. Where these basic principles are in evidence, it is argued, 'modern' society (as opposed to 'traditional', 'pre-modern' or 'post-modern' forms) can be said to exist. Whereas these macro-processes are found in every modern society, the 'basic institutions' through which they are concretely realized may differ from one modern society to another. As different modern societies actualize foundational processes (e.g. individualization) through a variety of sometimes contrasting organizational arrangements (e.g. economy, politics and law), the 'basic institutions' of modernity are thereby varied. While the foundational dynamics of modernity (e.g. individualization) remain the same from one modern society to another, the manner of their institutional configuration (e.g. economic, political and legal rights) may differ from one social context to the next.

Second, the notion of 'entangled Modernity' acknowledges that many of the processes of modernization currently at play across the globe are (owing both to historical origins and more recent formations) of a 'transnational' or 'border transcending' character. The cosmopolitan dynamics of existing modernization processes thereby comprise a 'dynamic intermingling and interaction between societies', the 'interconnectedness' of which constitutes a form of 'entanglement'. Of a macro-structural, mid-range institutional and micro-social character, this entanglement plays out across established national borders and traditional cultural boundaries through shared ('entangled') dynamics and processes which manifest in every dimension of modern society. Third, while the degree of interconnectedness and extent of entanglement inevitably differs from one group of societies to the next, this approach recognizes that some modern societies share intertwined historical paths or intermingling contemporary relations which involve a heightened level of both structural and socio-cultural embroilment. By virtue of their intensified interrelations and greater degrees of modern entanglement, societies with strong interconnections most readily permit an inclusive theorization identifying, analysing and interpreting shared features and common transformations which, allowing for caveats and qualifications, transcend traditional societal boundaries.

Fourth, the entangled modernity approach identifies the emergence of a progressively radicalized form of modern societal existence that has been appearing in various parts of the world, typically since the 1950s. Marked by the application of prefixes such as 'late-', 'hyper-', 'liquid-' and 'second-', the notion that modernity has entered a new, radicalized phase of its existence has become increasingly prevalent in recent decades (e.g. Bauman, 2005; U. Beck et al., 1994). By talking of 'second-' (Beck), 'liquid-' (Bauman), 'reflexive-' (Lash) or 'late-modernity' (Giddens), social theorists argue that certain modern societies have, over the course of recent decades, experienced a significant radicalization of their overarching macrostructural dynamics, mid-range institutional processes and everyday micro-social interactions. Exemplified by the impact of globalization and market-oriented dynamics, the radicalization of modernity's basic principles (e.g. differentiation and individualization) involves the concomitant transformation of the basic institutions of entangled modern societies (Beck and Grande, 2010).

With the vast majority of its membership in Brazil, Europe and North America, the entangled modernity traversed by contemporary *daimista* members of the new middle class is overwhelmingly that of Western modernity.[2] Rooted initially in the European colonial enterprise and its imperial co-optation of the Americas, entangled Western modernity has subsequently been shaped by industrializing and, latterly, commodity capitalism driven in large part, but no means solely, by North American concerns. Even allowing for particular historical profiles and contemporary regional variations, the interconnected trajectories, border-transcending dynamics and shared late-modern radicalization of the countries in which the bulk of *daimistas* reside engender much by way of a common socio-cultural terrain. For example, Western modernity is constituted, first and foremost, by a market-orchestrated, urban-industrial and techno-scientific complex underwritten by structural and social integration. Orchestrated by the imperatives of a market economy, a substantial majority of the population (or 'workforce') are typically concentrated within urban environments facilitating industrial and technologically driven modes of profit-oriented and competition-driven production. In structural terms, Western modernity is characterized by the universal, and usually centralized, application of economic, political, legal, educational and linguistic processes which impact upon all aspects of life. Structural integration is facilitated through infrastructural networks of transport (e.g. road, rail and air) and communication (e.g. mail, telephone and satellite). The social integration characteristic of Western modernity arises directly from the processes and networks of structural integration. Catalysed by the dynamics of urbanization and modern economic production, social integration is further enhanced by the modern individual's increased interaction with and mutual reliance upon an extended web of other human beings in both immediate and mediated forms. From basic goods (e.g. food, clothing and shelter), through institutional encounter (such as education, work and leisure) to mediated interaction (e.g. radio, television and internet), the average member of Western modernity both interacts with and relies upon a vast array of integrated networks and those who populate them. In socio-cultural terms, the shared ('common') knowledge which underwrites this diffuse interdependence is infused by a sense of the world and its nature as mutable and thereby pliant to human endeavour. Furthermore, the techno-scientific developments upon which Western modernity rests enable the enjoyment and cultivation of lifestyles which transcend pre-modern preoccupations with pursuing and securing the basic goods of material survival.

Realized through the process of differentiation, the typically complex nature of Western modernity is characterized by structural variegation and socio-cultural plurality. In structural terms, Western modernity has an almost vertiginous number of processes, mechanisms and institutions through which the day-to-day activities of its members occur. Be they economic, political, legal, employment-related, educational, recreational, communal or familial, the structures of modern society are numerous, variegated and highly specialized. At the same time, Western modernity exhibits a socio-cultural variety unprecedented in human history. On the one hand, social pluralization occurs in response to structural differentiation, as the variegated kinds of societal structures engender progressively diverse life-experiences for the different groups which populate the increasingly varied parts of the social system. The structural complexity of Western modernity is reflected in the sheer number of social categories, status groups or classes existing within it. On the other hand, social differentiation occurs through domestic and transnational migration, as different socio-cultural groups move (or are moved) from one place to another. The subsequent interaction of different social, racial, ethnic and linguistic groups further enhances the socially plural character of modern society. Although its implications are disputed, the process of societal differentiation involves the relativization of established knowledge, belief and value systems. Coupled with the increased presence of previously unavailable practices and symbols, the relativization of existing repertoires wrought by socio-cultural pluralization facilitates the construction of new and hybrid forms of practical-knowledge.

The process and consequences of societal differentiation are reinforced by Western modernity's characteristically constant, rapid and far-reaching transformation at both structural and social levels. In combination, the imperatives of urban-industrial and techno-scientific development involve the ongoing revision of economic, political, legal and educational structures to manage, if not keep pace with, the scale and rapidity of contemporary change. In socio-cultural terms, swift and widespread transformation fundamentally alters the hold which established traditions and practices are able to exert. Exacerbated by the rapid, large-scale and continued uprooting (disembedding) and formation (re-embedding) of practical-knowledge systems, the process of detraditionalization undermines the authority and hold of inherited forms of practice, knowledge, belief and morality. Whereas the erosive dynamics of detraditionalization involve the flipside formation of new traditions (retraditionalization), these are by and large of a less permanent and all-embracing nature.

Western modernity is progressively oriented to the individual. Comprising a diverse range of collective institutions and identities through which human life plays out (e.g. family, class, religion, sex and race), Western modernity is characterized by a weakening of the influence they have traditionally exerted over the individual. Born through the combination of aforementioned dynamics, the limitation of collective determination wrought by the modern process of individualization furnishes the individual with an enhanced degree of personal choice and expression. On the one hand, the erosion of collective determination manifests through an increased level of socio-cultural mobility, as the late-modern individual enjoys newfound latitude in, for example, matters of education, employment, leisure and personal relationships. On the other hand, the dynamics of individualization engender enhanced degrees of subjective expression, exhibited through broadened repertoires of, for example, sexuality, belief and lifestyle (e.g. self-presentation, diet and patterns of consumption).

The objective processes and subjective expressions of Western modernity have been further radicalized through structures and flows associated with the dual developments of globalization and commoditization. Although the growth of international exchange was integral to the rise of Western modernity (not least in respect of trade and workforce migration), the historically recent intensification of worldwide transnational processes is such that the term 'globalization' has been coined to signal this late-modern step-change (Waters, 2001). The techno-scientific advances of the late-modern period (e.g. travel, communications and information technology) enable the rapid and large-scale circulation of material goods, people, information, tastes, values and beliefs. Exemplified by recent financial crises and subsequent global slumps, such is the nature of this worldwide circulation that domestic structures and socio-cultural dynamics are now inextricably interwoven within a highly integrated network of transnational exchange. In the same vein, whereas market-orchestrated consumption has long been an important component of Western modernity, recent developments (not least the emergence and spread of neo-liberal, commodity capitalism) have radicalized established commercial processes and consumerist tendencies. The market enjoys an almost preeminent position within Western modernity, with structural, institutional and interpersonal dynamics undergoing progressive reformulation in the interests of the pursuit, exchange and enjoyment of an ever-increasing diversity of material and immaterial commodities. As with globalization, and exemplified by contemporary notions of commoditization, these typically late-modern developments engender new modes of subjectivity and associated valorizations of the material world.

The globalizing processes and market-driven dynamics of Western late-modernity constitute a geographically diffuse and evolving network of rapid and large-scale flows. The transnational entanglement of economic, legal, political, ethical and aesthetic structures and institutions connects localities and regions to a seemingly limitless number of otherwise disparate and faraway locations. At the same time, this globalizing network enables the border-transcending flow of goods, people, information, power, tastes and values at a vertiginous speed and scale which renders established spatio-temporal distinctions almost irrelevant. In tandem with aforementioned dynamics and processes, these networks and flows have far-reaching implications for the structural configuration of Western late-modernity, along with the modes of subjectivity whose behaviour, beliefs and values it encompasses. On the one hand, the dual processes of globalization and commoditization impact upon Western modernity by radicalizing aforementioned foundational dynamics of, for example, integration, differentiation, transformation and individualization. On the other, the radicalization of foundational structural dynamics catalyses the ongoing transformation of socio-cultural processes such as relativization, detraditionalization and subjectivization. Of a quintessentially late-modern provenance, the behaviour, beliefs and values of the new middle class perhaps best exemplify the contemporary practical-symbolic concerns of entangled Western modernity.

The entangled Western subjectivity of the new middle class

When detailing the principal contours of new middle-class subjectivity, the aforementioned literature relates it primarily to one or both of two constitutive dynamics. First, the subjective dispositions of the new middle class are explicated relative to its position as an intermediate class between a manual (lower, working or proletarian) class and a non-manual but also non-salaried (upper or bourgeois) class. Here, emphasis rests upon the contradictions, tensions and paradoxes engendered by a well-educated and professionally employed class which enjoys a relatively secure standard of living but is nevertheless preoccupied with its positional status relative to those considered worse or better off. Second, new middle-class subjectivity is treated as a characteristically late-modern phenomenon. As such, the practical-symbolic concerns of the new middle class are understood as forged through the radicalization of aforementioned modern dynamics and socio-cultural processes allied with, for example, commodity capitalism, the subjective turn, cultural and technological industries and globalization. In respect of their relevance to the topic at hand, three aspects of the new middle-class subjectivity are worthy of note: its pluralized and fluid character; individualized demeanour; and commoditized disposition.

The new middle class exhibits a relatively pluralized and fluid subjectivity which reflects, among other things, an informed appreciation of ongoing socio-cultural transformation and exposure to a varied range of world views and life-experiences. Cosmopolitan in nature and outlook, new middle-class subjectivity is generally tolerant of cultural, political or religious difference, comfortable with societal change and copes well with moral ambiguity. Individual subjectivity is customarily informed by the eclectic appropriation of practical regimes and symbolic resources from a broad spectrum of socio-cultural sources. Relatively self-assured in respect of the diverse tastes, values and behaviour it embodies, new middle-class subjectivity is nevertheless disposed to the ongoing revision of the practices and symbols on which it draws. In tandem with its individualized demeanour and commoditized disposition, the pluralized and fluid subjectivity of the new middle class manifests in a relativizing world view through which commitments and allegiances are readily rendered provisional.

The individualized demeanour of new middle-class subjectivity qualifies collective modes of belonging and corporate participation through their subordination to the desires and concerns of the late-modern self. Evaluated relative to their contribution to individual well-being, communal forms of behaviour are progressively voluntarized and self-oriented. Where it exists, new middle-class political activism tends principally to articulate a range of subjectively orchestrated concerns which trade traditional collectivist and emancipatory politics for a 'life politics' (or 'politics of lifestyle') preoccupied with obtaining societal conditions conducive to 'self-actualisation' (Giddens, 1991: 214). The political behaviour of the individualized new middle class manifests most explicitly as a 'politics of the first person' (Betz, 1992: 108). Not least owing to its socio-economic status, enhanced educational capital and informed world view, the individualized subjectivity of the new middle class is also highly reflexive in character. Here, reflexivity comprises a strategic and self-aware instrumentality through which the practical and symbolic concerns of the new middle class are pursued. On the one hand, new middle-class reflexivity includes a keen positional awareness characterized by the comparative dynamics of association, dissociation and 'distinction' vis-à-vis other groups occupying the late-modern landscape (Bourdieu, 1984). On the other, reflexivity involves the subjective dynamics of strategic self-presentation through which practical and symbolic resources are appropriated and displayed in the cause of personal development (*ad intra*) and individual advancement (*ad extra*); achievements frequently regarded as two sides of the same coin. Combined with its pluralized fluidity and commoditized character, individualized subjectivity manages the self as 'project' forged as a customized lifestyle permanently under construction and constantly in pursuit of aesthetic gratification (Featherstone, 2007).

The intimate association between new middle-class subjectivity and late-modern patterns of consumption is much discussed by the relevant literature. Lash and Urry, for example, call the new middle class 'the consumer *par excellence* of post-modern cultural products' (1987: 292), while Lee uses the phrase 'new consumption classes' (1993: 169). Likewise, Betz maintains that 'the very nature of the new middle class makes it especially disposed towards an economic, social and cultural system which puts heavy emphasis on consumption' (1992: 99). Sharing similar views to others treating the late-modern Brazilian context (e.g. A. Guerra et al., 2006: 17; Owensby, 1999: 245; Sorj, 2006: 52), O'Dougherty regards consumption as 'central' and 'foundational' to new middle-class 'self-definition' and 'identity' (2002: 11, 22). For many of these commentators, the commoditized subjectivity of the new middle class plays out through the positional class dynamics of differentiation (from *below*) and association (with *above*) which particular modes of consumption permit. The prestige and status associated with the acquisition of late-modern commodities (understood here as positional goods) is viewed as constitutive of new middle-class subjectivity and its pursuit of socio-cultural 'distinction' (e.g. Bourdieu, 1984; Wynne, 1998). At the same time, and no little indebted to its birth under commodity capitalism and exposure to late-modern culture industries, the subjective well-being of the new middle class is closely tied with what and how it consumes. Of an expectant and aspirational nature, new middle-class subjectivity valorizes consumption as both an integral component of the self-project and fundamental right to be protected and enjoyed.

Religious implications

The entangled context of Western late-modernity with which new middle-class subjectivity is so intimately connected comprises a range of macrostructural, mid-range institutional and micro-social dynamics and processes which impact upon the religious landscape inhabited by urban-professional *daimistas*. For example, and irrespective of debates about the actual religiosity of late-modern society and its occupants, recent decades have seen further structural secularization through which the state is reducing both its traditional involvement in the substantive regulation of religion and the established entanglement of secular and religious institutions. In addition to removing political-legal obstacles to new and alternative modes of religious belief and practice, the eradication of traditional mechanisms of support facilitate a leveller field on which non-mainstream religious groups may compete on a more equal footing. In the same vein, the disembedding effects of late-modern processes such as rapid transformation, individualization and migration are undermining the traditional influences of practices and beliefs inherited from prior generations. The detraditionalizing consequences of these developments are further exacerbated by the radicalization of established pluralizing dynamics (e.g. differentiation) through widespread exposure to novel tastes, goods, practices and values facilitated by the networks and flows of globalization. In combination with structural secularization, the dynamics of detraditionalization and relativizing effects of pluralization engender a socio-cultural terrain wholly conducive to the formation of ever more hybrid and mutable religious repertoires both within and outwith formal institutional contexts.

The increasingly hybrid and mutable religious repertoires characteristic of entangled Western late-modernity are paralleled by the progressively eclectic and flexible belief systems of their individual participants. Catalysed by aforementioned dynamics, the processes of individualization and subjectivization impact upon the religious landscape by reconfiguring the traditional balance of collective – individual relations. On the one hand, increased self-determination in matters religious involves the subjectivized formulation of idiosyncratic and fluid world views forged through the appropriation and fusion of otherwise diverse and disparate beliefs and practices. The subjectivized dynamics of religious bricolage are complemented by those of religious transit. No longer bound by religious commitments of a life-long and exclusive nature, beneficiaries of an increasingly diverse range of religious provision are more frequently actualizing their enhanced choice and mobility through consecutive or concurrent participation in any number of religious groups, movements or organizations. A further consequence of late-modern individualization, religious participants are more demanding in their expectations of the religious repertoires with which they engage. Although individuals still willingly commit to the demands and constraints of the repertoires engaged, the implications of subjectivization nevertheless qualify collective modes of belonging through their subordination to self-oriented preoccupations of an experiential, exploratory and expressive kind. Faced with increasingly pluralized, mobile and expectant participants, religious organizations are likewise affected by individualization. From definitions of membership and its attendant obligations, through organizational funding, to ritual content, structure and scheduling, religious institutions, like their secular counterparts, are constantly revising received modes of practice and understanding to better meet the highly subjectivized demands of the increasingly mobile and expectant late-modern self.

The pluriform character, individualized demeanour and commoditized disposition of the new middle class places it in an ideal position to optimize the macrostructural, mid-range institutional and micro-social dynamics currently reshaping the late-modern religious landscape. Not coincidentally, given their overwhelmingly new middle-class ethos, the institutional and subjective impact of these dynamics is best exemplified by the organizational repertoires and participatory profiles of new religious movements. In keeping with its now predominant urban-professional membership and the late-modern context it inhabits, Santo Daime is no exception. Shaped by the late-modern sensibilities of the new middle class and framed by the same macrostructural dynamics (e.g. detraditionalization, pluralization and individualization) as other new religious repertoires, Santo Daime exhibits similar organizational contours (e.g. hybridism, flexibility and variegation) and participatory patterns (e.g. bricolage, transit and expectancy). Chapters 2, 3 and 4 have gone some way to engaging these dynamics and their impact upon the beliefs and practices of the Santo Daime movement. In addition to contributing to contemporary debates about religion and the market, the remainder of this chapter complements preceding discussions by reflecting upon the *daimista* repertoire in relation to the commoditized subjectivity of the new middle class from which Santo Daime now draws the vast bulk of its membership.

The *daimista* repertoire and late-modern commoditization

Writing about Brazilian neo-Pentecostalism, Roger Roca rejects what he views as the naive application of 'foreign' theoretical models which attempt to explicate the relationship between money and religion articulated by this historically recent religious phenomenon. Formulated in view of the dominant neo-liberal economic paradigm and ongoing commoditization of modern Western society, Roca argues, foreign explanatory models dismiss the 'health and wealth' prosperity gospel of neo-Pentecostal groups such as the Universal Church of the Kingdom of God (UCKG) as a form of 'commodity fetishism' engendered by the capitalistic processes of globalization. Roca maintains, however, that extrinsic models such as these fail adequately to appreciate the actual processes at play in neo-Pentecostalism's attitude to wealth because they do not pay attention to the role traditionally played by money in the internal dynamics of the Brazilian religious landscape. Were this role to be properly appreciated, organizations such as the UCKG would not be dismissed as 'simply practising money fetishism' à la Western neo-liberal commoditization. Viewed instead as recapitulating long-standing dynamics intrinsic to the Brazilian religious field, he argues, the prosperity-oriented activities of groups like the UCKG can be regarded as re-appropriating money in a way which transforms it 'into an instrument of Divine agency'. Rather than exemplifying Western notions of 'money fetishism', when situated relative to the established dynamics of the Brazilian religious landscape, such practices are better understood as a modern form of domestic 'money-magic' (2007: 319–39).

Whereas Roca writes of Brazilian neo-Pentecostalism, one could just as fittingly identify Santo Daime as susceptible to misconstrual at the hands of 'foreign' analytical frameworks. Roca's critique of the application of extrinsic theories insufficiently sympathetic to processes and dynamics autochthonous to a local religious field is thereby an instructive one. Informed by the pragmatic and supernaturalist characteristics of popular religiosity mentioned in Chapter 1, the traditional *daimista* repertoire of the Amazon region articulates a relationship between religion and money which is not conducive to being theoretically captured by concepts formulated with commodity capitalism in mind. Although engaging with it by way of broader contextualization, this book is not, however, about the traditional *daimista* repertoire. Rather, this work concerns itself with the urban-professional practitioners of Santo Daime who, as members of the new middle class, are intimately associated with commodity capitalism and its commoditization of late-modern subjectivity. While many of the foundational practices and symbols employed by urban middle-class *daimistas* originate outwith the late-modern context, they are used and interpreted by individuals of a thoroughgoingly late-modern provenance. Mindful of their origin, the practices and symbols of Santo Daime are nevertheless of overriding interest here as they are appropriated, re-signified and transformed by urban-professional members of late-modern, commoditized society.

The commoditization of late-modern subjectivity, not least that of the new middle class from which the bulk of contemporary *daimistas* derive, arises from the growth of commodity capitalism and its seemingly all-pervasive consumer culture. Clearly, objects of a material and immaterial kind have long served humankind as commodities sought, acquired and employed in the course of everyday life (Miller, 2010). At the same time, consumption for need or pleasure is a practice as old as our species (Appadurai, 1986). The rise of consumer culture engendered by commodity capitalism, however, has transformed matters such that commodities and the manner of their consumption assume a significance beyond and different to that which existed before. The culture of consumption central to new middle-class identity, denotes, according to Slater, 'a social arrangement in which the relation between lived culture and social resources, between meaningful ways of life and the symbolic and material resources on which they depend, is mediated through markets' (1997: 8). Indeed, argues Slater, the all-embracing character of the late-modern market entails that 'values from the realm of consumption spill over into other domains of social action, such that modern society is *in toto* a consumer culture, and not just in its specifically consuming activities' (1997: 25). In the same vein, Zigmunt Bauman argues that the commoditization of modernity has produced a 'society of consumers' in which 'consumerism' dominates as 'the *principal propelling and operating force*' through which 'systemic reproduction, social integration, social stratification and the formation of individuals . . . and group self-identification' are coordinated (2007: 28, 53).

Lury identifies the following processes as 'some of the most significant' of consumer culture:

> 1 The organized interpenetration of economic and everyday life. 2 The increasing importance of the exchange of commodities . . . driven by the pursuit of profit. 3 The development of a series of ongoing relationships between different systems of exchange or regimes of value . . . in which activities are linked through a whole set of interlinking cycles of production and consumption . . . 4 The growth of a range of different forms of consumer politics . . . 5 The active role of the state in organizing collective and individual forms of consumption. 6 The use of goods in contemporary societies by specific groups . . . leading to forms of expertise and the creation of subcultures or lifestyles. 7 The political identification of freedom with individual choice. (2011: 5–6; see also Slater, 1997: 24–32)

Echoing others in respect of the all-embracing nature of consumer culture, Lury maintains that its infiltration of the 'economic', 'social', 'domestic' and 'psychological' levels of everyday life is such that 'it affects the construction of identities, the formation of relationships and the framing of events' (2011: 193). As Featherstone notes, the commoditization of late-modern existence involves far more than modified objective conditions which radically increase the availability, diversity and kind of commodities in existence. As much of a cultural as an economic phenomenon, commoditization also involves a thoroughgoing re-signification in which the world, its contents and humankind's relationship with them are symbolized and engaged in a radically new way (2007: 82, 112). More than this, the re-signification wrought by consumer culture includes the symbolic reconfiguration not only of the world and our relationship with it, but also of our very selves. As Bauman maintains, the commoditization of society entails the concomitant commoditization of human subjectivity such that '*everyone* needs to be, ought to be, must be a consumer-by-vocation' (2007: 55).

The 'consumer', Sassatelli argues, functions within late-modern society as a '*normative cultural identity*' (2007: 149). As such, consumer culture is about more than 'commoditization and affluence' or 'conspicuous consumption and the democratization of luxuries' (2007: 6). It is, perhaps most fundamentally, about the production of commoditized selves. In terms of its relationship with the world at large, the commoditized subject merges with the commodities furnished by its given socio-cultural environment to the extent that the objects provided 'often function as dynamic elements of an extended self' (Lee, 1993: 26). In effect, the commoditized self understands and values itself relative to the manner and extent of its ability to consume that which its social environment makes available. *To be is to consume*. At the same time, the commoditized self engendered by consumer culture looks upon itself as something amenable to being consumed. As Bauman observes, 'the most prominent feature of the society of consumers – however carefully concealed and most thoroughly covered up – is the *transformation of consumers into commodities*' (2007: 12). Likewise, for Lury, 'consumer culture is a source of the contemporary belief that self-identity is a kind of *cultural resource, asset or possession*' (2011: 26). As a consequence, commoditized subjectivity understands and values itself relative to its ability to serve as a commodity for the extraction of value. *To be consumed is to be*.

Late-modern religious consumption

Treatments of religion as infused by market dynamics, analogous to modern economic processes or subject to progressive commoditization have become increasingly common over the course of the last few decades. For the new religions scholar Paul Heelas, however, the use of market-oriented notions such as consumption and commodity are something of an academic fad. 'Like so many other terms associated with postmodern "thought"', he argues, 'the language of consumption has become a consumer good – one which has been consumed by many within the academy, perhaps taking them over' (2008: 181). More substantively, Heelas rejects the association between new spiritualities and late-modern forms of modern consumerism as an overly reductionist analysis which bypasses most of what contemporary spiritual repertoires have to offer. Heelas is correct in that an explicit focus upon contemporary religious practice as a form of laté-modern consumption risks an overly reductionist analysis of an otherwise complex, nuanced and multifaceted terrain. In the same way, such an explicit focus is also vulnerable to misrepresenting late-modern society and its occupants as overly determined by market forces. Furthermore, it risks offering a one-dimensional picture of consumption and thereby overlooking the variegated practical-symbolic dynamics involved in the production, pursuit, acquisition and enjoyment of late-modern commodities. As Sassatelli remarks, the apparent simplicity of the term 'consumer culture' runs the risk of being 'used as a fetish' which ignores both the 'contested genealogy of the subject-consumer and the complex economic and cultural processes which underpin consumption' (2007: 198).

Heelas is mistaken, however, to the extent that he fails to offer an adequate account of the manner and extent to which the commoditization of late-modern society impacts and infuses the beliefs and practices of those engaged in new religious repertoires; not least the new middle class forming the overwhelming majority of non-mainstream participants. Heelas' argument that consumption is an everyday part of life that should not be analytically overblown by contemporary treatments of religion thereby fails to take seriously the ways in which commodity capitalism has reconfigured the late-modern character of consumption. As Giddens maintains, the 'commodifying of consumption' wrought by commodity capitalism

> is not just a matter of the reordering of existing behaviour patterns or spheres of life. Rather, consumption under the domination of mass markets is essentially a novel phenomenon, which participates directly in processes of the continuous reshaping of the conditions of day-to-day life. (1991: 198–9)

Consequently, though consumption is indeed an everyday part of life, and while religion's association with market processes are by no means historically recent, the commoditization of human existence wrought by commodity capitalism marks a fundamental shift, the significance of which must be accounted for by those engaging religion in its contemporary, late-modern context.

Peter Berger (1967) and Thomas Luckmann (1967) were among the earliest academics to treat the appearance of market dynamics across the modern religious landscape. According to Berger, the combined dynamics of structural secularization and socio-cultural pluralism engender the 'permanent presence' of competition across the religious landscape through which 'religious groups are transformed from monopolies to competitive marketing agencies'. As 'religious tradition' can no longer be 'authoritatively imposed', it 'now has to be *marketed*' or '"sold" to a clientele that is no longer constrained to "buy"'.

> The pluralistic situation is, above all, a *market situation*. In it, the religious institutions become marketing agencies and the religious traditions become consumer commodities. And at any rate a good deal of religious activity in this situation comes to be dominated by the logic of market economics. (1967: 137)

The impact of the ingression of market dynamics into the religious field, Berger argues, is twofold. First, the marketization of religion requires structural changes to religious institutions which must now manage 'an exceedingly complex and expensive operation'. Internally, these structural changes manifest through the 'rationalization' of institutional practices, including the adoption of goal-oriented preoccupations and bureaucratically managed procedures. Externally, structural change requires a growing involvement in activities such as 'public relations', 'lobbying' and 'fund raising' with 'consumer clientele', government bodies and 'private agencies'. Second, the impact of market forces 'also extend to the religious contents' in that 'religious marketing agencies' must now take account of the 'dynamics of consumer preference' in what is an increasingly competitive environment populated by 'uncoerced consumers'. Among the various consequences arising from the new 'consumer controls over religious contents', two are worthy of note. First, because they are prone to the changing tastes of the market, religious contents are subject to a 'principle of changeability' which both erodes the fixity of established traditions and ties modern religious repertoires to the shifting patterns of contemporary 'fashion'. Second, and 'insofar as the world of the consumers in question' is both 'secularized' and 'privatized', religious products must downplay their 'supernatural elements' and instead emphasize their immanent (e.g. moral, therapeutic and material) benefits (1967: 140–5).

Sharing Berger's analysis of modern macrostructural dynamics (e.g. structural differentiation and socio-cultural pluralism) and their institutional impact (i.e. marketization), Luckmann nevertheless offers a complementary focus in his treatment of the individual as a now 'autonomous' religious consumer (1967: 104). The autonomous religious consumer arises, says Luckmann, from the convergence of three characteristically modern dynamics: (i) modernity's fragmentation of the traditionally homogeneous 'sacred cosmos' into '*assortments* of "ultimate" meanings' with little or no coherence between them; (ii) the disembedding of individuals from collective associations such that 'to an immeasurably higher degree than in a traditional social order . . . the individual is left to his own devices in choosing goods and services, friends, marriage partners, neighbors, [and] hobbies'; (iii) modern society's all pervasive 'consumer orientation' which 'is not limited to economic products but characterizes the relation of the individual to the entire culture' (1967: 98). In combination, these typically modern dynamics lead the individual 'to confront the culture and the sacred cosmos as a "buyer"' who 'may choose from the assortment of "ultimate" meanings as he sees fit'. More than this, however, such is modernity's estimation of the free-floating consumer that marketized religion bestows 'something like a sacred status' upon individual autonomy. As a consequence, religious expression is characterized by a 'mobility ethos' which is both 'individualistic' and 'manipulative' (i.e. instrumentally oriented). Assuming the nature of a 'lifelong quest' for the 'inner man', modern religiosity becomes orchestrated by the goal of 'self-expression and self-realization'. In contrast to the 'obligatory themes' of the traditional sacred cosmos, the modern religious 'consumer' moves freely among a 'heterogeneous assortment of possibilities'. Picking and choosing according to subjective tastes and idiosyncratic concerns, the modern individual constructs a 'syncretistic', 'eclectic' and *ad hoc* meaning-system whose 'thematic heterogeneity' consists 'of a loose and rather unstable hierarchy of "opinions" legitimating the affectively determined priorities of "private" life' (1967: 102–11).

Building upon the formative insights of Berger and Luckmann, more recent academic construals of religious belief and practice as infused by market dynamics, analogous to modern economic processes or prone to progressive commoditization comprise three mutually inclusive foci. First, emphasis rests upon the macrostructural dynamics (e.g. structural secularization, pluralization and marketization) of late-modern society which inform the increasingly competitive, commercially savvy and consumer-oriented behaviour of religious institutions. Despite its limitations, the religious economy model, for example, has done much to highlight the relevance of macrostructural conditions to the vibrancy or otherwise of the religious landscape (e.g. Chesnut, 2003; L. Guerra, 2003; Stark and Bainbridge, 1985). Contrasting higher levels of religious participation in the United States with those of Europe, religious economists argue that the historically lower levels of state interference and concomitantly higher levels of religious competition evident in the United States contribute to a more vibrant religious market than that in evidence in Europe, where state involvement with religion has traditionally been widespread and thereby suppressed competition between religious providers (e.g. Finke and Stark, 1992).

Second, analytical stress lies upon the institutions themselves and their ability and inclination to market (e.g. brand) their religious wares by optimizing prevailing societal conditions (e.g. political-legal constraints and public opinion) and mobilizing available resources (e.g. finance and personnel) in the most effective and efficient manner possible (e.g. Moore, 1994; Roof, 1999; Twitchell, 2007; Wiegele, 2005). The sophisticated character of contemporary 'religious marketing', for example, is dealt with at length by Einstein (2008). Here, Einstein asserts that 'religion is a product, no different from any other commodity sold in the consumer marketplace' with 'many forms of religion . . . being advertised and promoted in a way never seen before' (2008: 4). As with Berger and Luckmann, Einstein cites modernity's creation of a '*real* open market for religion' as fundamental to the growth of religious marketing. She also highlights the importance of 'media saturation' and the 'ubiquitous advertising that goes with it'. In combination, religious choice and information overload mean that 'religion must present itself as a valuable commodity, an activity that is worthwhile in an era of overcrowded schedules'. As a consequence, 'religion needs to be packaged and promoted. It needs to be new and relevant. It needs to break through the clutter'. In short, religion needs to establish itself as a 'brand' worthy of consumer attentions (2008: 12).

Third, focus rests upon the increasing number of free-floating (i.e. disembedded) and reflexively orchestrated (e.g. strategic, mobile and expectant) religious consumers endowed with a historically unrivalled freedom of choice in both its subjective and objective capacities (e.g. Amaral, 2000; Bellah et al., 1985; Roof, 1993). In his treatment of the 'spiritual marketplace', for example, Roof talks of the contemporary religious 'seeker' whose 'reflexive spirituality' embodies a 'quest culture . . . engendered by confrontation with pluralism, individualism, and modernity', along with its 'therapeutic culture and . . . explicit attention to the self' (1999: 39). 'Whatever else religion may be', he argues, 'in a mediated and consumption-oriented society it becomes a *cultural resource* broadly available to the masses.' As a consequence, authority and responsibility fall upon increasingly disembedded individuals to exercise their now 'considerable agency in defining and shaping what is considered to be religiously meaningful' (1999: 75). In addition to the other two analytical frames, the focus adopted by Roof makes a valuable contribution to understanding the marketization of the contemporary religious field along with its institutional impact and individual consequences. Exposed to the same marketized dynamics as other occupants of the late-modern religious landscape, Santo Daime might fruitfully be engaged through one or more of these complementary analytical foci. Given the concerns of the current study, however, focus rests instead upon the commoditization of late-modern subjectivity and its implications for understanding the contemporary *daimista* repertoire. Particularly as it concerns the self and its relations with the 'things of this world', the notion of mystified consumption goes some way to explicating certain commoditized aspects of the contemporary *daimista* repertoire.

Mystified consumption

In her treatment of late-modern consumer culture, Sassatelli uses the notion of 'de-commoditization' to describe a variety of 'practices social actors enter into' in their everyday dealings with 'the market' that re-signify 'standardized commodities' by transforming 'them into goods with personal meanings' (2007: 115). Whereas the act of material or immaterial consumption remains, the process of de-commoditization reframes the 'meaning and use' of the commodities consumed by relating their significance not to the act of consumption itself but to 'other forms of value' such as 'affection, relationships, symbolism, status, normality, etc.' (2007: 139). The act of 're-framing' thereby transposes commodity-use into a significant practice, the meaning of which is greater or other than that ordinarily associated with everyday consumption. According to Sassatelli, the process of de-commoditization occurs in a wide variety of different 'contexts of consumption' formed

> through rituals and practices of embodiment, marking, sharing, sacralization, etc. which personalize commodities, code them through lived experiences, socialize them via social gatherings of various kinds, restrict their possibility of being exchanged on the market, attach them to specific settings, and so forth. (2007: 142)

The process of de-commoditization is, though, 'paradoxical' in nature in that the re-signification enacted through different contexts of consumption permits the late-modern consumer to 'get close to commodities while distancing him or herself from their immediate hold'. In effect, while the meaning of the commodities consumed is reconfigured, the dynamics of de-commoditization do not actually 'overturn the commoditization process as such' (2007: 115, 142). Whereas Sassatelli champions de-commoditization as a potentially subversive process which resists (but does not ultimately negate) contemporary commoditization processes, it may well be argued that the symbolic mystification wrought by de-commoditization also catalyses commoditization through its portrayal of certain commodities and their particular modes of consumption as having greater significance than they might otherwise be afforded. By symbolizing commodities as, for example, rewards and benefits for labours expended, privileges and entitlements associated with status or aspects of a specific cultural or ethical lifestyle, de-commoditization legitimates their consumption as the just deserts of fairness and rank or the integral components of identity and morality. In so doing, de-commoditization not only valorizes particular modes of commodity consumption but also reinforces them.

Along with its traditional and non-mainstream counterparts, the religious repertoire of Santo Daime may justifiably be regarded as a context of consumption. Whether through formal ritual practice or its symbolic world view, Santo Daime frames contemporary consumption in a manner which re-signifies but does not ultimately overturn the late-modern processes of commoditization. Like all forms of belief and practice, however, the views, values and behaviour which comprise the *daimista* repertoire are fundamentally irreducible to being straightforward expressions of commodity consumption. Nevertheless, not least given the preponderance of members drawn from the new middle class so intimately associated with late-modern commoditization, *daimista* belief and practice is by no means exempt from the commoditizing forces and dynamics constitutive of entangled, Western late-modernity. As it pertains to Santo Daime, the contemporary process of de-commoditization may be understood as a form of mystified consumption which re-signifies commodity-use through practical-symbolic reference to both an overarching cosmic Whole and the mystical processes of self-realization unwritten by it. The two principal aspects of mystified consumption are those of 'commodicy' and 'prosumption'. While these two aspects very much overlap, the former relates primarily to *daimista* engagement with the 'things of this world' and the latter chiefly to ritual construals of the self.

Commodicy

The term 'commodicy' plays on two related concepts, the first articulated by Max Weber's sociological rendering of 'theodicy' and the second by Bourdieu's notion of 'sociodicy', itself an adaption of Weber. Traditionally employed in philosophical and theological discussions, the concept of theodicy (literally, 'justifying god') refers to attempts to rationalize beliefs in the existence and actions of divinity in light of the evil and suffering with which worldly existence is seemingly beset. Weber grounds the term sociologically by using it to describe a variety of religio-cultural articulations employed by different social strata to justify or rationalize the enjoyment or otherwise of 'honor, power, possession, and pleasure' (1991a: 271). According to Weber, theodicies of the 'fortunate' and 'disprivileged' are both internal by way of motivation and 'external' in orientation. On the one hand, theodicy meets the 'psychological' and 'rational' needs of 'inner interests' by offering 'reassurance' in respect of what an individual or group has (or does not have) by way of status and possessions. On the other, theodicy serves 'external' interests as a form of 'legitimation' by which 'those who are fortunate' (or 'disprivileged') justify their position 'in comparison with others' who are relatively worse (or better) off (e.g. 1965: 138–50; 1991a: 267–301). While Weber was reluctant to identify his reading of theodicy as a straightforward example of class 'ideology',

Bourdieu has no such reservations. Employing the term 'sociodicy', Bourdieu makes explicit reference to the ideological character of theodicy as a means by which socially 'dominant groups' justify their privilege both in respect of their own 'competence' and in relation to 'dominated' sectors of society (e.g. 'deserving' and 'undeserving poor') (1998a: 43). As it applies to Santo Daime, the term 'commodicy' describes the practical-symbolic legitimation employed by *daimistas* to justify the pursuit, acquisition and enjoyment of material and immaterial commodities. Three aspects of *daimista* commodicy are worthy of note.

First, the holistic characteristic of the *daimista* repertoire (detailed in preceding chapters) plays an important role in the re-signification of everyday commodities as material effects of an otherwise immaterial causation. As noted, the holistic perspective posits a universal force, principle or dynamic whose ubiquitous presence underlies every aspect of cosmic existence. The unmitigated nature of this ubiquity ensures that every individual component of the universe, no matter its status, is joined to it and, by virtue of cosmic mediation, to everything else in existence. Outlined in Chapter 3, the ontological implications of universal holism furnish the cosmically connatural subject with the energies needed for self-realization and underwrite the epistemological relativization which frames both repertorial hybridism and individual bricolage. It does more than this, however, because the ontological implications of holism also involve the fusion of material and immaterial horizons through which the dynamics and contents of the material dimension of existence are readily interpreted as adjuncts and manifestations of the immaterial sphere. The ontological fusion of material and immaterial horizons thereby invokes the experiential merging of the mundane and the spiritual.

Mediated by the overarching ubiquity of the cosmic Whole, the mundane and spiritual realms are now internally related to each other such that what pertains to one pertains to the other. As a consequence, the mundane sphere of existence is sacralized and the spiritual realm of reality materialized. In so being, the spiritual is rendered immanent by its grounding in material processes and the material sphere and its contents are valorized not only as legitimate means to spiritual expression but also as justifiable contributors to the absolute realization of the higher-self. On the one hand, the elision of material – immaterial horizons implicated by metaphysical holism overcomes secular modernity's dislocation of the mundane and spiritual spheres. On the other, the implicit categorical fusion of mundane and spiritual experiences rejects traditional readings of material goods as impediments to the religious quest. In combination, the ontological and experiential outworking of *daimista* holism valorizes the 'things of this world' through their signification as immaterially caused and of immediate spiritual relevance.

Second, *daimista* commodicy legitimates commodity-use through its linkage of private spiritual advance and its outward material manifestation through such things as enhanced status and psychophysical well-being. Chapter 2 treated this linkage when engaging the intimate association between the private spiritual goods (e.g. healing, purification and self-understanding) made available by the *daimista* ritual field and the public benefits distributed in the form of, for example, functional status and positional prestige. Likewise, and as quoted in Chapter 3, Padrinho Alfredo maintains that the 'combat' against 'illusion' is not helped by 'fearing progress, money and our own prosperity' but by learning to live in a way which permits spiritual 'growth' to furnish 'better health' and 'improved standards of living' (Polari, 1998: 13). The linkage between spiritual advance and access to the goods and benefits which contribute to psychophysical well-being draws on a variety of repertorial emphases already detailed. The meritocratic expectations of ritual practitioners, for example, inform a spiritual work ethic expectant of just deserts for religio-moral labours expended. At the same time, the aestheticized subjectivity of ritual actors anticipates the fruits of spiritual exertion manifesting through experiential and expressive dimensions conducive to its exploratory and presentational preoccupations. These emphases combine with Santo Daime's ameliorative concerns with self-betterment to give the contemporary *daimista* repertoire a distinctly this-worldly orientation in which the benefits accrued by ritual practice assume a tangible, immanent quality to be enjoyed as much in the here and now as in any future incarnation. Although few *daimistas* espouse a full-blown 'health and wealth' gospel, the linkage of spiritual development and psychophysical well-being involves an act of re-signification through which the material and immaterial commodities contributing to the latter are valorized as evidence of the former. Centuries apart, Calvinist preoccupations with the visible 'signs of election' identified by Weber nevertheless resonate strongly with late-modern *daimista* expectations in respect of the public, psychophysical manifestation of private, spiritual status (1965: 183; 1992: 115).

Third, and in keeping with Weber's 'theodicy' and Bourdieu's 'sociodicy', the legitimation furnished by *daimista* commodicy is of an indirect, implicit character. Detailed in prior chapters, the overwhelming majority of *daimistas* espouse a countercultural world view critical of mainstream society. In addition to its moral degeneracy and egocentricity, the rampant materialism of mainstream society is often highlighted. In conversation with a North American member, for example, she criticized the 'materialist consumption' and 'material preoccupations' of her frequently overweight fellow nationals as they wonder round the local 'theme park' with 'a coke in one hand and a burger in the other'. The day prior to this conversation, she also told me how 'downtime' from her 'international' healing ministry was spent in one of the four homes she owned in 'various parts of the world'. Of course, owning four homes in different parts of the world does not necessarily make my informant materialistic nor, indeed, does it invalidate her critique of mainstream, North American society. It does, however, highlight the dislocutory nature of her anti-materialist discourse. Like the dislocutory speech acts detailed in prior chapters, my informant's narrative rhetorically distances but does not actually debar her from enjoying the things of this world. Rather, the re-signification implicit in her world view categorizes the practical-symbolic possibilities engendered by worldly existence in a way which differentiates acceptable from unacceptable modes of material enjoyment. As with theodicy and sociodicy in general, the commodicy at play here includes an implicit aesthetics of distinction which underwrites particular forms of commodity-use by symbolizing them as categorically distinct (e.g. as rewards or aspects of countercultural identity) from the commoditized (e.g. greedy or base) practices of other groups and individuals. In tandem with its other two dynamics, the dislocutory character of *daimista* commodicy signifies commodity-use in a manner which discursively qualifies but does not practically foreclose on the patterns of material and immaterial consumption associated with new middle-class lifestyles across entangled, Western late-modernity.

Ritual prosumption

The term 'prosumption' was coined to describe the late-capitalist tendency to collapse the acts of production and consumption into a single process through which commodity value is both extracted and generated at one and the same time. Positioning the late-modern subject as 'prosumer' (i.e. producer and consumer), the act of prosumption optimizes capital efficiency by harnessing the creative energies of the consumer to an act of production which makes the process of consumption possible and, by way of adding value to it, more profitable. From self-service restaurants, petrol stations and banks, through self-assembly furniture and do-it-yourself health checks, to radio call-ins and user-populated websites, the prosumptive process merges the value-generative act of production with the traditionally value-extractive act of consumption (Zwick et al., 2008). The act of prosumption is an archetypal neo-liberal process in that its fusion of consumption and production maximizes profit through the minimization of corporate outlays and business overheads. Strange as it first may appear, the prosumptive process is actually perceived as enhancing rather than diminishing the status of the late-modern self (Ritzer and Jurgenson, 2010). Such is the case because the notion of the prosumer as both producer and consumer plays to the contemporary valorization of the late-modern individual as the central axis around which all else is held to revolve. Treating the subject as 'product, producer and consumer' in one, the act of prosumption embodies a paradigmatically late-modern modality of selfhood which both extols and exploits contemporary understandings of the individual as 'entrepreneur of the self' (du Gay) and 'virtuoso' of 'self-(re) creation' (Lazaretto) (see Hearn, 2008).

As an aspect of mystified consumption, ritual prosumption comprises five interrelated components, many of which have been delineated in preceding chapters. These components are: agency, site, benefit, repertoire and modality. In respect of *agency*, the act of ritual prosumption has at its core late-modern refractions of the sovereign self. While the individual subject inevitably draws upon objectively furnished components of a material (e.g. ritual artefacts) and immaterial (e.g. supernatural energies) kind, such appropriation is mediated through a subjectivized understanding of the self as the ultimate arbiter of authority and principal agent of transformation. Reflecting aforementioned notions of the late-modern subject as entrepreneur and virtuoso of the self, the ritual practitioner of contemporary Santo Daime is both master of the prosumptive act and artisan of the technical processes involved. Ritual prosumption is, first and foremost, an autopoietic act of self-creation. Noted above in relation to *daimista* commodicy, the *benefits* inherent to ritual prosumption are both private and public, immaterial and material. Whatever the benefits accrued, however, their acquisition and enjoyment are signified as spiritual goods obtained as the outcome (i.e. product) of a transitional process through which the ritual practitioner moves from point *a* (ego) to point *b* (higher-self). Explicated below, what makes this transformative process truly prosumptive is the self's role in effecting (as producer) and experiencing (as consumer) the transition (as product) from *a* to *b*.

The *site* in which ritual prosumption occurs is that of the human body understood as an integrated psychophysical unit. Certainly, the prosumptive act is effected through the body's engagement with its physical environment (e.g. ritual space, religious paraphernalia and cultic co-participants) and all it makes available by way of material and immaterial goods. At the same time, though, external relational dynamics are relativized by an emphasis upon the constitutive role of internal psychophysical processes (e.g. ego eradication) and the individual's management of them (e.g. discipline and firmness). What happens without is but a means to effecting what happens within. Building upon the aforementioned metaphysical continuity (connaturality) of the self and the universe at large, the body is posited as a medium through which cosmic energies and universal forces are accessed and ultimately harnessed by the self for the benefit of the self. It is here that the fourth aspect of spiritual prosumption makes its contribution. The *ritual repertoire* of Santo Daime is important because its form and content not only frame but also enable the prosumptive process. Positing the body as the site of self-realization, the *daimista* repertoire furnishes participants with the practical-knowledge necessary to accessing and appropriating the cosmic forces which, by virtue of its connaturality, reside deep within the subject. Although dependent upon an individual's successful acquisition and correct application of the requisite knowledge and skills, self-realization is nevertheless catalysed and guided by a ritual repertoire mediated through interpersonal processes and framed by communally enacted dynamics.

Underwritten by the epistemological implications of its holistic world view, the prosumptive character of the *daimista* repertoire is reinforced by its hybridism and flexibility. In the first instance, the relativizing effects of holism facilitate the conspicuous appropriation and concomitant hybridization of formerly diverse (if not objectively discordant) beliefs and practices. In the second, the epistemological contingency born of holistic relativism renders existing articulations of the sacred as contingent (thereby perpetually revisable) and ambiguous (so open to multiple interpretations). By maximizing optionality and enhancing polysemy, the combination of hybridism and flexibility caters directly for aforementioned late-modern preoccupations with increased choice and subjective determination. Personal choice and determination are further reinforced through the subjectivized emphases of the *daimista* repertoire. Orchestrated by self-oriented and mobile selves, the contemporary *daimista* repertoire allows for the religious transit and spiritual bricolage integral to the reflexive biographical quest of the late-modern 'seeker'. Comprising consecutive memberships of or concurrent participation within different groups, religious transit optimizes individual 'freedom' while feeding the eclectic appetite of the spiritual bricoleur.

The prosumptive character of the *daimista* repertoire further manifests through its aestheticized nature. Detailed in prior discussions, the aestheticized character of the *daimista* repertoire comprises an inward preoccupation with self-exploration coupled with outwardly expressive concerns. Informed by the metaphysical connaturality of the self, self-exploration is valorized as inner states are read as subjective correlates of objective metaphysical realities. Self-feeling thereby assumes an overarching cosmic significance. As it relates to ritual prosumption, the tendency to expressivity embodies two complementary dynamics. First, the additional ritual space allowed for increased expressivity permits greater self-assertion which (as the externalization of subjectively mediated reality) acts as a status claim or demand upon others for recognition and reward. Second, ritual facilitation of subjective expression permits the objectification of otherwise inner experiences which (by virtue of publicly broadcasting what was formerly private) enhances personal gratification by expanding the perceived reach of the self. In each instance, and coupled with its exploratory counterpart, expressivity involves an extension to the reach of individual subjectivity, inherent to which is an assumed enhancement of the self's purchase upon both itself and its external environment.

Ritual prosumption is further underwritten by the meritocratic-egalitarianism of the *daimista* repertoire. Among other things, the meritocratic ethos manifests in reciprocal understandings of agency which assume an equivalence of fair return for the psychophysical labours expended. This ritual work ethic combines with an egalitarianism born of the holistic belief that every individual has equal access to the same universal forces residing deep with the self. Although their egalitarianism makes urban-professional *daimistas* wary of established pecking orders, organizational hierarchy is ultimately accepted *on condition that* it can be climbed by those who are willing and able to make the necessary exertions. On the one hand, hierarchy is understood as a purely functional and thereby contingent arrangement, the graduated structure of which is relative to the individual endeavours of subjective agency. On the other, hierarchy (or, better, the individual's place in it) exists as an objective measure of subjective merit along with the authority and status thereby accrued.

In his critique of the culture of new capitalism, Richard Sennett cites Erving Goffman's notion of 'half finished frames'. Used by the advertising industry, half finished frames increase the allure of the products marketed by offering an incomplete scenario which the consumer is invited to complete by way of 'filling in the picture' (2006: 148–9). In so doing, the 'half finished' advertisement both energizes the consumer by calling upon her commoditized imagination and mobilizes him to action by asking that he put himself in the frame (as purchaser) and thereby complete the picture. Encapsulating the *modality* of its ritual prosumption, this concept lends itself to explicating something of the *daimista* repertoire's contemporary attraction. Such is the case because the benefits offered by the *daimista* repertoire are predicated on the rectification of an absence or realization of unfulfilled potential by which the subject moves from point *a* (i.e. where one is now as 'ego') to point *b* (where one should be as 'higher-self'). In the first instance, the individual is energized through her representation as a half finished frame in need of completion. In the second, the subject is mobilized through the promise of tangible private and public benefits (of a material and immaterial kind) which accrue as the picture is completed.

The half finished framing of the individual as a product in need of completion is complemented by two other key prosumptive dynamics. First, the *daimista* repertoire posits the self as the primary agent through which the act of self-completion is achieved. Fundamentally reliant upon the productive agency of the self, the transition from *a* to *b* is, first and foremost, a process of autopoiesis. Self-betterment is thereby not simply an end state to be achieved, but also a productive process by which the self produces itself through the concerted application of the practical-knowledge furnished by the doctrine of Santo Daime. Second, representation of the individual as both outcome (i.e. product) and agent (i.e. producer) of ritual prosumption is further nuanced by an understanding of the self as a reflexive consumer of all that it does and experiences. In and of itself, neither the act of moving (as producer) nor being moved (as product) from *a* to *b* is sufficient to satisfy the aestheticized demands of the reflexive self. Implicated by the aforementioned aestheticization of the late-modern self, the act of ritual prosumption is only fully consummated by the self's experience of itself as that which both produces and is produced through the transformative dynamics of sustained ritual practice. It is this combination of self as agent (producer), beneficiary (product) and aesthete (consumer) which marks the urban-professional repertoire of Santo Daime as a quintessentially prosumptive process.

Given all that has been treated in preceding chapters, it is plain to see that Santo Daime and its ritual repertoire are beyond theoretical reduction to a single line of analysis connected with the commoditized subjectivity of the new middle class from which the majority of *daimistas* now hail. Like so many religious world views, Santo Daime's engagement with the world is far too rich to be captured by a single concept or analytical focus. Nevertheless, and not least given its new middle-class status, it would be analytically naive to suppose that the contemporary *daimista* movement is wholly immune to the impact of commodity capitalism and its commoditization of the late-modern subject. Exemplified by the preceding dynamics of commodicy and prosumption, the de-commoditizing re-signification wrought by Santo Daime's mystification of late-modern consumption reframes but does not ultimately negate the impact of commoditized subjectivity upon its contemporary repertoire. Does the failure of mystified consumption to overturn the commoditizing forces of late-modernity make Santo Daime, or any other religion for that matter, any less religious? No. In fact, the opposite may well be true. By symbolizing their pertinence for the psychophysical well-being of the self, the re-signification undertaken by mystified consumption renders the world and its contents more rather than less meaningful from a religious point of view. As the following section argues by way of concluding this chapter, the act of re-signification inherent to mystified consumption goes some way to supporting Santo Daime's classification as a form of 'world-rejecting aestheticism'.

Classifying Santo Daime

Among the least contentious analytical observations that can be made about Santo Daime are: (i) it is a new religious movement; and (ii) it is an ayahuasca religion. In respect of the first observation, the relatively recent historical emergence of Santo Daime qualifies it, at least chronologically, as a new religious movement (see A. Dawson, 2011c: 113–30). The simple chronological criterion of appearing after a particular point in time, however, tells us little of substance about Santo Daime or in what ways it compares or contrasts with other religious phenomena of a novel or established status. In the study of Japanese new religions, for example, such has been the limitation of chronologically informed definitions that scholars now talk of 'new', 'new, new' and 'new, new, new' religious phenomena (see Clarke, 2000). That new religions are 'new' is of no particular academic insight. At the same time, and as the English scholar of new religions Eileen Barker maintains, 'one cannot generalise' about new religious movements. Such is the case, she argues, because the new religious landscape is highly variegated, with its occupants differing from each other in respect of, for example, 'their origins, their beliefs, their practices, their organization, their leadership, their finances, their life-styles and their attitudes to women, children, education, moral questions and the rest of society' (1999: 20). What is important, though, is what the emergence, consolidation and subsequent growth or decline of new religious phenomena like Santo Daime tell us about society in general and its religious landscape in particular. Goulart's study of the formation and establishment of Santo Daime, for example, offers much by way of insight into the socio-cultural changes then taking place in Amazonian society and their impact upon its popular religious terrain (2004). Likewise, it is hoped that the current study of Santo Daime goes some way to explicating aspects of the contemporary interface between entangled late-modernity and the religious beliefs and practices framed by it. It is, then, not Santo Daime's status as 'new' that counts but what its newness signifies as a practical-symbolic barometer of ongoing changes both to contemporary religiosity and its overarching societal context.

The analytical limitations associated with the unqualified category of newness apply also to approaches which define Santo Daime relative to the practical and symbolic origins of its ritual repertoire and religious world view. The simple definition of Santo Daime as an 'ayahuasca religion' is a case in point. Emphasis upon the importance of Daime as a ritual sacrament does indeed go some way to providing an insightful analytical linkage with Brazil's other ayahuasca religions of *A Barquinha* (The Little Boat) and *A União do Vegetal* (The Union of the Plant [UDV]). Among other things, this linkage enables an appreciation of the socio-cultural roots (e.g. Amazon region and popular religiosity) and repertorial emphases (e.g. alternate states, uniforms and music) which these religions hold in common (A. Dawson, 2007: 76–98). There are, however, important aspects of their respective contemporary repertoires which differentiate these religious world views in a manner and extent which goes significantly beyond simple differences in the practical-symbolic framing of ritual ayahuasca consumption. Whereas the shared roots and repertorial emphases of ayahuasca religiosity furnish much by way of common repertorial ground, the contemporary *daimista* movement embodies a range of belief and practice which, at key points, holds more in common with the non-mainstream and alternative repertoires of entangled late-modernity than it does with *A Barquinha* or the UDV.

Although focus upon repertorial origins gives valuable information about the different kinds of beliefs and practices at play, it does not in itself reveal much of sociological significance about the contemporary *daimista* movement. For example, the backward looking nature of concerns with repertorial derivation often result in the theoretical underappreciation of new developments and ongoing modifications to, along with their causes and implications for, inherited beliefs and practices. Furthermore, analyses that are overly preoccupied with issues of practical and symbolic derivation can too readily ignore relevant similarities between new religions of otherwise different socio-cultural origins. In the same vein, the simple analytical focus upon shared repertorial origins may result in practical-symbolic differences between groups with a common provenance being uncritically downplayed or wholly overlooked. In respect of the symbolic origins and practical provenance of *daimista* repertorial components, the socio-cultural dynamics of popular Amazonian religiosity are justifiably identified by academic analyses as furnishing its foundational and most formative rituals and beliefs. As with Roca's aforementioned study of neo-Pentecostalism and its typically Brazilian concerns with 'money-magic' (2007), attention to practical-symbolic origins and the ritual dynamics they engender is a wholly relevant and analytically indispensable approach to understanding important aspects of the contemporary *daimista* repertoire.

In a good many treatments of Santo Daime, however, the analytical stress placed upon its foundational beliefs and practices endows them with a determinative power that ultimately detracts from an appreciation of the ways in and extent to which the *daimista* repertoire is being transformed, albeit incrementally, at the hands of its urban-professional majority. This determinative emphasis upon foundational beliefs and practices also engenders the underappreciation of repertorial differences across the contemporary movement as a whole and the theoretical downplaying of practical-symbolic similarities with other, characteristically late-modern, alternative religious world views. On the one hand, these analytical oversights often reflect the insider (i.e. member) status of those writing upon Santo Daime and their concerns with narrating the orthodoxy, authenticity or loyalty to received practices and beliefs of those with whom they are dealing. On the other, they arise from the preoccupations of academics sympathetic to the ritual use of psychoactive substances and thereby keen to defend Santo Daime by underlining its traditional associations with established (and tolerated) indigenous repertoires and mixed-race religio-cultural heritage. In combination, these approaches inform a tendency to portray Santo Daime in a way which overplays the repertorial significance of practical-symbolic components (e.g. ayahuasca and shamanism) inherited from the Amazonian context relative to contemporary ritual emphases and spiritual concerns either of a non-traditional provenance (e.g. cannabis) or embodying a distinctly late-modern variation on an otherwise established theme (e.g. aspects of spirit mediumship).

Like other new religious movements, the hybrid, flexible and variegated nature of the *daimista* repertoire makes it difficult to classify. During fieldwork, for example, it was commonplace to hear long-standing Brazilian members of Cefluris defining Santo Daime as a 'Christian spiritual order', form of 'Christian mediumship' or 'millenarian Christianity'. Noted in opening chapters, popular Catholicism has certainly played a part in shaping Santo Daime. It would be analytically reductionist, however, to classify the *daimista* world view as Christian; not least given the discomfort that many contemporary members have with this epithet. Detailed by Chapter 3, Santo Daime is also decreasingly influenced by the end-world narratives of the traditional millenarian paradigm. The anti-reductionist qualification applies also to the foundational emphases of *vegetalismo*, Afro-Brazilian religiosity and European esotericism. As with Christianity, each of these influences is foundational but by no means individually definitive. Likewise, and irrespective of its growing importance, Santo Daime is far more than a religion of spirit mediumship. In the same vein, the growing impact of practices and beliefs arising from the late-modern alternative scene does not make Santo Daime, per se, a new-age religion or human potential movement. In short, or at least as it applies to thematic classification, the contemporary *daimista* repertoire is more than the sum of its individual parts.

The hybridism, flexibility and variegation of its contemporary repertoire thereby militate against any neat typologization of the *daimista* world view. Roy Wallis' influential threefold typology of new religious movements, for example, struggles adequately to classify the contemporary *daimista* repertoire. Wallis' typology merges the formative typological insights of Max Weber (1965) with the later classifications offered by Bryan Wilson (1970) and J. Milton Yinger (1970). Drawing these contributions together, Wallis proposes a threefold analytical schema encapsulating the 'ways in which a new religious movement may orient itself to the social world into which it emerges'. Defining these three typological orientations as 'world-affirming', 'world-rejecting' and 'world-accommodating', Wallis maintains that

> a new movement may embrace the world, affirming its normatively approved goals and values; it may reject that world, denigrating those things held dear within it; or it may remain as far as possible indifferent to the world in terms of its religious practice, accommodating to it otherwise,

and exhibiting only mild acquiescence to, or disapprobation of, the ways of the world. (1984: 4)

According to Wallis, 'world-rejecting' religions are characterized by their espousal of end-world millenarian scenarios, sectarian divisions between those outwith or within a community of spiritual purity and a strong communitarian ethic of self-sacrifice and service to established hierarchies. More indifferent than antithetical to the world at large, 'world-affirming' repertoires do not oppose society as such but nor do they concern themselves with its correction or reformation. Instead, esoteric emphases of self-mastery and individual enlightenment are employed both to harness the self's inner potential and to optimize her ability to benefit more readily from the opportunities, goods and experiences which the everyday world presents. Whereas the world-rejecting type expects the prevailing order to be replaced by a future reality, the world-affirming movement emphasizes the here and now as a means through which individual potential is realized. In contrast to both of these types, the 'world-accommodating' new religion pays little heed to rejecting or engaging with the given social order. Stressing the need for personal renewal, world-accommodating movements focus upon the spiritual development of the individual which is undertaken in experientially oriented ritual regimes and evidenced through heightened subjective states of a deeply intimate but publicly expressive nature. As should now be evident, Santo Daime's hybrid repertoire embodies aspects of each of Wallis' three ideal types in a fashion which undermines the attribution of any single emphasis as the dominant mode of worldly orientation. Furthermore, it does so in a variegated manner such that different communities across the movement embody elements of world-rejecting, world-affirming and world-accommodating orientations in a variety of ways and to varying extents.

A coincidence of opposites

The hybrid, flexible and variegated character of Santo Daime gives it a paradoxical quality which further inhibits neat classification. Detailed in prior chapters, for example, the *daimista* repertoire marries strict collective dynamics with strongly subjectivized emphases. On the one hand, the corporate ritual regime is characterized by its preoccupations with spatio-temporal order and practical-symbolic discipline. These preoccupations combine to engender an 'anatomo-chronological schema of behaviour' (Foucault, 1991: 152) through which individual ritual participants are regimented and disciplined relative to the overarching demands of collective cultic practice. On the other, individual cultic participants are charged with effecting their own self-realization by harnessing and focusing deep-seated subjective energies. Though framed by corporate ritual dynamics, the individual serves as the primary agent and ultimate arbiter of the subjectively orchestrated processes involved in ego eradication and the concomitant emergence of the higher-self. Noted above, the ritual dynamics of autopoiesis posit the individual cultic practitioner (i.e. ritual prosumer) as producer (self-creator), product (self-realization) and process (self-consumption) rolled into one. The paradoxical interface of collective – individual dynamics is further characterized by ongoing developments in the *daimista* repertoire highlighted in preceding chapters. As noted, contemporary members drawn from the new middle class are no less respectful of and committed to the established rituals and beliefs of the traditional *daimista* world view than prior generations. The reverence of urban-professional *daimistas* for inherited beliefs and practices is, however, matched by a late-modern sense of self. Albeit mostly unintentional, the highly subjectivized and self-oriented nature of contemporary *daimistas* is nevertheless resulting in the gradual modification of key aspects of the established repertoire. Chapter 2, for example, identifies the reconfiguration of the private – public dynamics of the *daimista* ritual field, Chapter 3 notes the qualification of the institutional-communal regime of validation by increasingly mutual and individualized concerns and Chapter 4 delineates the expansion of expressive modes of spirit mediumship.

The paradoxical quality of Santo Daime is further evinced by its complementary union of ascetical application and mystical contemplation. The practical-symbolic demands of *daimista* asceticism are exemplified by aforementioned notions of 'discipline' and 'firmness'. On the one hand, these notions refer (*ad extra*) to the need for constant synchronicity between individual deportment and the practical-symbolic demands of collective ritual practice. On the other, they encapsulate (*ad intra*) the interiorized focus of continued self-scrutiny and engagement in respect of identifying and eradicating the ego-related defects which give rise to personality flaws and moral frailties. Demanding enough on their own, the ascetical labours involved in exterior correlation and interior vigilance are made all the more onerous by the psychophysical impact of the ritual consumption of Daime and, at times, other psychotropic substances. Embodied by notions of 'vision' (*miração*), 'self-awareness' and 'expanded consciousness', for example, the alternate states engendered by Daime consumption may also involve periods of mystical contemplation. Here, the labours of ascetical application give way to a clarity and insight characterized by emotional calm, physical relaxation and psychical serenity. Among other things, these periods comprise intense focus upon and heightened sensitivity to both material and immaterial phenomena, prolonged reflection upon feelings, thoughts and activity and a strong appreciation of the interconnectedness of all things coupled with an acute awareness of solidarity with one's ritual co-participants. The paradoxical union of ascesis and contemplation is catalysed by the growing popularity of certain forms of spirit mediumship treated at length in the preceding chapter. Whereas traditional modes of ritualized alterity are characterized by their *inter*-subjective orientations in respect of human and non-human others, contemporary forms of alterity involve predominantly *intra*-subjective preoccupations. Captured by the idiomatic spectrum, the contemporary *daimista* repertoire offers cultic participants a highly variegated range of possibilities through which ritualized alterity may be invoked, explored and expressed in both ascetical and contemplative modes.

The earlier discussion of the de-commoditizing processes of mystified consumption likewise underlines the paradoxical nature of the contemporary *daimista* world view. As detailed, the de-commoditization wrought by mystified consumption frames the appropriation of both worldly goods and the self as complementary sources of commodity value. In combination, the dynamics of commodicy and prosumption re-signify material and immaterial commodities in a way which renders them not only spiritually meaningful (and thereby readily consumable) but also cosmically significant (and thereby status-bearing). The this-worldly orientation orchestrated by mystified consumption is, however, accompanied by an articulate and, at times, forceful world-rejecting discourse. The unrelenting materialism of contemporary society and its acquisitive and avaricious character are recurrent themes employed by *daimista* narrations of the world at large. Treated in the Chapter 3, the world and its contents are categorized as worthless, illusory and passing away. At the same time, the countercultural status of Santo Daime is further reinforced through the employment of apolitical narratives of outright rejection of or cultured indifference to the values and practices of mainstream society. As argued, however, such world-rejecting narrations are best regarded as dislocutory speech acts which, though qualifying the things of this world, do not actually foreclose on their use or enjoyment. Members of the new middle-class, urban-professional *daimistas* are imbued with a commoditized subjectivity which, though refracted by it, is neither ultimately overwritten nor wholly negated by conversion to Santo Daime. Rather than being antithetical to the pursuit and appropriation of late-modern commodities, dislocutory narratives and their world-rejecting tenor are more fruitfully viewed as part and parcel of the de-commoditizing dynamics of mystified consumption and its religious re-signification of the things of this world. In true paradoxical style, world-rejecting discourse and a this-worldly disposition are two sides of the same *daimista* coin.

To ascribe paradoxicality to the *daimista* world view is not to label it incoherent, contrary, illogical or contradictory. Far from it. It is, though, a means of highlighting the *both/and* quality of Santo Daime implicated in its hybrid, flexible and variegated character. To appropriate a phrase from the medievals, the *daimista* repertoire embodies a 'coincidence of opposites' (*coincidentia oppositorum*) which articulates seemingly contrasting, if not apparently exclusive, elements in a manner conducive to their creative interplay. Building upon foundational components inherent to popular Amazonian religiosity, the paradoxical tendencies of Santo Daime have been radicalized at the hands of an urban-professional constituency drawn from the new middle class spawned by entangled late-modernity. Constituted by the interplay of aforementioned (e.g. self-oriented, instrumental, meritocratic-egalitarian) dynamics, the paradoxical nature of the contemporary *daimista* repertoire underwrites a typically late-modern religious aesthetic characterized by, among other things, its eclectic, adaptable and multifaceted features. Oriented to the pursuit of absolute self-realization, Santo Daime's religious aesthetic exhibits a marked preoccupation with the nurture and management of heightened subjective experiences of both an ordinary and non-standard kind. This preoccupation imbues the religious aesthetic with a range of exploratory, expressive and expectant tendencies which call upon a range of components, not least psychotropic substances (valorized as entheogens), associational interactions (serving as objective magnifiers of subjective exertions), countercultural rhetoric (framing an apolitics of identity), material and immaterial commodities (re-signified through mystified consumption) and the individual self (operationalized as autopoietic ritual prosumer). In combination with aforementioned elements, these features give Santo Daime a paradoxical quality which, in respect of its orientation to society at large, might best be understood as a kind of 'world-rejecting aestheticism'.

World-rejecting aestheticism

The notion of 'world-rejecting aestheticism' is a play on terms established by Weber's classic typology of religious orientations to the world at large. In a chapter on 'Asceticism, Mysticism, and Salvation Religion', Weber identifies a number of worldly orientations which religions instantiate in their dealings with their respective societal environments (1965: 166–83). While the typology is justifiably criticized for being overly stereotypical and homogenizing in its representation of particular religions, it has nevertheless furnished subsequent generations of academics (see Wallis above) with a useful analytical framework for explicating the nature and implications of the worldly orientations adopted by religious organizations and movements. Weber's typology of worldly orientations is founded upon two primary distinctions. First, Weber distinguishes between 'ascetical' and 'mystical' modes of religious belief and practice. Ascetical forms of religion embrace an activist approach to salvation as something believed, at least in large part, to be pursued through private exertions and collective regimes orchestrated by concerns with spiritual probity, physical discipline and moral rectitude. In contrast, mystical modes of religion regard salvation as something sought after through quiet and restful contemplation to be nurtured and sustained by 'the absolute minimization of all outer and inner activity' (1965: 169). Second, Weber distinguishes between 'inner-' and 'other-worldly' kinds of religious disposition. Whereas 'other-worldly' emphases regard salvation as something best pursued at a distance from worldly processes and dynamics, 'inner-worldly' approaches regard qualified engagement with or presence in the world as not necessarily injurious to an individual's salvific prospects. For inner-worldly religion, it is not so much location as attitude that counts. Bringing these two sets of distinctions together, Weber offers an analytical model representing what he sees as the four most typical world views by which religions orient the socio-cultural engagement and economic-political activity (or otherwise) of their members. These four types are: 'inner-worldly asceticism', 'inner-worldly mysticism', 'other-worldly asceticism' and 'other-worldly mysticism'.

Inner-worldly mysticism is, for Weber, characterized by an 'acceptance of the secular social structure' tinged with resignation, indifference and humility 'before it'. While minimizing involvement in worldly institutions, the inner-worldly mystic does not see his social environment as necessarily antithetical to the contemplative task. In its other-worldly (here 'world-fleeing') form, mysticism links contemplative success with an outright abandonment of the world at large. No longer mired in the daily machinations of the mundane, the world-fleeing mystic is free to pursue salvific illumination unhindered by societal affairs. Like its other-worldly mystical counterpart, 'world-rejecting asceticism' views 'a formal withdrawal' from the world and an associated divestiture of all 'creaturely interests' as an ideal means of pursuing salvation. Here, though, the salvific pursuit involves multifarious corporal disciplines and ritual regimes such as those perfected by the monastic communities of both Eastern and Western traditions. In contrast, inner-worldly asceticism regards the religious presence in society as a 'vocation' (calling) through which individual application, the meeting of corporate obligations and resistance to worldly 'temptations' are seen as 'pleasing to god' and thereby a means to the 'grace' necessary for salvation. In the world but not of it, inner-worldly asceticism engages the things of this world with a self-discipline and sobriety that rejects emotional 'excess', 'sensual indulgence' and 'reliance upon natural joys and gifts'.

As foregoing discussions indicate, the paradoxical quality of Santo Daime problematizes its neat classification. Weber's fourfold typology, however, offers a useful foil for an attempt to capture the worldly orientation of the *daimista* repertoire in a manner which does justice to its paradoxical character. Describing the *daimista* world view as a form of 'world-rejecting aestheticism' is one such attempt. Noted at various points in preceding discussions, Santo Daime has a well-established discourse of world rejection. Although the spread and growth of the movement involves the increasing presence of gathered rather than alternative communities, Santo Daime's progressive congregationalization has not diminished its countercultural ethos and attendant world-rejecting narratives. Indeed, the discourse of world rejection may well be vitalized by the desire of contemporary *daimistas* both to identify with the idealized alternative lifestyles of foundational generations and to differentiate themselves from those (both *in* and *of* the world) among whom they live. Framing an apolitics of self-transformation (see Chapter 3), world-rejecting narratives continue to be an important symbolic component informing the countercultural identity of the contemporary *daimista* movement.

Upon describing 'world-rejecting asceticism' (on which the notion of world-rejecting aestheticism plays), Weber maintains that it is 'psychologically felt' as a 'negative' attitude of 'opposition to the world' and 'struggle against it'. Repudiating society at large, the world-rejecting ascetic nevertheless defines herself through 'an inner psychological relationship with it' (1965: 169). At least psychologically, the ascetic's rejection of the world is a paradoxical one. As well as precluding its designation as a form of world-rejecting asceticism, the replacement of 'asceticism' with 'aestheticism' is intended to explicate the paradoxical character of Santo Daime's world-rejecting orientation. In contrast to the world-rejecting ascetic, the rejection of the world articulated by the average *daimista* is by far more felt than it is actually realized. Drawn from the new middle class spawned by entangled late-modernity, urban-professional *daimistas* are imbued with a strongly aestheticized and commoditized subjectivity. In so being, the late-modern subjectivity of Santo Daime's urban middle-class membership associates the pursuit of absolute self-realization with experiential and expressive preoccupations reliant, among other things, upon the appropriation of material and immaterial commodities (re-signified through mystified consumption). Noted in prior discussions, the world-rejecting discourse employed by *daimistas* might thereby justifiably be regarded as a dislocutory speech act which qualifies (de-commoditizes) but does not ultimately foreclose on the use and enjoyment of the things of this world. Like the world-rejecting ascetic, the repudiation of mainstream society articulated by *daimista* counterculturalism is 'psychologically felt' as a genuine and heartfelt 'opposition to' and 'struggle against' the world at large. As such, it is constitutive of Santo Daime's religious world view and an integral component of *daimista* belief and practice as an apolitics of identity. Unlike world-rejecting asceticism, though, Santo Daime's repudiation of society at large involves for its urban-professional membership neither 'a formal withdrawal from the "world"' nor the outright denial of 'all creaturely interests' (1965: 166). The world-rejecting discourse of Santo Daime thereby retains an inherently this-worldly quality.

The this-worldly character of *daimista* world-rejecting narratives is not, however, identical with the 'inner-worldly' orientation identified by Weber. While sharing with inner-worldly mysticism an 'indifferent' attitude to societal affairs, the *daimista* world view is far from accepting, 'resigned' or 'humble' in respect of the 'secular social structure'. In the same vein, and although having a common concern with being in the world but not of it, Santo Daime differs from inner-worldly asceticism in two key respects. First, the *daimista* world view offers no theological rationalization of worldly engagement such as that furnished by the Protestant concept of 'vocation'. Second, the aestheticized character of urban-professional *daimistas* balks at the inner-worldly ascetic's 'rationally controlled patterning of life', refusal of 'natural joys and gifts' and 'avoidance of all surrender to . . . one's own moods and emotions' (1965: 173, 183). Exemplified by its use of psychotropics, the aestheticized repertoire of Santo Daime is worlds apart from the ritual regimes of inner-worldly asceticism. Although sharing certain aspects with the inner-worldly orientation in both its mystical and ascetical forms, the *daimista* world view sits comfortably with neither.

As an apolitics of self-transformation, the contemporary *daimista* repertoire combines, albeit paradoxically, a world-rejecting demeanour with an aestheticized this-worldly ethos. On the one, its world-rejecting discourse articulates a countercultural apolitics which valorizes the inner self and its ritual transformation over the public realm and active participation within it. On the other, its aestheticized subjectivity embodies a this-worldly orientation which (by way of mystified consumption) links self-transformation with the pursuit and appropriation of material and immaterial commodities. In so doing, Santo Daime's world-rejecting aestheticism couples a heartfelt symbolic denial of the world with the concerted enjoyment of its contents. In keeping with its paradoxical character, world-rejecting aestheticism fuses concerns of an other-worldly nature with preoccupations of a this-worldly bent. By no means the only reason for its spread across entangled Western late-modernity, the world-rejecting aestheticism of Santo Daime nevertheless speaks to its urban-professional membership in a manner both resonant with and conducive to its characteristic combination of this-worldly, self-transformative concerns and apolitical, countercultural demeanour.

Postscript

A new and exotic arrival to entangled, Western late-modernity, Santo Daime is doubly pathologized. First, and coupled with its unfamiliar ritual regime and hybrid religious world view, the sacramental status of ayahuasca (with its active ingredient, DMT) makes Santo Daime an object of bemusement and suspicion on the part of public opinion and state authorities alike. Articles in two of Britain's largest mainstream newspapers, for example, go some way both to capturing and reinforcing the mixture of perplexity and mistrust with which Santo Daime is commonly greeted by those initially hearing of or coming across this, now international, new religion. Although neither article is intentionally hostile to Santo Daime, the presentation and content of each does little, if anything, to frame matters in a manner conducive to reasoned reflection on the part of its readers. Published in November 2005, an article in *The Telegraph* opens with the headline 'Now let us hallucinate', while a piece in *The Times* (April 2008) is framed by the headline 'Santo Daime: the drug-fuelled religion'.[1] Among the words reproduced in respect of Santo Daime, those of 'bonkers', 'insanity', 'bizarre', 'exotic drugs rituals', 'the ultimate religious high', 'people getting off their heads', 'hallucinogenic Class A drug' and 'trafficking' stand to the fore. Inevitably, the alarmist term 'cult' is mobilized, with Santo Daime's concern with ritual order and discipline described as 'very controlling'. Both articles note the traditional practice of wetting a newborn's lips with Daime, while mention is also made of birthing mother's consuming small doses of the sacrament. In the same vein, *The Times* article in its newspaper format is accompanied by a large photograph showing a child in *Céu do Mapiá* taking a glass of Daime at the point of ritual despatch. Irrespective of content, the correlation of image and headline speak volumes.

As well as sensationalizing Santo Daime, each of these articles conveys, more or less implicitly, the message that *daimista* belief and practice is not for the ordinary (i.e. 'normal') man in the street; let alone, his pregnant wife and child. Indeed, a number of informants subjected to police operations against Santo Daime recount this attitude as typical of the officers and state officials involved in the initial execution of search and arrest warrants. The same informants also maintain, however, that the perplexity and suspicion demonstrated by state operatives is very quickly dispelled subsequent to investigation of and engagement with Santo Daime and its followers. For example, a European community leader arrested and convicted of 'possession of a controlled drug' (i.e. DMT) 'for the purpose of selling or otherwise supplying it to another' told me how the specialist drug enforcement officers involved in the initial arrest soon became openly 'apologetic' when realizing that they were not dealing with the kind of felon and associated criminal activity with which they are usually occupied. Whereas this purported change of attitude did not prevent my informant's eventual criminalization, recent decisions to legalize Santo Daime in Holland and the US state of Oregon are viewed by *daimistas* as signs of hope that, irrespective of what bemusement and mistrust remains, their religious beliefs and practices will ultimately enjoy judicial protection in all parts of the world.

The second act of pathologization comes indirectly at the hands of social-theoretical critiques of non-mainstream religious repertoires exhibiting the kind of self-oriented, aestheticized, this-worldly and apolitical characteristics treated in prior chapters as typical of the contemporary *daimista* world view. Viewed as symptoms of the overarching failings of late-modern society (e.g. individualism, materialism and political privatism), the repertorial dynamics of alternative religious world views are dismissed as exacerbating an already sorry state of affairs. Lasch, for example, links the individualization of late-modern society with a 'revival of ancient superstitions, a belief in reincarnation, a growing fascination with the occult, and the bizarre forms of spirituality associated with the New Age movement' (1979: 245). Symptomatic of the 'disintegration of public life' wrought by late-modern individualism, he argues, the 'new therapeutic sensibility' of alternative repertoires reflects a 'contemporary narcissism' comprising an 'intense preoccupation of the self' underwritten by 'the ideology of personal growth' (1979: 25, 31, 51). Beck and Beck-Gernsheim likewise link late-modern processes of individualization with the emergence of what they call 'the market for the answer factories, the psycho-boom, the advice literature'. Disoriented by the 'erosion' of established patterns of collective support, the now disembedded and 'overtaxed individual' looks to escape his late-modern fate through a 'flight into magic, myth, metaphysics' composed of 'that mixture of the esoteric cult, the primal scream, mysticism, yoga and Freud which is supposed to drown out the tyranny of possibilities but in fact reinforces it with its changing fashions' (2002: 7). Writing nearly a decade later, Beck couples his earlier critique of alternative religious subjectivism with a rejection of its materialist pandering to the individualized predilections of late-modern commoditized subjectivity. Here, Beck dismisses 'esoteric or New Age offerings' which embody 'a kind of masochistic self-interest that satisfies its religious needs in the wellness offerings of the religious-esoteric world-consumer society in a manner that at once condemns and confirms that society' (2010: 153).

Bauman is also critical of 'postmodern' ritual repertoires which he regards as catering for 'the orgasmic experience of . . . sensation-gatherers' and their 'search for "peak-experiences"'. Such is the self-oriented nature of these alternative repertoires that Bauman questions their legitimate consideration as 'essentially religious' (1998: 70–2). As part of his later indictment of consumer society's 'subjectivity fetishism' (2007: 14), Bauman criticises the 'self-referential' and 'inward-looking' agendas peddled by 'certified and/ or self-proclaimed' purveyors of 'self-discovery' who 'guide us into the dark dungeons of our souls where our authentic selves are supposed to stay imprisoned and from where they are struggling to escape into the light'. Impacted by the subjectivizing dynamics of late-modern individualization, he maintains,

> We seem to have little choice but to look for a hint as to how to wander deeper and deeper into the 'inside' of ourselves . . . I look for the 'real me' which I suppose to be hidden somewhere in the obscurity of my *pristine* self, unaffected (unpolluted, unstifled, undeformed) by outside pressures. I unpack the ideal of 'individuality' as *authenticity*, as 'being true to myself', being the 'real me'. (2005: 17)

For Bauman, the subjectivized discourse of 'self-reforming selves' both mediates and reinforces what he sees as the corrosive civic effects of late-modern individualization (2000: 11). The interiorized preoccupations and apolitical ethos of alternative repertoires not only embody a 'culture of disengagement' but also rationalize on spiritual grounds the 'political apathy . . . ignorance and indifference' by which it is accompanied (2005: 62, 126). As such, the apolitics of self-transformation articulated by non-mainstream world views constitutes the 'citizen's worst enemy' through its refusal to acknowledge 'society' and its institutions as 'simultaneously' the 'cradle' and 'destination' of individual well-being (2000: 37; 2005: 18).

The double pathologization to which Santo Daime is subjected arises from the application of normative expectations in respect of what religion should look like and what it should do. With regard to non-academic opinion, the first act of pathologization arises from Santo Daime's unfavourable comparison with mainstream religion (not least Christianity) which furnishes the normative template by which public opinion and state authority are guided. Whereas Santo Daime has many of the same features as its traditional and mainstream counterparts, its ritual repertoire also has elements which are strikingly, and for some alarmingly, different. Santo Daime is thereby perceived as an aberration from the standard model. The second act of pathologization exemplified by aforementioned academic critiques is grounded ultimately in functional understandings of religion which define their object relative to a range of particular societal tasks which bona fide belief and ritual practice are expected to undertake. A long-standing academic of new religiosity, Wilson embodies this approach by arguing that the eclecticism and subjectivized character of 'new cults' 'reduces religion to the significance of pushpin, poetry, or popcorns', thereby making them 'inconsequential for modern society'. Engaging religion through the typically functionalist trope of societal integration, Wilson rejects the significance of 'new cults' because 'they add nothing to any prospective reintegration of society and contribute nothing towards the culture by which a society might live' (1979: 96). Beck's earlier dismissal of alternative religious paradigms likewise reflects a functional understanding of religion as 'a particular mode of experience with which to establish social ties, networks and biographies that transcend national and ethnic boundaries' (Beck, 2010: 189). On both counts, Santo Daime is pathologized because it fails to meet a range of pre-given, normative expectations in respect of what religion should look like (modelled on traditional, mainstream paradigms) and what it should do (as a form of social integration or civic enhancement).

In contrast to aforementioned social-theoretical critiques of alternative religious repertoires, the approach employed throughout preceding chapters is informed by what is popularly termed 'methodological atheism' (Berger, 1967: 180) in the sociology of religion or 'methodological agnosticism' (Smart, 1973: 54) in religious studies. As such, the foregoing treatment of Santo Daime both avoids evaluating the *daimista* world view as either true or false and refuses to adjudge whether it instantiates a form of religion which is good or bad for society at large. However, if the approach taken helps dispel the bewilderment and suspicion exhibited by public opinion or political authority in respect of Santo Daime, so much the better. Likewise, if it qualifies the often uninformed and one-dimensional treatment of alternative religious paradigms at the hands of mainstream social theorists, this is something to the good. Though welcomed, such outcomes are nevertheless not primarily intended by what has gone before. After all, this book is not an apology (in the classical sense of *apologia*) for Santo Daime. Indeed, there are many *daimistas* who will balk at the portrayal of 'the doctrine' by preceding discussions, seeing them as doing more harm than good. Rather, Santo Daime has been engaged with a view to understanding its beliefs and practices against the overarching backdrop furnished by the interface between contemporary modes of religion and late-modern, urban-industrial society.

To this end, a number of typically late-modern dynamics have been identified as impacting upon the contemporary *daimista* repertoire and incrementally transforming the traditional beliefs and practices bequeathed by the foundational communities of the Amazon region. Among the late-modern dynamics identified, those of individualization, pluralization, rapid and large-scale transformation, globalization and commoditization stand to the fore. Prior discussions also argue that these dynamics impact upon Santo Daime as they are refracted through a now dominant urban-professional constituency, the overwhelming majority of which hails from the new middle class of entangled, Western late-modernity. Combined with already established components and emergent processes related with the movement's ongoing expansion, the refraction of typically late-modern dynamics through urban middle-class members engenders a number of orchestrating principles by which the contemporary *daimista* repertoire is characterized. Noted throughout prior discussions, the six most important of these repertorial characteristics are: the *subjectivized* valorization of the individual as the ultimate arbiter of religious authority and the primary agent of spiritual self-transformation; an *instrumental* (i.e. strategic and reflexive) religiosity oriented to the goal of absolute self-realization; a *holistic* world view which connaturally grounds the individual self in an overarching cosmic whole and relativizes belief systems as contingent expressions of otherwise universal truths; an *aestheticized* demeanour characterized by strong experiential preoccupations manifest through inward self-exploration and outer self-expression; a *meritocratic-egalitarianism* which is both expectant of rewards for efforts expended and qualifies traditional hierarchical structures; and a *this-worldly* ethos which looks for the benefits of spiritual transformation as much in the here and now of this life as in the there and then of any future incarnation.

Paralleling the organizational diversification wrought by Santo Daime's progressive internationalization, these orchestrating principles combine to produce an increasingly hybrid, flexible and variegated repertoire populated by polysemic and mobile selves forged, among other things, through bricolage and transit (see Chapter 1). While traditional preoccupations with spatio-temporal order and practical-symbolic regulation remain in force, the chief characteristics of the contemporary *daimista* repertoire constitute it as a dynamic ritual field driven as much by the competitive pursuit of private and public benefits as by inherited modes of collective regimentation (see Chapter 2). Pursuit of the private and public goods distributed through the ritual field of force comprises an apolitics of self-transformation which has superseded the more traditional apolitics of social transformation informed by popular Brazilian millenarianism. Exemplifying the shift from a chiefly communitarian to a principally subjectivized emphasis, the now dominant apolitics of self-transformation complements the established institutional-communal regime of validation with increasingly mutual and self-oriented concerns (see Chapter 3). This shift in emphasis is treated in Chapter 4 in relation to particular forms of spirit-oriented practice, the growing popularity of which furnishes a vehicle for the incremental modification of the established *daimista* repertoire. Embodying novel modes of expressivity and alterity, contemporary forms of spirit mediumship render inherited beliefs and practices more conducive to meeting the experiential, exploratory and expectant preoccupations of Santo Daime's urban-professional membership. The urban-professional profile of the contemporary *daimista* movement is explicated in Chapter 5 as deriving from a new middle-class identity which is intimately associated with entangled, Western late-modernity. Developing the notion of dislocutory speech act introduced in Chapter 3, the contemporary *daimista* repertoire is engaged as a de-commoditizing context of religious consumption which orients the self and its relations with society at large by means of a typically paradoxical world-rejecting aestheticism.

Exemplified by the foregoing treatment of Santo Daime, the late-modern processes of individualization and subjectivization do not necessarily entail the end of collective forms of religious association. They do, though, involve the recalibration of established modes of participation and belonging in a way which relativizes corporate dynamics through their subordination to the subjectivized needs and aspirations of the late-modern individual. Likewise, the detraditionalizing processes associated with the rapid and large-scale transformation effected by late-modernity do not automatically negate the contemporary valorization of inherited belief and ritual practice. They do, however, involve the reconfiguration of tradition as established symbols and practices are interpreted and enacted by subjectivized selves within ever more hybrid, flexible and variegated religious repertoires. In the same vein, the radical pluralization of society and ensuing socio-cultural relativization need not engender disorientation and crisis on the part of the late-modern subject in search of religious meaning. Indeed, they may well contribute towards the formation of mobile, confident and expectant selves who thrive religiously on the contemporary coincidence of enhanced optionality in both its objective (i.e. what, where and how) and subjective (why and by whom) dimensions. Finally, the commoditization of consciousness wrought by commodity capitalism and late-modern culture industries equates neither with rampant materialism nor the total eclipse of the sacred. It does, though, involve the practical-symbolic transformation of the self and its worldly relations in a way which infuses religious belief and behaviour with commoditized sensibilities through which the spiritual quest is unavoidably refracted. Irreducible to processes and dynamics such as these, the new world religion of Santo Daime is nevertheless shaped by and imbued with them. As with other new religious phenomena, that Santo Daime is influenced by the typically late-modern forces treated in preceding chapters diminishes neither its legitimacy nor spiritual significance relative to mainstream religious paradigms where these processes and dynamics may well be more attenuated (but on the rise) or less apparent (but just as real).

Orchestrated by an urban-professional majority and fully integrated within the alternative religious scene, Santo Daime is now as much a religion of entangled, Western late-modernity as it is of the Amazon region in which it was originally conceived. Does this make the contemporary *daimista* movement any less spiritually authentic or religiously meaningful than the traditional repertoire of its mixed-race Amazonian founders? No it does not. Indeed, the ongoing transformation of *daimista* belief and practice is very much in keeping with both the formative historical developments under Master Irineu and the subsequent modifications wrought by Padrinho Sebastião and the early Cefluris community. Inevitably involving changes and additions to inherited belief and practice, the hybridism, flexibility and progressive variegation of the contemporary *daimista* repertoire nevertheless embody a religious ethos much in tune with what has gone before.

Notes

Introduction

1 Cefluris stands for the 'Raimundo Irineu Serra Eclectic Centre of the Universal Flowing Light' (*Centro Eclético da Fluente Luz Universal Raimundo Irineu Serra*). Following convention, Cefluris and other Brazilian acronyms are reproduced in lower-case text.

Chapter 1

1 Of a relatively mild character, the psychoactive effects of *Banisteriopsis caapi* are caused by the three beta-carboline alkaloids, harmine, harmoline and tetrahydroharmine (Callaway, 2005).

2 The human enzyme monoamine oxidase (MAO) normally renders the DMT contained in *Psychotria viridis* physiologically ineffective to oral ingestion. The MAO-inhibiting properties of *Banisteriopsis caapi*, however, disrupt this process and thereby enable the body's chemical absorption of DMT. As a result, the psychoactive effect of the ayahuasca brew is intensified (McKenna et al., 1984).

3 Other accounts include an eagle perching on Clara and her gift of an orange (symbolizing the world) to Irineu Serra (see Goulart, 2004: 29–36; MacRae, 1992: 62–4).

4 I'm indebted to Matthew Meyer for some of this information.

5 Both studies identify the native culture of the Tupi-Guarani as the most influential source of indigenous elements embodied by the respective beliefs and practices they examine (Galvão, 1955: 8; Maués and Villacorta, 2004: 25)

6 For example, the Rio Branco community founded by Irineu Serra and today led by his widow Peregrina Gomes Serra rejects spirit possession as a legitimate form of *daimista* ritual practice and comprises a relatively affluent congregation drawn from the city's (mainly white) professional and upper classes.

7 Santo Daime's founding community is known today as Ciclu-Alto Santo. Ciclu (*O Centro de Iluminação Cristã Luz Universal*) signifies 'The Universal Light Christian Illumination Centre' and 'Alto Santo' (literally, Holy Height) was the name subsequently given to the centre's location in the neighbourhood of Custódio Freire, a borough of modern-day Rio Branco (Gregorim, 1991: 65–7).

8 Despite widespread speculation (reviewed by Goulart, 2004: 61–2), the meaning of the term 'Juramidam' (sometimes rendered *Juramidá*) has never been fully clarified. Along with others, MacRae suggests that the term may mean 'followers' or 'soldiers' (*midam*) of 'God' (*Jura*) or refer to Christ as the 'son' (*midam*) of the 'Father' (*Jura*) (1992: 67–70). Certainly, by the time of his death, Irineu Serra was closely associated with, if not viewed as the reincarnation of, Jesus Christ; with many *daimistas* today regarding the term 'Juramidam' as synonymous with Master Irineu, while the members of Santo Daime are the 'family' or 'people' of Juramidam.

9 The most significant of these key personnel were Germano Guilherme, Antônio Gomes, João Pereira and Maria Damião. The collection of hymns received by these individuals is known as the 'Hymnal of the Dead' (*Hinário dos Mortos*) (Gregorim, 1991: 70). The hymnal is sung at the festivals of Holy Week and All Souls, and is part of the official calendar of all of the most important branches of Santo Daime.

10 Perhaps indicative of his earlier exposure to popular esoteric sources, Irineu Serra adopted the twin-beamed Cross of Caravaca as Santo Daime's most explicit Christian symbol. Associated in popular Catholicism with the cult of Saint Helen, the Cross of Caravaca takes its basic form from the Christian cross but adds a short horizontal beam that runs parallel above the original, and longer, crossbeam. Known in Santo Daime as 'the cruzeiro', the two-sparred cross is said to represent both Jesus Christ (via the original crossbeam) and Master Irineu (by way of the second crossbeam which runs above the original).

11 Mota de Melo was also very much influenced by the mystical esoteric writings of Jorge Adoum (1897–1958), not least his work 'I am' (*Eu Sou*).

12 Two related points are here worthy of note. First, the initial interest of the 'southerners' in Santo Daime represented part of their broader quest to explore the psychedelic experiences engendered by the ingestion of psychoactive 'power plants' (*plantas de poder*) such as ayahuasca, the peyote cactus, the fly agaric mushroom and the cannabis leaf popularized by the writings of, for example, Castaneda (1968), Harner (1972) and Leary (1968). On account of its relative scarcity, ayahuasca was regarded as one of the more desirable power plants and was sought out by Mortimer and his companions as part of a subjectively oriented search for new and more exotic experiences. Second, Mota de Melo's openness to adopting cannabis as a sacrament alongside that of Daime is best viewed against a wider cultural backdrop of popular religious practices in which 'sacred plants' (and the spirits to which they give access) have played a staple role. At the same time, Mota de Melo was both unaffected by the social stigma connected with cannabis at play across urban-industrial contexts and committed to the ritual consumption of a plant already prone to persecution.

13 Umbanda is sometimes referred to as 'southern Umbanda' (*Umbanda do sul*) to distinguish it from more diffuse forms of popular Afro-Amazonian religiosity likewise termed 'umbanda' which existed in the north of Brazil prior to the arrival and progressive dominance of their southern cousin from the 1960s onwards (see Furuya, 1994).

14 Although not universally applied, it is Cefluris custom to include the term 'Heaven' (*Céu*) within the name of those communities officially designated a 'church' (*igreja*). This usage reflects the millenarian influences examined in Chapter 3.

15 T. K. Schmidt (2007) offers a detailed ethnography of Mapiá informed by over a year's worth of fieldwork (the bulk of which was carried out in 1999), while Goulart (2004), Groisman (1999) and Arruda et al. (2006) furnish briefer descriptions. A. Dawson (2010) reflects upon some of the methodological implications of participant observation subsequent to time spent at Mapiá in 2007.

16 The continuing importance of Umbanda is, among other things, reflected in contemporary representations of the supernatural entity originally introduced to Master Irineu as Clara who is now commonly portrayed in Cefluris communities as the Umbanda spirit Iemanjá (also rendered Yemanjá). Originally a goddess (*orixá*) of the Afro-Brazilian religion of Candomblé, Iemanjá was appropriated by Umbanda as a spirit-guide who now has considerable significance for the movement. As with many of the deities of Candomblé, Iemanjá has a hybrid identity forged from the syncretism of African elements (e.g. goddess of the sea) and Catholic components (e.g. Our Lady of Seafarers) (Voeks, 1997). Reflecting this hybrid identity, contemporary *daimista* portrayals of the Virgin Mary/Iemanjá show a brown-skinned and often sensuous female form with long, dark hair topped by a crown, arms outstretched in welcome and wearing a long, flowing blue dress backlit by the moon.

17 Of these founding communities, only *Flor das Águas* no longer exists. Former members of this community, however, subsequently went on to found the influential churches of *Céu de Maria* (Heaven of Mary) and *Céu da Nova Era* (Heaven of the New Age) in the state of São Paulo.

18 Although in existence for more than a decade, the acronym Iceflu is rarely used outside of official documentation. Most members and, indeed, a not insignificant tranche of official materials continue to use Cefluris in reference to the movement headed by Padrinhos Alfredo and Alex.

19 In the same vein, the continuing vulnerability of *daimista* communities to state action both within and outwith Brazil furnishes a strong motive for groups to remain officially allied with Cefluris and thereby enjoy the protective umbrella of its formal institutional auspices.

20 The date of the Argentinian ritual was acquired through www.bialabate.net, the Spanish date was obtained from López-Pavillard (2008: 74), the Belgian date from personal correspondence with Marc Blainey (December 2011) and the date of the first Santo Daime ritual in the United States was given in interview (29 March 2010) by Jonathan Goldman, leader of the 'Church of the Holy Light of the Queen' in Ashland, Oregon.

21 The clandestine character of much Santo Daime practice outside of Brazil makes the size of the international membership of Cefluris extremely hard to judge. Whereas group numbers in less well-established contexts may be counted on one hand, aggregate numbers in countries where Santo Daime has been present for some time or is less prone to police action run into the hundreds. By way of a rough guesstimate, I suspect regular world-wide participation in Cefluris rituals outside of Brazil to involve between 4,000 and 6,000 people.

Chapter 2

1 Outside of Brazil, those charged with maintaining ceremonial order are, among other things, called 'guardians' or 'helpers'.

2 Although of a more general and abstract kind, Catherine Bell's treatment of ritual theory and practice likewise uses Foucault (and Bourdieu). Exemplified by her view that the efficacy of ritual power relies upon 'misrecognition' by those subjected to it, like Foucault (and, to a lesser extent, Bourdieu), Bell underestimates the active role of subjective agency in constituting ritual as an efficacious event (1992).

3 The hexagonal orientation and star-shaped table are modifications to *daimista* ritual space made subsequent to the break with Alto Santo.

4 Indicative of popular religious roots influenced by indigenous belief systems, and around before the later introduction of the guitar, the maraca has been used to keep time during hymn singing since the very beginnings of Santo Daime. Again reflective of popular religious influences, the maraca is idealized as a spiritual weapon employed in the battle between good and evil (see Chapter 3). Unlike musical instruments which may be played only by those licensed to be at or near the central table, the maraca may be used in all parts of the ranks.

5 Reflecting the influence of traditional millenarianism (see Chapter 3), the Circle of Regeneration and Faith (CRF) to which Irineu Serra belonged before founding Santo Daime employed military themes along with ranks stretching from private to marshal. Although military-style ranks were subsequently introduced to Santo Daime, they were later abandoned on account of the antagonism and discord they generated (Silva, 1983).

6 I'm indebted to Matthew Meyer for the latter point regarding height.

7 The ability to fulfil the official ritual calendar is the key criterion informing the classificatory distinction between a 'point' (from 'point of light') and a 'church'.

8 The term *hinário* refers both to a particular kind of ritual and to specific collections of hymns. This is potentially confusing as some *hinário* rituals may involve singing from more than one collection of hymns. To distinguish the ritual from the collection, I use the capitalized 'Hymnal' to designate the actual ceremony and the lower-cased 'hymnal' to refer to a collection of hymns.

9 The proximity of Padrinho Sebastião's death (20 January 1990) to the Feast of Saint Sebastian (19 January) entails the celebration of his passing at the Hymnal originally scheduled for this Saint's Day.

10 The term 'entheogen' was coined in the late 1970s and initially referred to psychoactive plants (e.g. ayahuasca, fly agaric mushroom, San Pedro cactus) ritually employed to stimulate spiritual or mystical experiences (Ruck et al., 1979). Literally meaning 'engendering the god within', the term 'entheogen' is now applied to a wide variety of psychotropic agents of both natural and pharmaceutical origin.

11 *Daimistas* usually concur when I describe Daime as also tasting somewhat foul. Indeed, and although frowned upon by traditionalists within the

movement, an increasingly common practice is the sucking on a sweet immediately after swallowing a dose of Daime.

12 Numerous accounts of the individual experiences provoked by the ritual consumption of ayahuasca are available through a variety of media, not least the internet. Combining personal experimentation, fieldwork and insights from cognitive psychology, Shanon's book *The Antipodes of the Mind* remains the most critically informed treatment of 'the ayahuasca experience' in the Brazilian context (2002).

13 The remaining types do not readily apply to *daimista* activity in Holland where the legal status of cannabis engenders a different socio-cultural dynamic and thereby less guarded approach than that prevailing in other contexts.

14 Aware of the accusations made by dos Lakatos (2007) about the presence of hard drugs (e.g. cocaine and heroin) within Cefluris, I can only say that I have neither witnessed nor heard mention of their use by *daimistas* and, indeed, would be extremely surprised if such accusations proved to be true.

15 Along with many of its non-official (but still highly influential) hymnals, all of Santo Daime's official hymnals (i.e. those sung at the 19 Hymnal rituals scheduled by the official calendar) are available at www.nossairmandade. com and www.Daime.org.

16 The female equivalent of Padrinho, Madrinha means 'godmother'.

17 Including short treatments of the Alto Santo and Cefluris communities, Labate and Pacheco (2010) provide a useful overview of some important features of Brazilian ayahuasca music.

18 The march (4/4 time), waltz (3/4 time) and mazurka (3/4 time, with the second or third beat accentuated) provide the respective rhythms of the three dance steps used in the danced Hymnal (*bailado*).

19 See, for example, hymns 108 (re. Santa Maria) and 131 (re. Ogum Beira Mar) of Padrinho Alfredo's *The Little Key*. Within the same hymnal, hymn 28 celebrates the 'Mushroom King' (*Cogo-Rei*). The hymnals of Padrinho Alex Polari (*Nova Anunciação* – 'New Announcement'), his wife Sônia Palhares (*Firmado na Luz* – 'Grounded in the Light') and Alfredo's brother Padrinho Valdete (*O Livrinho do Apocalipse* – 'The Little Book of the Apocalypse') are among the most popular non-official hymnals. The hymnal *O Chaveirinho* ('The Little Locksmith') by Padrinho Glauco Villas Boas – close friend of Padrinho Alfredo and leader of *Céu de Maria* until his untimely death in March 2010 – both celebrates and was received under the influence of Santa Maria.

20 Texts (including English translations) of the principal liturgical components of Santo Daime rituals are available at www.nossairmandade.com.

21 Dietary (e.g. alcohol and certain kinds of meat) and sexual (i.e. sex and menstruation) restrictions up to three days before and after ritual activity were established practices within aforementioned *vegetalista* traditions (Luna, 1986). Traditional strictures relating to dietary and sexual abstinence before and after ritual activity are, however, being progressively eroded as Santo Daime expands beyond the Amazon region. The vast majority of those encountered during fieldwork made little or no mention of sexual

abstinence and regarded traditional dietary restrictions not so much as ritual obligations but as useful words of advice intended to lessen the bodily discomforts associated with Daime consumption.

22 The practical regulation of movement within and between ritual spheres has doctrinal and pastoral motives. In addition to the doctrinal motives outlined in this section, the pastoral reasons for managing individual transit during ritual activity relate most immediately to personal well-being. Daime is a psychoactive substance which impacts psychophysical functions in a variety of ways and to varying extents depending on the modes of its consumption and the physical and mental health of the individual. While the pre-ritual screening of initiates varies in content and quality across the movement, during actual ritual practice those responsible for managing ceremonial activity pay considerable attention to those in their charge.

23 The manner in and zeal with which inspectors undertake their roles vary from community to community and person to person. During danced Hymnal rituals (*bailados*), for example, my hands had a tendency to swell up some hours into the ceremony. To alleviate both the swelling and pain caused by the stretching of the skin, I would ask permission to leave inner ritual space for the liminal area where, before returning to my place, I would run cold water over my hands until my conditions began to ease. Within the overwhelming majority of communities where this happened, I was granted permission to leave the ranks and take the time needed to cool my hands down; while in others, I was allowed to leave ritual space but close attention was paid to the time I was absent from the ranks. Within one community, however, an inspector refused my request to leave inner ritual space and, instead, brought in a bucket of water in which I cooled my hands while squatting on the edge of the ceremonial arena at the back of my section.

24 Communities differ as to the amount or character of the ritual participation required before a neophyte is allowed to assume the uniform and thereby be classed as a member. Prior to becoming a member, the non-uniformed are asked to wear white or lightly coloured clothing and avoid sporting 'hot' colours such as red.

25 An English-language description of the white and blue uniforms, accompanied by a drawing of the female uniform, is available at www.santoDaime.org/admin/novidades/oficios_fardas_i.htm.

26 Such is the cultural capital associated with those from Mapiá (*mapienses*) that most of the larger communities in Brazil finance the presence of one or more *mapienses*. Occupying prestigious positions at ritual events, *mapienses* with the strongest association with Padrinho Sebastião and his family are the most revered.

Chapter 3

1 Although the terms 'millenarianism' and 'millennialism' are more often than not used interchangeably, the latter word is closely associated with prophecies inspired by scriptural references from Jewish and Christian traditions (see Robbins and Palmer, 1997: 9–10).

2 Exemplified by the periodic, pre-conquest migrations to the coast by Tupi-Guarani tribes in search of the *Land without evil*, millenarian preoccupations existed prior to the arrival of Portuguese settlers and the subsequent spread of Luso-Catholic versions of the millenarian paradigm (Ribeiro, 1992: 71). Later manifestations of millenarianism among indigenous peoples tended to reflect the influences of the Luso-Catholic paradigm, the *santidades* (holy ones) of the early colonial period being a classic example; as are the millenarian outbreaks among the Baniwa, Canela and Krahó peoples in the late nineteenth and early twentieth centuries. Oro's treatment of the 'Brotherhood of the Holy Cross' (*Irmandade da Santa Cruz*) which emerged in the state of Amazonas in 1972 offers a more recent example (1989).

3 Allowing for the fact that the greater number of popular Catholic millenarian movements have been lost to history, the most famous recorded examples are generally identified as: the movement led by Silvestre José dos Santos between 1817 and 1820 which founded the 'City of Earthly Paradise' in the Rodeador mountains in the north-east state of Pernambuco; the movement led by João Ferreira in the mid- to late 1830s which established the 'Enchanted Kingdom of Vila-Bela' at Pedra Bonita in central Pernambuco; the founding in the early 1900s of the 'Holy City of Juazeiro' in the north-east state of Ceará by followers of the prophet Cícero Romão Baptista (Padre Cícero); the movement led by Antônio Vicente Mendes Maciel ('the Counsellor') which existed between 1893 and 1897 and founded the 'Holy City of Canudos' (known also as 'Belo Monte') in the north-east state of Bahia; the Contestado movement of the early 1900s led initially by the healer and prophet José María in the contested border regions of the southern states of Paraná and Santa Catarina; the movement of Calderão established in the mid-1930s in the north-east state of Ceará and headed by a succession of 'saints' (*beatos*), the first of whom was José Lourenço (Levine, 1992: 218–25). While the most famous examples of popular Catholic millenarianism in Brazil are drawn from the nineteenth and early twentieth centuries, similar movements continued to emerge throughout the twentieth century (see Negrão, 2001: 9; Pessar, 2004; Queiroz, 1965: 363–4).

4 Landes' comments that 'millennial thinking, however spiritually put, is political thinking' and that 'millennialism is a deeply politically subversive form of social mysticism' are perhaps somewhat overblown and do not readily apply to the Brazilian context (2006: 4, 6).

5 Although treating contemporary movements, Walliss offers a helpful overview of six major factors (three 'endogenous' and three 'exogenous') 'predisposing millenarian groups to violence' (2004: 13–36).

6 Indicative of the softening of millenarian discourse under way across the Brazilian leadership, the following comments by Padrinho Alex Polari are typical of the contemporary revision of earlier apocalyptic predictions: 'Today, much is said about a collapse, a kind of apocalypse, an end of the world. However, before manifesting itself physically with a volcanic eruption or tsunami, I think that the apocalypse will begin in a psychical form . . . It will be difficult to find a solution for the planetary crisis other than that of a spiritual revolution' (Nogueira, 2012).

7 Instances in which psychophysical or material benefits do not appear are typically accounted for by one or a number of elements which form part of

Santo Daime's overarching 'theodicy' (see Weber, 1991a: 270–6). Here, 'bad karma' inherited from past lives and of too great an amount to be worked off in this life alone is often cited as a cause. In addition, the 'will of the Daime' might be referenced to indicate that a greater plan precludes the enjoyment of this-worldly benefits. Subjective moral failings and religious weaknesses are also seen as a common source of an individual's failure to participate fully in the fruits of Santo Daime's spiritual efficacy.

8 Although now of an 'elective', 'intentional' and 'voluntary' nature, the ongoing relevance, if not need, of collective modes of religious participation is variously underwritten through reference to, for example: their overcoming of 'rootlessness' and provision of support mechanisms (Flory and Miller, 2000: 245); meeting the need to belong to something greater than oneself (Roof, 1993: 261); offering 'confirmation' and 'communion' (McGuire, 2008: 229); furnishing 'validation' (Hervieu-Léger, 2001: 167); and remedying 'estrangement' (Wuthnow, 1998: 166).

Chapter 4

1 While ritualized engagement with animal spirits is an important part of many indigenous and traditional *vegetalista* practices involving ayahuasca, in keeping with Amazonian *caboclo* customs (Galvão, 1955: 91–117), Padrinho Sebastião and the early Cefluris community treated interaction with animal spirits with suspicion, believing it likely to do more harm (e.g. bad luck and illness) than good (see Arruda et al., 2006: 146). It was only subsequent to the ingression of middle-class non-mainstream adepts that interaction with animal spirits gained in popularity. During fieldwork with a community in south Brazil, for example, an informant told me of a recent exchange between him and the 'Giant Cobra spirit during a vision (*miração*)'. Walking from his home to the church building, this individual had earlier come upon a cobra lying in the path ahead of him. Although the snake soon moved away, my informant was anxious lest any future encounter result in harm either to him or the snake. Consequently, during the next ritual event he 'summoned up' the Giant Cobra spirit and entered into a pact whereby he would strive to avoid snakes and, in turn, the spirit would ensure that the snakes stayed out of his way.

2 *Daimistas* also use esoteric notions of astral projection to describe ecstatic modes of supernatural encounter involving disembodied trips to other dimensions of space and time or different parts of the contemporary world.

Chapter 5

1 As with its European and North American usage, the term 'new middle class' (*nova classe média*) is employed by Brazilian social scientists in a variety of ways. In contrast to those using the term to describe the new social groups spawned by the neo-liberal reforms of the mid-1990s (e.g. Neri, 2010),

I follow others in associating the term with the mid-sector groups which emerged subsequent to the dramatic urban-industrializing push initiated by President Juscelino Kubitschek in the mid-1950s (e.g. A. Guerra et al., 2006; O'Dougherty, 2002). Forged by much the same forces (e.g. commodity capitalism) as its European and North American counterparts, the new middle class of Brazil has a great deal in common with other mid-sector members of late-modern society.

2 For discussions about the 'modern' character of Brazil, see: Martins (2000), Oliven (2001), Ortiz, (1988, 2000), Sorj (2006), Tavolaro (2008) and Wanderley (2007).

Postscript

1 By Alex Bellos, *The Telegraph* article is available at: www.telegraph.co.uk/news/uknews/1503447/Now-let-us-hallucinate.html. *The Times* article by Steve Boggan is available at: http://women.timesonline.co.uk/tol/life_and_style/women/the_way_we_live/article3699397.ece.

Bibliography

Adoum, J. n.d. *Eu Sou: Breviário do Iniciado e Poder do Mago*. São Paulo: Editora Pensamento.

Amado, J. 1978. *Conflito Social no Brasil: A Revolta dos 'Mucker,' Rio Grande do Sul, 1868–1898*. São Paulo: Edições Símbolo.

Amaral, L. 2000. *Carnaval da Alma: Comunidade, Essência e Sincretismo na Nova Era*. Petrópolis: Editora Vozes.

Ammerman, N. 1997. *Congregation and Community*. New Brunswick: Rutgers University Press.

Appadurai, A., ed. 1986. *The Social Life of Things: Commodities in Cultural Perspective*. Cambridge: Cambridge University Press.

Araújo, W. S. 1999. *Navegando sobre as Ondas do Daime: História, Cosmologia e Ritual da Barquinha*. Campinas: Editora da Unicamp.

—2004. 'A Barquinha: Espaço Simbólico de uma Cosmologia em Construção', in B. C. Labate and W. S. Araújo, eds, *O Uso Ritual da Ayahuasca*, 2nd edn. Campinas: Mercado de Letras, 541–55.

Arruda, C., Lapietra, F. and Santana, R. J. 2006. *Centro Livre: Ecletismo Cultural no Santo Daime*. São Paulo: All Print Editora.

Austin, J. L. 1962. *How to Do Things with Words*. Cambridge: Harvard University Press.

Azzi, R. 1978. *O Catolicismo Popular no Brasil: Aspectos Históricos*. Petrópolis: Editora Vozes.

Balzer, C. 2004. 'Santo Daime na Alemanha. Uma Fruta Proibida do Brasil no "Mercado das Religiões"', in B. C. Labate and W. S. Araújo, eds, *O Uso Ritual da Ayahuasca*. Campinas: Mercado de Letras, 507–37.

Barker, E. 1999. 'New religious movements: their incidence and significance', in B. Wilson and J. Cresswell, eds, *New Religious Movements: Challenge and Response*. London: New York, 15–31.

Bastide, R. 1985. *As Religiões Africanas no Brasil*. Livraria Pioneira Editora.

—2001. *O Candomblé da Bahia: Rito Nagô*. São Paulo: Companhia das Letras.

Bauman, Z. 1998. 'Postmodern religion?' in P. Heelas, ed., *Religion, Modernity and Postmodernity*. Oxford: Blackwell, 55–78.

—2000. *Liquid Modernity*. Cambridge: Polity Press.

—2005. *Liquid Life*. Cambridge: Polity Press.

—2007. *Consuming Life*. Cambridge: Polity Press.

Beck, U. 2010. *A God of One's Own: Religion's Capacity for Peace and Potential for Violence*. Cambridge: Polity Press.

Beck, U. and Beck-Gernsheim, E. 2002. *Individualization: Institutionalized Individualism and Its Social and Political Consequences*. London: Sage.

Beck, U. and Grande, E. 2010. 'Varieties of second modernity: the cosmopolitan turn in social and political theory and research'. *British Journal of Sociology*, 61.3, 409–43.

Beck, U. and Sznaider, N. 2006. 'Unpacking cosmopolitanism for the social sciences: a research agenda'. *British Journal of Sociology*, 57.1, 1–23.

Beck, U., Giddens, A. and Lash, S. 1994. *Reflexive Modernization: Politics, Tradition and Aesthetics in the Modern Social Order*. Cambridge: Polity Press.

Behrend, H. and Luig, U. 1999. 'Introduction', in H. Behrend and U. Luig, eds, *Spirit Possession, Modernity and Power in Africa*. Madison: University of Wisconsin Press, xii–xxii.

Bell, C. 1992. *Ritual Theory, Ritual Practice*. New York: Oxford University Press.

Bell, D. 1999. *The Coming of Post-Industrial Society: A Venture in Social Forecasting*, rev. edn. New York: Basic Books.

Bellah, R. N., Madsen, R., Sullivan, W. M., Swidler, A. and Tipton, S. M. 1985. *Habits of the Heart: Individualism and Commitment in American Life*. Berkeley, CA: University of California Press.

Berger, P. L. 1967. *The Sacred Canopy: Elements of a Sociological Theory of Religion*. New York: Anchor Books.

—1979. *The Heretical Imperative: Contemporary Possibilities of Religious Affirmation*. New York: Anchor Press.

—1988. *The Capitalist Revolution: Fifty Propositions about Prosperity, Equality, and Liberty*. New York: Basic Books.

Berger, P. L. and Luckmann, T. 1966. *The Social Construction of Reality: A Treatise in the Sociology of Knowledge*. London: Pelican.

Berger, P. L., Davie, G. and Fokas, E. 2008. *Religious America, Secular Europe? A Theme and Variations*. Aldershot: Ashgate.

Besnier, N. 1996. 'Heteroglossic discourses on Nukulaelae spirits', in A. Howard and J. M. Mageo, eds, *Spirits in Culture, History, and Mind*. New York: Routledge, 75–98.

Betz, H.-G. 1992. 'Postmodernism and the new middle class'. *Theory, Culture and Society*, 9, 93–114.

Blancarte, R. J. 2000. 'Popular religion, catholicism and socioreligious dissent in Latin America: facing the modernity paradigm'. *International Sociology*, 15.4, 591–603.

Boddy, J. 1994. 'Spirit possession revisited: beyond instrumentality'. *Annual Review of Anthropology*, 23, 407–34.

Bourdieu, P. 1984. *Distinction: A Social Critique of the Judgement of Taste*. London: Routledge.

—1991. *Language and Symbolic Power*. Cambridge: Harvard University Press.

—1993. *Sociology in Question*. London: Sage.

—1998a. *Acts of Resistance: Against the New Myths of Our Time*. Cambridge: Polity Press.

—1998b. *Practical Reason: On the Theory of Action*. Cambridge: Polity Press.

Bourdieu, P. and Wacquant, L. J. D. 1992. *An Invitation to Reflexive Sociology*. Cambridge: Polity Press.

Bourgogne, G. 2011. 'One hundred days of ayahuasca in France: the story of a legal decision', in B. C. Labate and H. Jungaberle, eds, *The Internationalization of Ayahuasca*. Berlin: LIT Verlag, 353–63.

Bourguignon, E. 1976. *Possession*. San Francisco, CA: Chandler and Sharp.

Brown, D. D. 1994. *Umbanda: Religion and Politics in Urban Brazil*. New York: Columbia University Press.

Brown, M. F. 1997. *The Channeling Zone: American Spirituality in an Anxious Age*. Cambridge: Harvard University Press.

Burris, V. 1995. 'The discovery of the new middle classes', in A. J. Vidich, ed., *The New Middle Classes: Life-Styles, Status Claims and Political Orientations*. London: Macmillan, 15–54.

Butler, J. 1997. *Excitable Speech: A Politics of the Performative*. London: Routledge.

Callaway, J. C. 2005. 'Various alkaloid profiles in decoctions of *banisteriopsis caapi*'. *Journal of Psychoactive Drugs*, 37.2, 1–5.

Camargo, C. P. 1961. *Kardecismo e Umbanda: Uma Interpretação Sociológica*. São Paulo: Livraria Pioneira Editora.

Canclini, N. G. 1995. *Hybrid Cultures: Strategies for Entering and Leaving Modernity*. Minneapolis: University of Minnesota Press.

Crapanzano, V. 2006. 'Postface'. *Culture and Religion*, 7.2, 199–203.

Casanova, J. 2006. 'Rethinking secularization: a global comparative perspective'. *The Hedgehog Review*, 8.1/2, 7–22.

Castaneda, C. 1968. *The Teachings of Don Juan: A Yaqui Way of Knowledge*. California: University of California Press.

Cavalcanti, M. L. V. de C. 1983. *O Mundo Invisível: Cosmologia, Sistema Ritual e Noção de Pessoa no Espiritismo*. Rio de Janeiro: Zahar Editores.

Cemin, A. B. 2004. 'Os Rituais do Santo Daime: "Sistemas de Montagens Simbólicas"', in B. C. Labate and W. S. Araújo, eds, *O Uso Ritual da Ayahuasca*. Campinas: Mercado de Letras, 347–82.

Chesnut, R. A. 2003. *Competitive Spirits: Latin America's New Religious Economy*. Oxford: Oxford University Press.

Clarke, P. B. 2000. *Japanese New Religions in Global Perspective*. London: Curzon Press.

Cohn, N. R. C. 1970. *The Pursuit of the Millennium: Revolutionary Millenarians and Mystical Anarchists of the Middle Ages*. London: Paladin.

Comaroff, J. 1985. *Body and Power, Spirit of Resistance: The Culture and History of a South African People*. Chicago: Chicago University Press.

Consorte, J. G. and Negrão, L. N. 1984. 'Os "Borboletas Azuis" de Campina Grande: Um Movimento Messiânico Malogrado', in J. G. Consorte and L. N. Negrão, eds, *O Messianismo no Brasil Contemporâneo*. São Paulo: FFLCH/USP-CER, 301–428.

Couto, F. de La R. 2004. 'Santo Daime: Rito da Ordem', in B. C. Labate and W. S. Araújo, eds, *O Uso Ritual da Ayahuasca*. Campinas: Mercado de Letras, 385–411.

Crapanzano, V. 1977. 'Introduction', in V. Crapanzano and V. Garrison, eds, *Case Studies in Spirit Possession*. New York: Wiley and Sons, 1–39.

D'Andrea, A. A. F. 2000. *O Self Perfeito e A Nova Era: Individualismo e Reflexividade em Religiosidades Pós-Tradicionais*. São Paulo: Edições Loyola.

Da Matta, R. 1996. 'Understanding messianism in Brazil: notes from a social anthropologist'. *Encuentros*, 17, 1–13.

Dawson, A. 2005. 'The Gnostic Church of Brazil: contemporary neo-esotericism in late-modern perspective'. *Interdisciplinary Journal of Research on Religion*, 1.8, www.religjournal.com/.

—2007. *New Era – New Religions: Religious Transformation in Contemporary Brazil*. Aldershot: Ashgate.

—2008. 'Religious identity and millenarian belief in Santo Daime', in A. Day, ed., *Religion and the Individual: Belief, Practice, Identity*. Aldershot: Ashgate, 183–95.

—2010. 'Positionality and role-identity in a new religious context: participant observation at Céu do Mapiá'. *Religion*, 40, 173–81.

—2011a. 'Consuming the self: new spirituality as "mystified consumption"'. *Social Compass*, 58.3, 1–7.

—2011b. 'Introduction: possession and invocation in contemporary context', in A. Dawson, ed., *Summoning the Spirits: Possession and Invocation in Contemporary Religion*. London: I.B. Tauris, 1–20.

—2011c. *Sociology of Religion*. London: SCM Press.

—2011d. 'Spirit, self and society in the Brazilian new religion of Santo Daime', in A. Dawson, ed., *Summoning the Spirits: Possession and Invocation in Contemporary Religion*. London: I.B. Tauris, 143–61.

—2012a. 'Making matter matter: the Santo Daime ritual of *feitio*', in N. Tassi and D. Espirito Santo, eds, *Making Spirits: Materiality and Transcendence in Contemporary Religion*. London: I.B. Tauris, 229–52.

—2012b. 'Spirit possession in a new religious context: The *umbandization* of Santo Daime'. *Nova Religio*, 15.4, 60–84.

Dawson, L. L. 1998. *Comprehending Cults: The Sociology of New Religious Movements*. Toronto: Oxford University Press.

Della Cava, R. 1970. *Miracle at Joaseiro*. New York: Columbia University Press.

Dos Lakatos, G. 2007. *Santo Daime Revelado: Drogas, Fraudes e Mentiras*. Curitiba: Editora Corpo Mente.

Durkheim, É. 1961. *Moral Education: A Study in the Theory and Application of the Sociology of Education*. New York: Free Press.

Einstein, M. 2008. *Brands of Faith: Marketing Religion in a Commercial Age*. London: Routledge.

Eisenstadt, S. N. 2000. 'Multiple modernities'. *Deadalus*, 129.1, 1–29.

Evans-Pritchard, E. E. 1956. *Nuer Religion*. New York: Clarendon Press.

Ezzy, D. 2011. 'The ontology of good and evil: spirit possession in contemporary witchcraft and paganism', in A. Dawson, ed., *Summoning the Spirits: Possession and Invocation in Contemporary Religion*. London: I.B. Tauris, 179–97.

Faivre, A. 1986. 'Esotericism', in M. Eliade, ed., *Encyclopedia of Religions*. New York: Macmillan, 156–63.

—1992. 'Introduction: I', in A. Faivre and J. Needleman, eds, *Modern Esoteric Spirituality*. London: SCM Press, xi–xxii.

Faivre, A. and Needleman, J., eds. 1992. *Modern Esoteric Spirituality*. London: SCM Press.

Featherstone, M. 2007. *Consumer Culture and Postmodernism*, 2nd edn. London: Sage.

Finke, R. and Stark, R. 1992. *The Churching of America, 1776–1990: Winners and Losers in Our Religious Economy*. New Brunswick: Rutgers University Press.

Firth, R. W. 1967. *Tikopia Ritual and Belief*. Boston: Beacon Press.

Flory, R. W. and Miller, D. E., eds. 2000. *GenX Religion*. London: Routledge.

—2008. *Finding Faith: The Spiritual Quest of the Post-Boomer Generation*. New Brunswick: Rutgers University Press.

Foucault, M. 1991. *Discipline and Punish: The Birth of the Prison*. London: Penguin.

Franco, M. C. P. and Conceição, O. S. da. 2004. 'Breves Revelações sobre a Ayahuasca. O Uso do Chá entre os Seringueiros do Alto Juruá', in

B. C. Labate and W. S. Araújo, eds, *O Uso Ritual da Ayahuasca*. Campinas: Mercado de Letras, 201–27.

Furuya, Y. 1994. 'Umbandização dos Cultos Populares na Amazônia: a Integração ao Brasil?' in H. Nakamaki and A. P. Filho, eds, *Possessão e Procissão: Religiosidade Popular no Brasil*. Osaka: National Museum of Ethnology, 11–59.

Galvão, E. E. 1955. *Santos e Visagens: Um Estudo da Vida Religiosa de Itá, Amazonas*. São Paulo: Companhia Editôra Nacional.

Gaonkar, D. P. 2001. 'On Alternative Modernities', in D. P. Gaonkar, ed., *Alternative Modernities*. London: Duke University Press, 1–23.

Geertz, C. 1973. *The Interpretation of Cultures*. New York: Basic Books.

Giddens, A. 1973. *The Class Structure of the Advanced Societies*. London: Hutchinson University Library.

—1991. *Modernity and Self-Identity: Self and Society in the Late Modern Age*. Cambridge: Polity Press.

Giumbelli, E. 2002. 'Zélio de Moraes e As Orígens da Umbanda no Rio de Janeiro', in V. G. da Silva, ed., *Caminhos da Alma: Memória Afro-Brasileira*. São Paulo: Summus, 183–218.

Goulart, S. 2004. 'Contrastes e Continuidades em uma Tradição Amazônica: As Religiões da Ayahuasca.' Unpublished Doctoral Thesis. State University of Campinas, Brazil.

Gouldner, A. W. 1979. *The Future of Intellectuals and the Rise of the New Class*. London: Continuum.

Gregorim, G. 1991. *Santo Daime: Estudos sobre Simbolismo, Doutrina e Povo de Juramidam*. São Paulo: Ícone.

Groisman, A. 1996. 'Santo Daime: Notas sobre a 'Luz Xamânica' da Rainha da Floresta', in E. J. M. Langdon, ed., *Xamanismo no Brasil: Novas Perspectivas*. Florianópolis: Editora da UFSC, 333–52.

—1999. *Eu Venho da Floresta: Um Estudo sobre o Contexto Simbólico do Uso do Santo Daime*. Florianópolis: Editora da UFSC.

—2004. 'Missão e projeto: motivos e contingências nas trajetórias dos agrupamentos do Santo Daime na Holanda'. *Revista de Estudos da Religião*, 1, 1–18.

Guerra, L. D. 2003. *Mercado Religioso no Brasil: Competição, Demanda e a Dinâmica da Esfera da Religião*. João Pessoa: Idéia.

Guerra, A., Pochmann, M., Amorim, R. and Silva, R., eds. 2006. *Classe Média: Desenvolvimento e Crise. Atlas da Nova Estratificação Social no Brasil*, Vol. 1. São Paulo: Cortez Editora.

Guimarães, M. B. L. 1992. 'A "Lua Branca" de Seu Tupinamba e de Mestre Irineu: Estudo de Caso de um Terreiro de Umbanda'. Unpublished Masters Thesis, Federal University of Rio de Janeiro, Brazil.

Haber, R. 2011. 'The Santo Daime Road to Seeking Religious Freedom in the USA', in B. C. Labate and H. Jungaberle, eds, *The Internationalization of Ayahuasca*. Berlin: LIT Verlag, 301–17.

Habermas, J. 1984. *The Theory of Communicative Action: Reason and the Rationalization of Society*, Vol. 1. Boston: Beacon Press.

Hammer, O. 2001. *Claiming Knowledge: Strategies of Epistemology from Theosophy to the New Age*. Leiden: Brill.

Hanegraaff, W. J. 1996. *New Age Religion and Western Culture: Esotericism in the Mirror of Secular Thought*. Leiden: Brill.

Harner, M. 1972. *The Jivaro*. New York: Doubleday.

Hearn, A. 2008. '"Meat, mask, burden": probing the contours of the "branded self"'. *Journal of Consumer Culture*, 8.2, 197–217.

Heelas, P. 1996a. 'Cultural studies and business cultures', in A. Godley and O. M. Westall, eds, *Business History and Business Culture*. Manchester: Manchester University Press, 77–98.

—1996b. *The New Age Movement: The Celebration of the Self and the Sacralization of Modernity*. Oxford: Blackwell.

—2008. *Spiritualities of Life: New Age Romanticism and Consumptive Capitalism*. Oxford: Blackwell.

Heelas, P. and Woodhead, L. 2005. *The Spiritual Revolution: Why Religion Is Giving Way to Spirituality*. Oxford: Blackwell.

Hervieu-Léger, D. 2001. 'Individualism, the validation of faith, and the social nature of religion in modernity', in R. K. Fenn, ed., *The Blackwell Companion to Sociology of Religion*. Oxford: Blackwell, 161–75.

Howard, A. and Mageo, J. M. 1996. 'Introduction', in J. M. Mageo and A. Howard, eds, *Spirits in Culture, History, and Mind*. New York: Routledge, 1–10.

Inglehart, R. 1990. *Culture Shift in Advanced Industrial Society*. Princeton, NJ: Princeton University Press.

Junior, A. M. A. 2007. 'Tambores para a Rainha da Floresta: A Inserção da Umbanda no Santo Daime'. Unpublished Masters Thesis, Catholic Pontifical University of São Paulo, Brazil.

Kenyon, S. M. 2011. 'Spirits and slaves in Central Sudan', in A. Dawson, ed., *Summoning the Spirits: Possession and Invocation in Contemporary Religion*. London: I.B. Tauris, 58–73.

Kramer, F. 1993. *The Red Fez: Art and Spirit Possession in Africa*. London: Verso.

Labate, B. C. 2004. *A Reinvenção do Uso da Ayahuasca nos Centros Urbanos*. Campinas: Mercado de Letras.

—2005. 'Dimensões Legais, Éticas e Políticas da Expansão do Consumo da Ayahuasca', in B. C. Labate and S. L. Goulart, eds, *O Uso Ritual dos Plantas de Poder*. São Paulo: Mercado de Letras, 397–457.

—2011. 'Comments on Brazil's 2010 resolution regulating ayahuasca use'. *Curare*, 34.4, 298–304.

Labate, B. C. and Feeney, K. 2012. 'Ayahuasca and the process of regulation in Brazil and internationally: implications and challenges'. *The International Journal of Drug Policy*, 23, 154–61.

Labate, B. C. and Pacheco, G. 2004. 'Matrizes Maranhenses do Santo Daime', in B. C. Labate and W. S. Araújo, eds, *O Uso Ritual da Ayahuasca*. Campinas: Mercado de Letras, 303–44.

—2010. *Opening the Portals of Heaven: Brazilian Ayahuasca Music*. Berlin: LIT Verlag.

Laderman, C. and Roseman, M., eds. 1995. *The Performance of Healing*. New York: Routledge.

Lambek, M. 1981. *Human Spirits: A Cultural Account of Trance in Mayotte*. Cambridge: Cambridge University Press.

Landes, R. 2004. 'Millennialism', in J. R. Lewis, ed., *The Oxford Handbook of New Religious Movements*. Oxford: Oxford University Press, 333–58.

—2006. 'Millenarianism and the dynamics of apocalyptic time', in K. G. C. Newport and C. Gribben, eds, *Expecting the End: Millennialism in Social Historical Context*. Waco: Baylor University Press, 1–23.

Langdon, E. J. M. 1996. 'Introdução: Xamanismo – Velhas e Novas Perspectivas', in E. J. M. Langdon, ed., *Xamanismo no Brasil: Novas Perspectivas*. Florianópolis: Editora da UFSC, 9–37.

Lange, H. and Meier, L., eds. 2009. *The New Middle Classes: Globalizing Lifestyles, Consumerism and Environmental Concern*. Dordrecht: Springer.

Lasch, N. 1979. *The Culture of Narcissism: American Life in an Age of Diminishing Expectations*. New York: Norton.

Lash, S. 1994. 'Reflexivity and its doubles: structure, aesthetics, community', in U. Beck, A. Giddens and S. Lash, eds, *Reflexive Modernization: Politics, Tradition and Aesthetics in the Modern Social Order*. Cambridge: Polity Press, 110–73.

Lash S. and Urry, J. 1987. *The End of Organized Capitalism*. Cambridge: Polity Press.

Leary, T. 1968. *The Politics of Ecstasy*. New York: G. P. Putnam's Sons.

Lederer, E. and Marschak, J. 1995. 'The New Middle Class', in A. J. Vidich, ed., *The New Middle Classes: Life-Styles, Status Claims and Political Orientations*. London: Macmillan, 55–71.

Lee, M. J. 1993. *Consumer Culture Reborn: The Cultural Politics of Consumption*. London: Routledge.

Lefebvre, H. 1991. *The Production of Space*. Oxford: Blackwell.

Levine, R. M. 1992. *Vale of Tears: Revisiting the Canudos Massacre in Northeastern Brazil, 1893–1897*. Berkeley, CA: University of California Press.

Levy, R. I., Mageo, J. M. and Howard, A. 1996. 'Gods, spirits, and history', in J. M. Mageo and A. Howard, eds, *Spirits in Culture, History, and Mind*. New York: Routledge, 11–28.

Lewis, I. M. 2003. *Ecstatic Religion: A Study of Spirit Possession and Shamanism*, 3rd edn. London: Routledge.

López-Pavillard, S. 2008. 'Recepción de la Ayahuasca en España'. Unpublished Masters Thesis, Complutensian University of Madrid, Spain.

López-Pavillard, S. and de las Casas, D. 2011. 'Santo Daime in Spain: a religion with a psychoactive sacrament', in B. C. Labate and H. Jungaberle, eds, *The Internationalization of Ayahuasca*. Berlin: LIT Verlag, 365–74.

Lucas, P. C. 2011. 'New age millennialism', in C. Wessinger, ed., *The Oxford Handbook of Millennialism*. Oxford: Oxford University Press, 567–86.

Luckmann, T. 1967. *The Invisible Religion: The Problem of Religion in Modern Society*. New York: Macmillan.

—1990. 'Shrinking transcendence, expanding religion?' *Sociological Analysis*, 50.2, 127–38.

Luna, L. E. 1986. *Vegetalismo: Shamanism among the Mestizo Population of the Peruvian Amazon*. Stockholm: Almqvist and Wiksell International.

Lury, C. 2011. *Consumer Culture*, 2nd edn. Cambridge: Polity Press.

Luz, P. 2004. 'O Uso Ameríndio do Caapi', in B. C. Labate and W. S. Araújo, eds, *O Uso Ritual da Ayahuasca*. Campinas: Mercado de Letras, 37–68.

Mabit, J. 2004. 'Produção Visionária da Ayahuasca no Contexto dos Curandeiros da Alta Amazônia Peruana', in B. C. Labate and W. S. Araújo, eds, *O Uso Ritual da Ayahuasca*. Campinas: Mercado de Letras, 147–80.

MacRae, E. 1992. *Guiado pela Lua: Xamanismo e Uso Ritual da Ayahuasca no Culto do Santo Daime*. São Paulo: Editora Brasiliense.

—1998. 'Santo Daime and santa maria – the licit ritual use of ayahuasca and the illicit use of cannabis in a Brazilian Amazonian religion'. *The International Journal of Drug Policy*, 9, 325–38.

Magnani, J. G. C. 2000. *O Brasil da Nova Era*. Rio de Janeiro: Jorge Zahar Editor.

Mardin, S. 2006. *Religion, Society and Modernity in Turkey*. Syracuse: Syracuse University Press.

Martin, B. 1981. *A Sociology of Contemporary Cultural Change*. Oxford: Basil Blackwell.

Martins, J. de S. 1981. *Os Camponeses e a Política no Brasil*. Petrópolis: Editora Vozes.

—2000. 'The hesitations of the modern and the contradictions of modernity in Brazil', in V. Schelling, ed., *Through the Kaleidoscope: The Experience of Modernity in Latin America*. London: Verso, 248–74.

Maués, R. H. and Villacorta, G. M. 2004. 'Pajelança e Encantaria Amazônica', in R. Prandi, ed., *Encantaria Brasileira: O Livro dos Mestres, Caboclos e Encantados*. Rio de Janeiro: Pallas, 11–58.

McGarry, M. 2008. *Ghosts of Futures Past: Spiritualism and the Cultural Politics of Nineteenth-Century America*. Berkeley, CA: University of California Press.

McGuire, M. B. 2008. 'Toward a sociology of spirituality: individual religion in social/historical context', in E. Barker, ed., *The Centrality of Religion in Social Life: Essays in Honour of James A. Beckford*. Aldershot: Ashgate, 215–32.

McKenna, D. J., Towers, G. H. N. and Abbot, F. 1984. 'Monoamine oxidase inhibitors in South American hallucinogenic plants: tryptamine and β-carboline constituents of ayahuasca'. *Journal of Ethnopharmacology*, 11, 189–206.

Mello e Souza de, L. 2003. *The Devil and the Land of the Holy Cross: Witchcraft, Slavery, and Popular Religion in Colonial Brazil*. Austin, TX: University of Texas Press.

Menozzi, W. 2011. 'The Santo Daime legal case in Italy', in B. C. Labate and H. Jungaberle, eds, *The Internationalization of Ayahuasca*. Berlin: LIT Verlag, 379–88.

Milanez, W. 1988. *Oaska: O Evangelho da Rosa*. Campinas: Sama Editora.

Miller, D. 2010. *Stuff*. Cambridge: Polity Press.

Mills, C. W. 2002. *White Collar: The American Middle Classes*, fiftieth anniversary edn. Oxford: Oxford University Press.

Monteiro, D. T. 1974. *Os Errantes do Novo Século: Um Estudo sobre o Surto Milenarista do Contestado*. São Paulo: Livraria Duas Cidades.

Moore, R. L. 1994. *Selling God: American Religion in the Marketplace of Culture*. New York: Oxford University Press.

Moreira, P. and MacRae, E. 2011. *Eu Venho de Longe: Mestre Irineu e seus Companheiros*. Salvador: EDUFBA.

Mortimer, L. 2000. *Bença Padrinho!* São Paulo: Editorial Céu de Maria.

Moura da Silva, E. 2006. 'Similaridades e Diferenças entre Estilos de Espiritualidade Metafísica: O Caso do Círculo Esotérico da Comunhão do Pensamento (1908–1943)', in A. C. Isaia, ed., *Orixás e Espíritos: O Debate Interdisciplinar na Pesquisa Contemporânea*. Uberlândia: EDUFU, 225–40.

Myscofski, C. A. 1988. *When Men Walk Dry: Portuguese Messianism in Brazil*. Atlanta, GA: Scholars Press.

Negrão, L. N. 1984. 'Um Movimento Messiânico Urbano: Messianismo e Mudança Social no Brasil', in J. G. Consorte and L. N. Negrão, eds, *O Messianismo no Brasil Contemporâneo*. São Paulo: FFLCH/USP-CER, 21–300.

—2001. 'Revisitando o messianismo no Brasil e profetizando seu futuro'. *Revista Brasileira de Ciências Sociais*, 16, 119–29.

Neri, M. C., ed. 2010. *A Pequena Grande Década: Crise, Cenários e a Nova Classe Média*. Rio de Janeiro: CPS/FGV.

Netto de, J. P. 1988. *Religion of the Third Millennium*. São Paulo: Legião de Boa Vontade.

Nogueira, B. T. 2012. 'Alex Polari: "O mundo só vai mudar quando a gente perceber que somos mais do que matéria . . . somos luz"'. *Revista Trip*, 208, http://revistatrip.uol.com.br/revista/208.

O'Dougherty, M. 2002. *Consumption Intensified: The Politics of Middle-Class Daily Life in Brazil*. Durham: Duke University Press.

Oliveira de, P. A. R. 1985. *Religião e Dominação de Classe: Gênese, Estrutura e Função do Catolicismo Romanizado no Brasil*. Petrópolis: Editora Vozes.

Oliven, R. G. 2001. 'Cultura e Modernidade no Brasil'. *São Paulo em Perspectiva*, 15.2, 3–12.

Ong, A. 1987. *Spirits of Resistance and Capitalist Discipline: Factory Women in Malaysia*. Albany, NY: State University of New York Press.

Oro, A. P. 1989. *Na Amazônia um Messias de Índios e Brancos: Para uma Antropologia do Messianismo*. Petrópolis: Editora Vozes.

Ortiz, R. 1985. *Cultura Brasileira e Identidade Nacional*. São Paulo: Editora Brasiliense.

—1988. *A Moderna Tradição Brasileira*. São Paulo: Editora Brasiliense.

—1994. *Mundialização e Cultura*. São Paulo: Editora Brasiliense.

—2000. 'Popular culture, modernity and nation', in V. Schelling, ed., *Through the Kaleidoscope: The Experience of Modernity in Latin America*. London: Verso, 127–47.

Otten, A. H. 1990. '*Só Deus é Grande': A Mensagem Religiosa de Antônio Conselheiro*. São Paulo: Edições Loyola.

Owen, A. 1989. *The Darkened Room: Women, Power, and Spiritualism in Late Victorian England*. London: Virago Press.

Owensby, B. P. 1999. *Intimate Ironies: Modernity and the Making of Middle-Class Lives in Brazil*. Stanford: Standford University Press.

Passos, J. D. 2006. 'Pentecostalismo e modernidade: conceitos sociológicos e religião popular metropolitana'. *Revista Nures*, 2.2, www.pucsp.br/revistanures/revista2/artigos_joao_decio.pdf.

Pessar, P. R. 2004. *From Fanatics to Folk: Brazilian Millenarianism and Popular Culture*. Durham: Duke University Press.

Polari de Alverga, A. 1996. 'Seriam os Deuses Alcalóides?' www.santodaime.org/arquivos/alex1.htm.

— ed. 1998. *O Evangelho Segundo Sebastião Mota*. Céu do Mapiá: Cefluris Editorial.

—1999. *Forest of Visions: Ayahuasca, Amazonian Spirituality and the Santo Daime Tradition*. Rochester: Park Street Press.

Queiroz de, M. I. P. 1965. *O Messianismo no Brasil e no Mundo*. São Paulo: Dominus Editôra.

Rhode, S. A. and Sander, H. 2011. 'The development of the legal situation of Santo Daime in Germany', in B. C. Labate and H. Jungaberle, eds, *The Internationalization of Ayahuasca*. Berlin: LIT Verlag, 339–51.

Ribeiro, R. 1992. 'Brazilian messianism'. *Luso-Brazilian Review*, 29.1, 71–81.

Richman, G. D. 1990/1. 'The Santo Daime doctrine: an interview with Alex Polari de Alverga'. *Shaman's Drum*, Winter, 31–41.

Ritzer, G. and Jurgenson, N. 2010. 'Production, consumption, prosumption: the nature of capitalism in the age of the digital "prosumer"'. *Journal of Consumer Culture*, 10.1, 13–36.

Robbins, T. and Palmer, S. J. 1997. 'Patterns of contemporary apocalypticism in North America', in T. Robbins and S. J. Palmers, eds, *Millennium, Messiahs and Mayhem: Contemporary Apocalyptic Movements*. New York: Routledge, 1–27.

Roca, R. S. 2007. '"Dinheiro vivo": money and religion in Brazil'. *Critique of Anthropology*, 27.3, 319–39.

Roof, W. C. 1993. *A Generation of Seekers: The Spiritual Journeys of the Baby Boom Generations*. New York: HarperCollins.

—1999. *Spiritual Marketplace: Baby Boomers and the Remaking of American Religion*. Princeton, NJ: Princeton University Press.

Ruck, C. A. P., Bigwood, J., Staples, D., Ott, J. and Wasson, R. G. 1979. 'Entheogens'. *Journal of Psychoactive Drugs*, 11.1/2, 145–6.

Santos, J. L. dos. 2004. *Espiritismo: Uma Religião Brasileira*. Campinas: Editora Átomo.

Sassatelli, R. 2007. *Consumer Culture: History, Theory and Politics*. London: Sage.

Sassi, M. 1979. *O Que é O Vale do Amanhecer*. Brasília: Editora Vale do Amanhecer.

Schmidt, T. K. 2007. *Morality as Practice: The Santo Daime, an Eco-Religious Movement in the Amazonian Rainforest*. Uppsala: Uppsala University Press.

Schmidt, V. H. 2006. 'Multiple modernities or varieties of modernity?' *Current Sociology*, 54.1, 77–97.

Searle, J. 1969. *Speech Acts: An Essay in the Philosophy of Language*. Cambridge: Cambridge University Press.

Seigel, J. 2005. *The Idea of the Self: Thought and Experience in Western Europe since the Seventeenth Century*. Cambridge: Cambridge University Press.

Senn, F. 1984. *Joyce's Dislocutions: Essays on Reading as Translation*. Baltimore: The Johns Hopkins University Press.

Sennett, R. 2006. *The Culture of the New Capitalism*. New Haven: Yale University Press.

Sered, S. S. 1994. *Priestess, Mother, Sacred Sister: Religions Dominated by Women*. New York: Oxford University Press.

Shanon, B. 2002. *The Antipodes of the Mind: Charting the Phenomenology of the Ayahuasca Experience*. Oxford: Oxford University Press.

Shaw, R. 2002. *Memories of the Slave Trade: Ritual and the Historical Imagination in Sierra Leone*. Chicago: University of Chicago Press.

Silva, C. M. da. 1983. 'O Palácio de Juramidan. Santo Daime: Um Ritual de Transcendência e Despoluição'. Unpublished Master's Thesis, Federal University of Pernambuco, Brazil.

Simmel, G. 1997. *Essays on Religion*. New Haven: Yale University Press.

Slater, D. 1997. *Consumer Culture and Modernity*. Cambridge: Polity.

Smart, N. 1973. *The Science of Religion and the Sociology of Knowledge.* Princeton, NJ: Princeton University Press.

Smith, F. M. 2006. *The Self Possessed: Deity and Spirit Possession in South Asian Literature and Civilization.* New York: Columbia University Press.

Sorj, B. 2006. *A Nova Sociedade Brasileira*, 3rd rev. edn. Rio de Janeiro: Jorge Zahar Editor.

Spohn, W. 2003. 'Multiple modernity, nationalism and religion: a global perspective'. *Current Sociology*, 51.3/4, 265–86.

Stark, R. and Bainbridge, W. S. 1985. *The Future of Religion: Secularization, Revival, and Cult Formation.* Berkeley, CA: University of California Press.

Stoll, S. 2002. 'Religião, ciência ou auto-ajuda? trajetos do espiritismo no Brasil'. *Revista de Antropologia*, 45.2, 361–402.

Stoller, P. 1989. *Fusion of the Worlds: An Ethnography of Possession Among the Songhay of Niger.* Chicago: University of Chicago Press.

—1995. *Embodying Colonial Memories: Spirit Possession, Power, and the Hauka in West Africa.* New York: Routledge.

Strathern, A. and Lambek, M. 1998. 'Introduction. Embodying sociality: Africanist-Melanesianist comparisons', in M. Lambek and A. Strathern, eds, *Bodies and Persons: Comparative Perspectives from Africa and Melanesia.* Cambridge: Cambridge University Press, 1–28.

Talmon, Y. 1966. 'Millenarian movements'. *European Journal of Sociology*, 7, 159–200.

Taussig, M. 1987. *Shamanism, Colonialism, and the Wild Man: A Study in Terror and Healing.* Chicago, IL: Chicago University Press.

Tavolaro, S. B. F. 2008. '"Neither traditional nor fully modern . . ." two classical sociological approaches on contemporary Brazil'. *International Journal of Politics, Culture and Society*, 19, 109–28.

Taylor, C. 1992. *Sources of the Self: The Making of Modern Identity.* Cambridge: Cambridge University Press.

—2007. *A Secular Age.* Cambridge: Harvard University Press.

Troeltsch, E. 1931. *The Social Teaching of the Christian Churches*, Vol. 1. London: George Allen and Unwin.

Tupper, K. W. 2008. 'The globalization of ayahuasca: harm reduction or benefit maximization?' *The International Journal of Drug Policy*, 19, 297–303.

—2009. 'Ayahuasca healing beyond the Amazon: the globalization of a traditional indigenous entheogenic practice'. *Global Networks*, 9.1, 117–36.

Tupper, K. W. and Labate B. C. 2012. 'Plants, psychoactive substances and the international narcotics control board: the control of nature and the nature of control'. *Human Rights and Drugs*, 2.1, 17–28.

Twitchell, J. B. 2007. *Shopping for God: How Christianity Went from in Your Heart to in Your Face.* New York: Simon and Schuster.

Van den Plas, A. 2011. 'Ayahuasca under International Law: the Santo Daime churches in the Netherlands', in B. C. Labate and H. Jungaberle, eds, *The Internationalization of Ayahuasca.* Berlin: LIT Verlag, 327–38.

Vidich, A. J. and Bensman, J. 1995. 'Liberalism and the new middle classes', in A. J. Vidich, ed., *The New Middle Classes: Life-Styles, Status Claims and Political Orientations.* London: Macmillan, 281–99.

Voeks, R. A. 1997. *Sacred Leaves of Candomblé: African Magic, Medicine, and Religion in Brazil.* Austin, TX: University of Texas Press.

Wafer, J. 1991. *The Taste of Blood: Spirit Possession in Brazilian Candomblé*. Philadelphia, PA: University of Pennsylvania Press.

Wallis, R. 1984. *The Elementary Forms of the New Religious Life*. London: Routledge & Kegan Paul.

Walliss, J. 2004. *Apocalyptic Trajectories: Millenarianism and Violence in the Contemporary World*. Bern: Peter Lang.

Wanderley, L. E. W. 2007. 'Modernidade, Pós-modernidade e Implicações na Questão Social Latino-Americana', in T. Bernardo and P. A. Resende, eds, *Ciências Sociais na Atualidade: Realidades e Imaginários*. São Paulo: Paulus, 47–85.

Waters, M. 2001. *Globalization*, 2nd edn. London: Routledge.

Weber, M. 1965. *The Sociology of Religion*. London: Methuen & Co.

—1991a. 'The social psychology of the world religions', in H. H. Gerth and C. W. Mills, eds, *From Max Weber: Essays in Sociology*, new edn. London: Routledge, 267–301.

—1991b. 'The sociology of charismatic authority', in H. H. Gerth and C. W. Mills, eds, *From Max Weber: Essays in Sociology*, new edn. London: Routledge, 245–52.

—1992. *The Protestant Ethic and the Spirit of Capitalism*. London: Routledge.

Wessinger, C. 2011. 'Millennialism in cross-cultural perspective', in C. Wessinger, ed., *The Oxford Handbook of Millennialism*. Oxford: Oxford University Press, 3–24.

Wiegele, K. L. 2005. *Investing in Miracles: El Shaddai and the Transformation of Popular Catholicism in the Philippines*. Honolulu: University of Hawaii Press.

Wilson, B. R. 1970. *Religious Sects: A Sociological Study*. London: Weidenfeld and Nicolson.

—1979. *Contemporary Transformations of Religion*. Oxford: Clarendon Press.

Wuthnow, R. 1994. *Sharing the Journey: Support Groups and America's New Quest for Community*. New York: The Free Press.

—1998. *After Heaven: Spirituality in America since the 1950s*. Berkeley, CA: University of California Press.

Wynne, D. 1998. *Leisure, Lifestyle, and the New Middle Class: A Case Study*. London: Routledge.

Zwick, D., Bonsu, S. K. and Darmody, A. 2008. 'Putting consumers to work: "co-creation" and new marketing govern-mentality'. *Journal of Consumer Culture*, 8.2, 163–96.

Index